ACTING IS A
JOB

ACTING IS A JOB

Real-Life Lessons about the Acting Business

Jason Pugatch

ALLWORTH PRESS
NEW YORK

10 09 08 07 06   5 4 3 2 1

Published by Allworth Press
An imprint of Allworth Communications, Inc.
10 East 23rd Street, New York, NY 10010

Cover design by Derek Bacchus
Interior design by Mary Belibasakis
Page composition/typography by Claude Martinot
Cover photo: © Michael Gerry

ISBN: 1-58115-438-0

Library of Congress Cataloging-in-Publication Data

Pugatch, Jason.
    Acting is a job: real-life lessons about the acting business/Jason Pugatch.
        p. cm.
    Includes index.
    ISBN 1-58115-438-0 (pbk.)
    1. Acting—Vocational guidance.   I. Title.

PN2055.P84 2006
792.02'8023—dc22
2006001955

Printed in Canada

For my parents

ACKNOWLEDGEMENTS

I owe not only a considerable debt of gratitude, but many, many free lunches, to Ethan Angelica, my extraordinary research assistant. Thanks are due to Jamee Freedus as well, for additional research.

Sky Spiegel, Rose Kernochan, and Val Day, each of whom believed in this project, encouraged me to press forward, and helped me navigate the maze of the publishing industry.

Each and every actor interviewed for this book. Without your forthrightness, this book would not be complete. And indeed, many thanks to the casting directors, agents, playwrights, directors, and producers who spoke with me so candidly.

My own agents, whom I will not name in order to protect the innocent. Every actor should have relationships like these.

Nicole Potter-Talling, Tad Crawford, and the entire team at Allworth Press, who have (thus far) left me to my own devices.

TABLE OF CONTENTS

INTRODUCTION
ACTING IS A JOB

> ". . . No matter how much (or how little) acting
> experience you may have, you can start pursuing an acting
> career right now . . . and this book shows you how."
> —*Breaking Into Acting for Dummies*

If you believe that quote, stop reading now. Close the cover, put this book back on the shelf, and have a wonderful career. Write me when you've made it.

If you think that acting, like other professional careers, may take at least a modicum of craft, talent, looks, luck, skill, emotional stability, guidance, patience, and endurance, then read on.

First, there are the stereotypes. Take your pick. Actors are:

A. Lazy
B. Dumb
C. Overpaid for their work
D. Waiters

Well, you can't win 'em all.

Certainly some actors have no training, some have no talent, some are stupid, and some of them make a lot of money. You could probably cross out my laundry list of prerequisites, with the exception of luck and endurance, and have an accurate accounting of the necessary skills an actor must have. Luck and endurance are the two most important factors in an acting career.

There's another buzzword. Career. Not a day on a soap opera, not three days of extra work that got you your SAG card. A career. The daily event to which people devote their working lives. A career is a very difficult thing for an actor to have.

For an actor, it's also difficult to judge whether you actually have a career. You're a lawyer when you're arguing in court: You have a career. You're a doctor when you're looking in someone's ear with a scope: You have a career. You're a teacher when you're explaining Euclidian geometry: You have a career. You're an actor when you're performing on stage, in television, or in a film.

But you do not have a career.

Acting is a perpetually freelance business that fools people into thinking better of it. It entices with celebrity culture, awards shows, and superstar salaries. But it is, at its core, a job-to-job industry.

The winter after I turned twenty-six, I did not have a career. Success was fleeting, and though I had done some bit parts on television and a commercial, career longevity was a long way off. I wondered if an MFA in acting from a recognized graduate program was a good idea, so I sought counsel from a former college professor. Expecting a conversation on the value of education, the art of acting, and the great skills I could inherit through study, I broached the subject of going back to school.

My teacher's response was pointed and simple.

"Unless you're a model," he said, "there's no work for you until you're thirty."

I am not a model.

I went to school. In the first month of training, we were forced to perform and outperform each other constantly. Acting schools are a weird blend of summer camp and the military. You're with the same incestuous group of people all the time. You're laughing, crying, emoting, moving, breathing, dancing, and drinking together. Between class, rehearsal, and performance, you're in the theater sixteen hours a day. You're exhausted and constantly competing for roles, stage time, and validation.

One day, after an especially gruesome display of acting, our Russian professor wore a particularly grim expression. He rubbed his chin with his hand, looked disapprovingly at the actors on stage, and spoke to the translator.

We anxiously awaited the interpretation. What deep secret was about to span the generational divide? What performance nut would be cracked today?

What did our master decree?

"Acting," he sighed, "is hard."

Fast-forward two years. MFA in hand, New York showcase complete, I'm fortunate enough to be taking agent meetings in New York. At one, I sit down with a woman whom I had met prior to school. I remembered this; she did not. Her pitch to me—and she did not stop talking our entire time together—was that she could take someone off the street, any good-looking young someone, and make him a star. That's what the business is about, she said. Looks.

Two years of training, some fifty-odd thousand dollars of debt, and I was right back where I started.

Acting is hard. Unless you're a model.

Do ugly actors who are good make it in this business? Yes. Do beautiful actors without a modicum of talent make it? Yes. Is there a hard and fast rule, rhyme, or reason to any of this? No.

Here's what there is. There is belief in yourself. There is a support network. There is the fact that endurance and patience are perhaps the most important skills an actor can have. And, most importantly, there is a need for you to be well informed.

Misperceptions prevail. Actors, with visions of Hollywood stardom, Broadway careers, or even a simple life of consistent employment, have been misled by an industry that sustains itself by leeching off the dreams of the uninformed. Each new generation of actors, and the general public they entertain, has no idea of the actual happenings in an actor's daily life. Sure, everyone knows that acting is hard, but do they know about twenty-hour days filled with temping, ramen soup lunches, and late-night rehearsals in unheated East Village studios? Have they heard what an audition is really like? How come my son didn't get that commercial, they wonder. Why did my daughter move from Houston to New York only to get a job back in Houston? How hard can it really be to find employment? What do you mean, I'm not "good looking"?

If you are the parent, friend, or relative of an actor, or you're anyone else outside the industry, you are more than likely lost in a haze of generalizations about the acting trade. Never fear—most actors are too. The impetus for writing this book came from my own parents and relatives, who would, at every Thanksgiving dinner, brag about my recent appearance on this soap opera or that television show. (The conversations about this always lasted far longer than my appearance on whatever show they were discussing.) Seeing a face on TV is exciting, and it pays well for a day's work. Yet I never managed to convince people that a day as a crime scene investigator on *Law & Order* did not a career make. I wasn't going to suddenly be discovered. I was not moving to a life of perpetual employment as a crime scene investigator on all the *Law & Order* spin-offs, or *Cold Case, CSI, CSI: Miami,* or *CSI: NY.* It just doesn't work that way.

Meanwhile, I was taking pride in the work I was doing in the downtown New York theater scene, working long into the night in chilly, converted school-houses on the Lower East Side. While I found this both romantic and artistically fulfilling, those who had to sit through performances, still wearing their winter coats, had another way of thinking about it.

"Soon," they said, "you'll get your break."

This gap in understanding about what it means to be an actor will have shrunk by the time you finish this book. Think of it as a handbook—a reference tool for the future months and years of auditions, callbacks, unions, shoots, per diems, scale rates, day player jobs, and, with any luck, residuals you will pocket. You will hear from working actors who have climbed and fallen and climbed again. They have been gracious enough to share their stories with me, and with you, in the greater hope of diffusing the fog that hovers over this business. There will be an equal amount of optimism and pessimism, because that's what life in this industry is like. Admittedly, this is a New York–centric guide. However, the rules of this maddening game can be applied to both coasts.

You will not find a formula for success within these pages. This book is not, like so many of the actors' guides out there, trying to sell the dream. It is not a dissection of the acting business that, when you've finished reading, will provide magical answers, a key to stardom or success, or a way to cash in quickly. It is a dose of realism in a hyperfantastic world—information for the admittedly uninformed. It's the book I wish someone had handed me when I started out in New York.

Because when you know what to expect in the acting world; when you are prepared for audition rooms and callbacks and working on a set and the agent interview; when you know which regional theaters are prestigious, which acting schools are valid; and when you have a community around you that also understands these things, then you'll have a head start on the game.

Then you'll have a fighting chance.

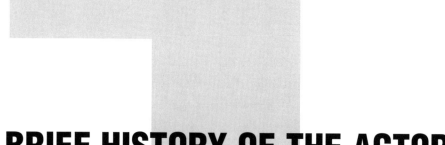

A BRIEF HISTORY OF THE ACTOR

(*or* How to Respond to the Statement, "I'm Doing a Restoration Comedy, Mom")

"I deny that I ever said actors are cattle. What I said was,
'Actors should be treated like cattle.'"
—Alfred Hitchcock

It's been an uphill battle for the actor for some time. Two thousand, five hundred and forty years, to be precise.

The general frustrations of the profession are nothing new. Financial strife, poor societal standing, endless travel to other regions, and the celebrity factor were not invented by griping unions, background players, and *People* magazine. The sordid history of the actor is one large pile of precedent, a warning for all who will follow: You want to live in the fringes society, be our guest—just don't expect us to care when the curtain goes down.

Ours is a lengthy history. We predate doctors and lawyers and science and Jesus. We have been banned, restored, outlawed, and revered. To appreciate this history, one must unveil the historical plight of the actor. As the saying goes, If you don't know where you're coming from, can you know where you're headed?

The development of the actor through history, and the consequent, complementary movements within the theater; from the theater into film; film into television; and, dare I say, television into reality television, is pertinent to understanding the place of the working actor in the world today. Where once the theatrical event was an act of worship performed for the gods, it has become an industry—a full-fledged business dedicated, in the commercial sector, to entertainment with a capital E!

The journey from the first Greek chorus to *A Chorus Line* is revealing as a roadmap for the profession. The permutations of the actor, from one part of an ensemble collective to individual star, are a trip worth taking. What follows in this chapter is the barest of bones, a Cliffs Notes of theatrical history. It is

534 BC First play contest held in Athens

knowledge that most actors have culled throughout their schooling, and that most lay audience members suffer without. Certainly, there are scholars who devote themselves to this kind of thing, so if you're truly interested in being able to carry out a four-course dinner party–length conversation, you're going to want to consult a better guide than what I've laid out here. But if you want to get a handle on why they're all talking at the same time in a Greek tragedy, but not in Ibsen; what trials actors have endured throughout history; and, as the title of this chapter suggests, why your child is unforgiving in expecting you to know about, and laugh during, a restoration comedy, then this chapter will give you a head start.

The Greeks: Fathers of It All

The Greeks set precedent for a tradition of art and commerce within the acting profession. They fathered the professional guidelines when it comes to matters of pay, practice, managing, and performing.

Greek performance served as both a form of worship to the gods and a way of addressing principal societal issues. The earliest Greek plays were character-less tragedies narrated by the *chorus*, a body of actors that spoke, sang, and moved as a whole unit. The chorus was nothing to shake a stick at: They underwent a nearly year-long training program and were held to exacting standards of diet and exercise as they practiced choreography, dancing, and singing. For years, the chorus was responsible for delivering the entire play, until one day, an actor named Thespis took on the role of a deity, and in doing so, became the first solo actor. This is why, when trying to be pretentious, we in the profession refer to an actor as a *thespian*.

The three major Greek playwrights are Aeschylus, Sophocles, and Euripides. They often retold the same stories their predecessors had tackled years earlier. As character development increased, the chorus adapted, often taking the role of a recognizable group that helped the audience place themselves within the play. In *Medea*, for example, the choral body is representative of the women of the town. Postmodern performance likes to play around with the chorus far more than any Grecian would have. Where contemporary theater might place three or four punk-rock chicks near Medea's home, the Greeks were far more likely to rely on a group of people all speaking in unison.

The evolution of character in Greek drama continued when Aeschylus introduced the second character, and thus, the concept of dialogue. Individuals

471BC Aeschylus introduces the second actor

were soon carrying on conversations with each other, rather than leaving the bulk of the work to the chorus. Later, Sophocles would introduce a third character, further rocking dramatic structure in the process. With this new influx of individual voices, plots began to take shape. Characters became more human, capable of individual emotional response in reaction to the gods.

Actors were paid decent wages during this period, and the state saw to it that they were not exploited by managers, a role handled today by the Screen Actors Guild. But we can thank the Greeks for another tenet of today's acting history: They are the original founders of type. Tragic actors and comic actors were sequestered from each other. They honed their performance skills for the material they performed, and judgments of their personal character landed steadfastly alongside such determinations. Tragic actors, i.e., those who performed in tragedies, attained positions at court and were often used as ambassadors for the state. A decree granted them safe passage:

> *Actors are to be given the security of person and property and exemption from arrest at the time of war. . . . They are allowed to travel in the line of duty between countries at war, and are exempt from military service.**

In this light, Sean Penn's prewar trip to Iraq actually has some precedence.

Comic actors, on the other hand, with their bawdy style and wild costumes, weren't even allowed to perform in the same festivals as tragedians until 486 BC, nearly fifty years after the festival of Dionysus began. Mimes . . . well, pity the poor mimes. They were relegated to performing on the street, the same way that today, well . . . mimes perform on the street. They were the kind of actors that other actors spat on, talked down to, and used to boost their own feelings about themselves as performers, the same way actors today, well . . . use mimes as the brunt of jokes. Today's equivalent to the mime would be something like, well . . . a mime. This begs the question, If a mime shoots another mime in an empty forest and there's no one around to hear it, does anybody care?

Right now, Marcel Marceau is poking an imaginary pin into an invisible voodoo doll that looks just like me.

---

* Mendel Kohansky, *The Disreputable Profession: The Actor in Society* (Westport, CT: Greenwood, 1984). Kohansky's research is cited throughout this chapter.

468 BC Sophocles introduces the third actor

Leaving the mime to his own silent fate, then (that was the last one, I swear), it should be noted that the division between comic and tragic actors has not faded into the sunset over the past three thousand years. An actor recently told me of a casting director who wouldn't see him for a sitcom because he didn't have enough comedy on his resume. He did, however, just finish playing Romeo at the Guthrie Theater in Minneapolis, one of the largest and most renowned regional theaters in the country. So, as you can see, much about the acting industry has changed since 486 BC.

Romans and Christians: A Very Brief History

There's a reason you haven't heard about the Roman theater: They didn't have much. Nor did they produce any truly memorable playwrights. A good death match with a lion was spectacle enough—tragedy and comedy all wrapped into one. Cicero was the Mark Burnett (renowned reality TV producer) of his time, using gladiators as protagonists, lumping real actors in with the sporting events. Suffice it to say, this conflation of all forms of entertainment didn't benefit the actor, and things began to go horribly wrong.

The actor's swift decline in status was soon put into law. Justinian code stated that "He who appears on the stage in order to act is marked with infamy." *Infamia*, in this case, being a legal term that stripped a person of particular civic and personal rights. Little rights, like living. While a Roman farmhand might be given twenty lashes for adultery, any man catching an actor in the act with his wife was allowed to kill him on the spot.

Religion and theater have always had a turbulent courtship. With the rise of Christianity, theater was parked under the religious tent. But Christian doctrine frowned upon spectacle, and further condemnation followed. Emperor Justinian II issued another ban on theater in 692 AD. There was nothing left for excommunicated performers but to pick up their wares and travel.

And so it is the Romans we have to thank for the advent of the regional theater. With animosity toward performers mounting, actors took to the provinces, packing up and forming touring troupes. Though outcasts in religious and legal doctrine, minstrels, jugglers, mimes, and acrobats enjoyed continued popularity with the nobility. They were the Paris Hiltons of their time: outlandish, verboten, and eminently entertaining.

And then . . . well, as far as the actor's development goes, not much. Until the Italians.

411BC Aristophanes' *Lysistrata* produced

The Italians, the French: Commedia dell'Arte and the Comédie-Française (Women Start Reading Here)

The proud tradition of male-only performance was dealt a stunning blow in 1545 when women began performing in the theater. "These Italians," Harold Pinter wrote in *Betrayal*, "so free and easy." In the mid-sixteenth century, traveling troupes of improvisational comic storytellers roamed the highways and street fairs of Italy. Called the Commedia dell'Arte, this form of improvisational comedy plotted around loose storylines was revolutionary. Comedy had never seen such unpracticed success.

The shows included a cast of stock characters: archetypes upon which many of today's comic characters are built. Pantalone, the bitter, rich miser, Zanni, the clown, and the Innamorati, or lovers, wrestled along plot lines consisting of such elements as lovers separated by a mean, slightly lecherous father; clowns who screwed things up and then came to the rescue; and doctors who knew little of medical practice other than the enema, and who practiced in full disregard of the Hippocratic oath. In the Commedia dell'Arte, broad farce was encouraged.

The Commedia would greatly influence comedic styles in both England and France in the coming centuries. Molière and his troupe, which would eventually work under the nom de plume of the Comédie-Française, mined much of their material from the Commedia players. In plays drawn from the same characterizations, mishaps and base immorality were, this time, fully scripted by the playwright. These two pylons of theater history are joined by another commonality: their commitment and reliance on an ensemble company of actors. In a little-known one-act play called *The Versailles Impromptu*, Molière casts his actors as themselves, and for forty-some minutes they argue over what type of show they are going to put together for the king in order to win a contract for continued performance. It is evident that in the time since, and most likely the time before, nothing has changed: The leading ladies are still cheating on their husbands, the leading man is still complaining about not having enough lines, and the playwright is still doing rewrites up until curtain.

The theater revolved around troupes and companies well into the middle of the twentieth century. These collectives of actors worked together time after time, learning each other's rhythms and styles, strengths and weaknesses. Certainly, they were on to something that the American theater neglects today, as few professional acting companies remain, even in the regional repertory.

1548 Molière's company opens • **1576** James Burbage builds his theater

The Brits: Renaissance, Shakespeare, and Restoration

During the English Renaissance, actors were brought out of the gutter to a position of vague repute. Public theaters, however, were still classed alongside such popular amusements as bear baiting. Theaters attracted audiences from all walks of life, among them soldiers and sailors on leave and in search of entertainment. Higher-priced balcony seats were filled by students and intellectuals, while the plebes occupied the standing-room area on the floor. They soon became known as groundlings, and actors had to fight, literally at times, to keep their attention. Industry cropped up around the theater—namely prostitution and larceny. Theaters were not allowed inside city limits. Most companies traveled, leading to the coining of one of the more apt phrases on the acting profession: "Take down the wash, the actors are coming."

Try as it might, the theater's association with moral turpitude continued. Actors whose companies might be performing before the court one day would be back dodging tomatoes the next. It's nothing like performing in an episode of *Law & Order* one day and returning to an Off-Off-Broadway show or temp job the next. So much has changed since the mid-sixteenth century.

By 1572, an act of Parliament required licensing of companies and plays. In 1576, the great Shakespearean actor James Burbage, perhaps the first true celebrity actor, built the first permanent theater in London. Producers, actors, and playwrights became shareholders in this and other companies. Actors in the Elizabethan period made about sixty pounds a year, twice as much as a schoolmaster. Shareholders could be expected to bring in about 150 pounds a year. Shakespeare, as an actor, playwright, and shareholder, cleared two to six hundred pounds a year.

All was trooping along well until 1642. Parliament, succumbing to pressure from the Puritans, enacted a law banning theater. Calling performances "spectacles of pleasure, too commonly expressing lascivious mirth and levity," it declared its participants "rogues, and punishable."

First the Romans, now the English. Actors can't catch a break.

It took eighteen years, but upon Charles II's ascension to the throne, the ban on theater was lifted, restoring it to a rightful place as entertainment in a somewhat civilized society. And so the bawdy, lewd, comic-oriented period of theater known as the Restoration began. It was a welcome return. For the first time, women graced the English stage in great numbers. The sexually and otherwise repressed society, now free from Puritan rule, took a cue from the French and began having some fun. The period produced some notable comedies, including Congreve's *The Way of the World* and Wycherley's *The Country Wife*.

With material paving the way for great comic performances, focus in the theater began to shift from the play to the actor. The first female star of the stage, Nell Gwynn, was, somewhat ironically, born in a brothel. She began as an orange girl in a theater and was eventually spotted by producers and given a small role in a production. A crowd favorite, she worked her way up to lead roles, eventually performing in her greatest real-life triumph as Charles II's mistress. What Nell apparently knew then, as the world of public relations teaches us today, is that a little relationship status never hurt anyone's career.

The Nineteenth Century: From Melodrama to Modern Drama

The nineteenth century fully cemented the actor's status as reigning celebrity of the day. For the first fifty years, no memorable plays were produced and no great writers emerged in the theater. Great actors, however, did. Edmund Kean, described by the critic George Henry Lewes as possessing "lionlike power and lionlike grace," was known as the greatest Shakespearean actor of his time.

America, that jealous stepsister, fostered no exception to the celebrity status afforded to actors. A theatrical community that had begun with the simple pleasures of vaudeville was soon importing English actors to star in plays. Theatergoers certainly took their stars seriously, as became evident in New York City one April afternoon. American actor Edmund Forrest and English actor William Macready were both scheduled to play Macbeth that night, Forrest at the Bowery Theatre and Macready at the Astor Place Opera House. A lingering dispute between the two only fueled the fire—Forrest had, in observing Macready's interpretation of Hamlet in London, hissed at him mid-performance from his seat in the balcony. Anti-English sentiment only incited matters further (this is now monitored by Actors' Equity, which negotiates with British Equity for transatlantic actor crossings). Crowds began to gather in protest outside the Astor Place Opera House and fighting ensued to a point where the army was summoned. When the smoke cleared, thirty-one were dead.

It was a striking event, considering Americans' dispassion for the theater on the whole today, and perhaps the only time Americans took their theater seriously.

Plays were, as the Astor Place riots illustrate, star-driven vehicles. Lead actors were paid far more than anyone else in the cast and were also, in essence, the directors of the shows in which they performed. At this time in theater history, no position of director existed. The autonomy given leading men is evident in one of Macready's diary entries, where he writes, sans irony, "The actors were very attentive and behaved very well."

There were only eight or nine rehearsals per production, and shows ran in a rotating repertory, much the way the Russian theater continues to operate today. The reason for this was primarily financial. A leading actor was prepared to perform in ten shows at a time, in order to accommodate lesser numbers of audience members. The crowds might have been thin, but they were loyal when it came to following their stars.

The way in which roles were acted was also quite different from what we consider acting to be today. Traditional training emphasized the passions—remorse, grief, jealousy—and stereotyping as appropriate approaches for playing a role. Actors referred to playing such types as the *lines of business*, breaking characters down into such roles as hero and heroine, villain, old man and good man. It was rare, as it continues to be to this day, that an actor would cross from one *line of business* to another.

In Europe in the latter half of the nineteenth century, the era of the actor was shifting to the era of the playwright. It began with Heinrich Ibsen, who is, as it was pounded into my head in high school, the father of modern drama.

Ibsen was the first of his generation to begin writing realistic plays. His debut, *Catalina*, appeared in 1850, and was followed by some of the more profound and recognized modern drama even to this day. He introduced the female (and pre-feminist) heroine to the stage in *A Doll's House*, roiling Scandinavia in the process. August Strindberg, Ibsen's Swedish rival, was working in a similar vein in *Miss Julie*, the tale of an aristocrat who seduces her father's valet.

In England, Oscar Wilde carried forward the tradition of the restoration comedy into more contemporary time. George Bernard Shaw, a critic turned playwright, began writing in the latter nineteenth century as well. Shaw was rather contemptuous in his ideas of actors, feeling on the whole that they were given far too much credit for the roles they played, with audiences unduly attributing the life of the play to the imagination of the actor.

From the late nineteenth into the early twentieth century, these writers produced new plays, challenging and transforming the presentational aesthetic that

1777 Sheridan's Restoration comedy *School for Scandal* produced

ruled the stage with more naturalistic plots and characters. Yet while some of the greatest realism in the history of the theater was being written, it is likely that it wasn't being performed as such. That is, until the Russians came along.

From Stanislavski to Brando

In the East, a remarkable development was underway.

Two men, Constantine Stanislavski and Vladimir Nemirovich-Danchenko, sat down one day over coffee at the Slavic Bazaar in Moscow. An artist and a theater manager, respectively, their intentions were as bold as the Bolsheviks'. They intended a revolution in the theater. They sat, brandishing ideas for a new company, finally creating a manifesto that would stand as the central dictum for the Moscow Art Theatre. If there is any one institution that can be named as the primary influence on the actors and acting we see today, this is the one.

The Russian Manifesto

At their meeting at the Slavic Bazaar, Stanislavski and Nemirovich-Danchenko came up with a manifesto for their new theater. In addition to one of the most famous lines ever written, "There are no small parts, only small actors," were the following:

- Today Hamlet, tomorrow an extra, but even an extra must be an artist.

- The playwright, the actor, the scenic designer, the dresser, and the stagehand all serve one purpose: to express the playwright's main idea.

- The theater begins with the cloakroom.

- Every violation of the creative life of the theater is a crime.

- Arriving late at the theater, laziness, capriciousness, hysteria, ignorance of parts, and repeating the same thing twice are all equally harmful and must be rooted out.*

The first studio of the Moscow Art Theatre was inaugurated in 1897. It consisted of a company of actors, a playwright, several directors, and a lot of ego.

*Adrian Cairns, *The Making of the Professional Actor: A2 History, an Analysis and a Prediction* (London: Peter Owen, 1996).

1814 Edmund Kean makes his London debut • **1879** Ibsen's *A Doll's House* produced

Together, they worked in a theater a stone's throw from the Kremlin. Anton Chekhov, a trained doctor turned writer, wrote plays for the company. He examined the intricacies and pain of Russian provincial life in ironic, subtle comedies. In *The Seagull, Three Sisters*, and *The Cherry Orchard*, to name a few, he demanded a realism not yet seen on the stage. In a true case of chicken or egg, one could even argue that, as a writer writing for a company of actors all undergoing the same training, he was writing plays for the Stanislavski system.

The system Stanislavski invented was a method of acting that relied on the tenets of emotional truth, physical action, and the importance of ensemble. As he and Nemirovich-Danchenko had laid out when founding the theater, there were to be no small parts, only small actors. The cast was more important than any individual within the cast: It was a system without stars. Years later, one actress in the company recalled how an actor's refusal to play in a crowd scene caused him to be fired from the show and banned from the company for four years.* Stanislavski utilized observation and sense memory and made terms like *intention, superobjective,* and *obstacle* the central tenets of acting. He believed that life on the stage must be just that. His ideas revolutionized a profession that was accustomed to a more presentational and affected style of performance: Stand facing the audience, use a booming voice, and hit your consonants. Stanislavski proposed something altogether different: Truth.

Were it not for a trip to America in 1923, when the Moscow Art Theatre toured the country, the system might never have crossed the Soviet borders and we might never have had a Marlon Brando, James Dean, or Jessica Tandy. As the actors of the Moscow Art Theatre performed across the United States, Americans grew aware that they were witnessing something extraordinary. The Russians became darlings of the tabloids and gossip pages. After a performance of *Uncle Vanya,* the *Chicago Daily Tribune* wrote that they had seen "acting better than may be seen elsewhere in all the world."

And the Beat Goes On

An anecdote about something called the "beat" has floated around the theater community for years. The "beat," in acting terms, is a descriptor of a malleable unit of time. It can be a moment ("that beat isn't working"), a few seconds ("wait a beat before saying that"), or a whole section of a scene (to divide a scene into beats).

* Ibid

As the story goes, Stanislavski was speaking to an American audience about his acting method. He kept referring in English to "bits" of the scene, as in "This *bit* with the seagull should be funnier," and "Wait a *bit* before saying that." Stanislavski was, of course, speaking in a thick Russian accent, and as his audience heard him refer to bits over and over again, with the short I pronounced as a long E, they thought they had grasped a radical new concept: the "beat."

Theater professionals and teachers flocked to the Moscow Art Theatre shows like Freudians to a hysteria convention. Among them were Lee Strasberg and Stella Adler, two of the most famous American acting teachers in history. When the tour ended, several members of the Moscow Art company remained in the states as defectors, and began teaching acting. Strasberg and Adler began studying with de facto (and defecting) members of the Moscow Art Theatre. Each eventually went out on his or her own, using Stanislavski's method as a base for training.

Strasberg began teaching his own interpretation of the Stanislavski method. It relied heavily on the emotional elements of the training. Accounts of Strasberg's misinterpretation of the Stanislavski system vary. Adler herself noted Strasberg's "excessive use of affective memory exercises"* after she spent time in Paris studying with Stanislavski in his later years. Stanislavski wasn't finished tooling with his method and, upon his return to Russia, he continued to develop his acting technique, never fully refining it until the mid 1940s. Sadly, and falsely, Stanislavski's method and The Method are commonly confused with each other. In fact, they differ immensely.

The notion of ensemble did, however, lead Strasberg to join with Harold Clurman and Cheryl Crawford to found the Group Theatre, a company of actors that carried the Russian acting revolution forward into the American theater. Pursuing this naturalistic style of acting, the Group began producing their own plays. A young actor in the company, Clifford Odets, began writing for them, and his *Awake and Sing* heralded the company's arrival as a major force in the American theater. Though short-lived, the Group Theatre and its members—Stella Adler and Sanford Meisner, among others—would fan out

* Ibid.

upon their departure and teach an entire generation of actors. Their roll call reads like a best-actor nomination at the Oscars: Pacino, Brando, Newman, and Streep all studied with former Group members.

These actors soon brought an entirely new way of performing to Broadway. Gone was the presentational style that ruled the day. There was now a new form of acting taking place, far closer to the performance style we know of as "American acting" today. Actors were sweating in the Southern heat of Tennessee Williams dramas, swirling whiskey to the melodramatic chords of Eugene O'Neill. Most everything the Russians had shown was beginning to stick. And Hollywood took note.

Brando and the Chicken

There's an acting class tale that, in its various incarnations, exemplifies the quality of the naturalistic style of acting that was taking form in America in the fifties. Details vary from version to version, but the one I know goes like this:

One day, Stella Adler led an acting class where she would call out a character and a situation and all the students in the class would impulsively react. (This is actually a well-known acting game.) In one moment, she instructed everyone in the class to become a chicken at the barnyard, and the flock of students began clucking and pecking their way around the room. Then she told her breed, "There's a nuclear bomb heading straight toward you."

The room erupted into an abandon of poultry madness. Chickens running every which way, screaming with fear. All of them, that is, except one young student, who sat patiently on his egg, as he had been doing the whole class.

Adler ended the exercise and then asked the young man why, when everyone else went mad, he had remained on his egg.

"Because I'm a chicken," the young Marlon Brando replied. "What does a chicken know about nuclear bombs."

The Film Age

We are now fully in the age of the film actor, and it has affected every part of the American acting experience, from style to economics. Stylistically, the

1932 Clurman, Crawford, and Strasberg found the Group Theatre

latter half of the twentieth century, and the dawn of the twenty-first, have embraced the naturalism of O'Neill and Williams. The movies have become America's greatest export, and have become the end goal for actors in search of careers. Film and television provide a bounty of wealth, both economically and in terms of prestige, beyond that of the theater.

Great living playwrights struggle to get productions mounted against the backdrop of Disney and a new wave of jukebox musicals, where books are written to accommodate the catalogue of the Beach Boys *(Good Vibrations)* or Elvis *(All Shook Up)*. Film and television have placed an unfair burden of expectation on the theater while outbidding it in search of talent. Rather than carving out an individual, and independent, niche, the theater has attempted to compete with the movies. Budgets rise for special-effects-laden shows. Thankfully, there are still critics and avid theatergoers who exalt plays that are mounted with two actors and a sofa, such as Caryl Churchill's recent coup, *A Number*. It is, after all, imagination that drives our work.

Ever since Andy Warhol's proclamation about the universal fifteen minutes of fame, everyone thinks he is an actor, or at least that he can make a television appearance. Personalities sell ad space better than good acting does, and so reality television has taken up timeslots once devoted to half-hour comedies and hour dramas. Less work for the actor, more airtime for anyone willing to endure life on a reality show.

Yet with hundreds of films in production, new media flourishing, and advertisers hiring actors for commercials in record numbers, one might say that things for the actor have never been better. Laundry isn't hidden upon our arrival; gone are the days of infamia. But then a closer look reveals some cracks in the system. Where are our most prolific modern playwrights? Have they all gone the way of the screenwriter? Meanwhile, who is willing to take a risk on the many untested voices, and the actors who bring these voices to life in workshops that are never given full productions? For the working actor, especially the New York actor—with an increase in celebrity casting in the theater, an overstocked lineup of reality television, and a film industry looking for names to get financing—where is the work? How far from touring Commedia troupes and traveling bands of Elizabethan players are we? Perhaps more importantly, how far do we want to be?

1947 Tennessee Williams's *A Streetcar Named Desire* produced

It is here that we begin, early in the twenty-first century. Our protagonist, the young actor, U-Haul freshly unpacked into a cozy (tiny) two-bedroom (converted one-bedroom) apartment somewhere in Queens (nine stops in on the 7 train), has begun a new expedition. There's an acting career about to begin; a buzz of excitement as auditions and agents and jobs await. And so our man, or woman, sits down on the futon couch doubling as a bed, a stack of monologue books piled high, and this week's *Backstage* waiting to be circled in red pen. What will the future hold?

The history of the actor is about to march forward. And so we begin.

1953 Beckett's *Waiting for Godot* produced

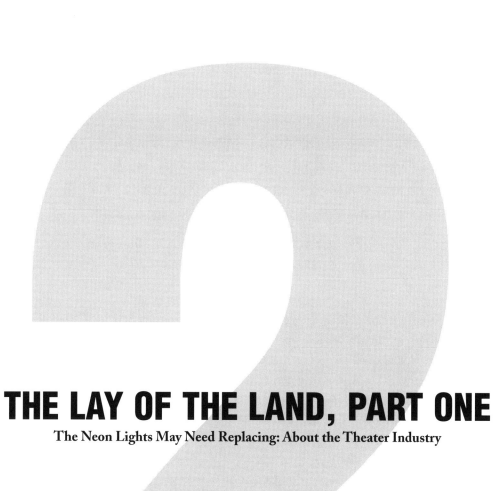

THE LAY OF THE LAND, PART ONE

The Neon Lights May Need Replacing: About the Theater Industry

"With the exception of a few minor film appearances, Mr. Combs, 34, has had no real experience as an actor. But he has willingly embraced a situation that many people have experienced only as a terrifying nightmare: appearing on a Broadway stage with very little preparation. Learning in a few months what others take years to study and master—and doing so for such a large role in a major revival— has, he says, been the most difficult challenge of his life."

—From *the New York Times'* review of Sean (Diddy) Combs's Broadway debut in *A Raisin in the Sun*.

It's December. You're home for the holidays at your parents' Christmas party. People mingle, drink eggnog. When they ask, or even if they don't, your mother is fond of telling guests that her child is an actor. They shudder, gasp, or make waiter jokes. Later, they corner you to get you talking about acting. The conversation probably goes something like this:

"So your mother tells me you're an actor."

"That's right," you respond.

"Oooh. What kind?"

My disdain for this question cannot be measured. I have been asked it on countless occasions and have yet to understand what it means.

There is a general misperception in the world that actors have the choice of specifying fields. Only actors with network offers, soap contracts, and movie deals have this luxury. "What kind?" asks whether you do theater, film, or television, implying that you have some input in the matter. Chances are that though you are trying to do all three, you have yet to do more than a smattering of work in any. Entering the acting profession is a little different from entering the legal profession. Where you come out of law school specializing in corporate law, you don't come out of acting school specializing in soap operas. That is, if you came out of school at all. You really don't get to specialize until you've hit a certain mark of success—and the vast majority of actors will take any job that comes their way. Call it "selling out" if you want—it's the truth.

The other problem is that there are so many different styles, venues, and subdivisions within theater, film, and television that there is no easy answer to the question, "What kind of actor are you?"

Most actors begin on stage. It may be a high school stage or a summer camp stage or the black-box stage of an acting class, but they are treading the boards nonetheless. The stage and the theater are where tradition lie. Historically speaking, film and television are baby siblings in the acting world. Granted, they grabbed the bulk of the inheritance money, but they remain newer forms. The tradition of acting, its schools and teachers, hail predominantly from the theater.

New York is the epicenter of the theater world, the tributary from which all shows flow. So let's map it out. Within New York there are three geographically titled divisions of the theater world: Broadway, Off-Broadway, and Off-Off-Broadway.

Broadway

Millions are invested, made, and more often than not, lost on Broadway shows. There is a small network of producers who control the productions, the theaters, or both: the Shuberts, the Nederlanders, and the Jujamcyn organizations are the major players. Contractually, Broadway is defined as "an area bounded by Fifth and Ninth Avenues from 34th Street to 56th Street and by Fifth Avenue and the Hudson River from 56th Street to 72nd Street . . . (or a) theatre having a capacity of more than 499 seats . . . unless Equity otherwise consents in writing."

Actors who appear in Broadway shows are employed under the League Production Contract. The language in the contract talks of real estate and seats for sale, so Broadway as a venue really boils down to money. The more a theater can seat, the better its venue, and the more tickets available to sell, the more the producers can afford to pay the actors—or so the logic goes. Very few shows perform on the Great White Way itself; most are on side streets. There are rows and rows of theaters, many aging and in need of renovation.

Broadway is a tourist industry. Fifty-five percent of all Broadway theatergoers are tourists, while only 18 percent of all audiences are New York City residents. It caters to the out-of-towner. The taste buds of the tourist are presumed to yearn for a fluffier style of theater—and so in past years we've been treated to such gems as *Mamma Mia!* and the overall Disneyfication of Broadway. It's not all bad. *The Lion King* was an artistic achievement. Julie Taymor, a longtime "downtown artist," was given a blank check and the artistic license to do something phenomenal—and she did. But *Beauty and the Beast* did not, nor did *Aida*, which the *New York Times* called "the new Disney cartoon pretending to be a Broadway musical." These shows have now become commercial props, shuffling casts in and out and, though selling at a decent rate, creating a rather stagnant atmosphere on Broadway.

For the most part, Broadway now steers completely clear of new writers. If a new play appears on Broadway, either its writer has met with great commercial success and validation in the past, or the play has transferred from a successful run somewhere else, most likely Off-Broadway. Broadway suffers from a serious drought of new plays because of the financial risk in mounting a show. The new play is to Broadway what the independent film is to movies—a risky, artistic investment. As a result, new writers are having a harder time being discovered—and many are going to write for film and television. Even an established playwright like Arthur Miller had difficulty getting new work produced on Broadway. His new plays always premiered in London.

New musicals are done far more often than new plays on Broadway, and they have usually previewed out of town before coming to New York. A show is often mounted in Washington, D.C., or San Diego before reaching Broadway. This is known as a tryout. Tryouts give everyone involved the chance to gauge audience reaction before the big money is at stake. In past years, several shows on the road to Broadway died during this process. *Bounce*, a new Sondheim musical, went no further than Washington, D.C., and *Children of a Lesser God*, to have starred Hilary Swank (Oscar winner for *Boys Don't Cry* and *Million Dollar Baby*) collapsed as well.

So if there are few new plays on Broadway, what plays are there? Revivals. Revivals do exactly what their name suggests—bring the dead back to life (which is true of some audience members as well). Plays that have proven to do well in the past are remounted with celebrity casts. We see a lot more Williams and O'Neill today than audiences did in their time. Why? The writing's been validated, the stars will attract audiences, and money will be made. They hope.

Off-Broadway

In a reaction to many of the inherent problems with Broadway, a move away from Broadway began to take shape in the late sixties. Many of today's celebrities—Pacino, Hackman, and Duvall—got their start performing in such shows. Off-Broadway is still, though increasingly to a lesser extent, the place where up-and-coming and established playwrights find their audiences. The theaters are smaller, as is the profit margin. Many of the straight plays that end up on Broadway originate in Off-Broadway theaters. Only once they have proved that they can gather a crowd do they make the transfer to a Broadway house.

Actors' Equity Association Off-Broadway Agreement

The agreement covers:

Productions presented in the borough of Manhattan unless Equity otherwise consents in writing, but may not be used in any theatre located in an area bounded by Fifth and Ninth Avenues from 34th Street to 56th Street and by Fifth Avenue and the Hudson River from 56th Street to 72nd Street, nor may it be used in any theatre having a capacity of more than 499. It is agreed that the Off-Broadway contract is not applicable where the primary intent is the development of a play or musical through the collaborative authorship of the Playwright and/or Director, and the Actors.

Off-Broadway theaters are a mix of for-profit and not-for-profit venues, and this is an important distinction to understand. Shows such as *Stomp, Blue Man Group*, and *De La Guarda* have been enjoying successful multiyear commercial runs Off-Broadway. Commercial Off-Broadway differs in both tone of production and the contract under which performers are paid. Producers of commercial Off-Broadway shows are trying to make money. Nonprofit Off-Broadway shows are generally put on by theater companies or by venues devoted to producing work not for the purposes of making money, but for the overall progression of the theater as an art form. Nonprofit theaters, some of them very prestigious (the Public, the Signature Theatre Company, Playwrights Horizons, and MCC among them), pay actors far less than commercial contracts (such venues as Dodger Stages, the Daryl Roth, and Union Square Theatre). As an audience member, you would be hard-pressed to tell the difference in quality between the two.

Off-Broadway is an ever-expanding landscape. Whereas the term once referred to a literal geographical area, it now reaches as far downtown as the Village and as high as Harlem. More than anything, it is newspapers and magazines that determine whether a show is given an Off-Broadway listing, as opposed to its uglier stepsister, Off-Off-Broadway. Being dubbed an Off-Broadway show will increase the likelihood of press attending, thereby giving shows a better shot at garnering an audience.

Because the move away from Broadway's inherent commercialism dictated the delineation of an Off-Broadway landscape, it is the foremost breeding ground for new plays. There are established companies that have become renowned for producing and importing new and important work. Many of these companies run development programs as well, and have thus negotiated different contracts with Equity to allow their work to continue. Red ink is commonplace, but the work is often brilliant. Broadway hits such as *Proof* and the musical *Rent* began in not-for-profit Off-Broadway theaters.

Though Off-Broadway began as an artistic proving ground, its finest products were eventually capitalized on by Broadway producers; thus, the entire world of Off-Broadway theater now harbors a recessed thought of a Broadway transfer in the corner of its collective mind. While Off-Broadway was once a place where actors could get their footing and collaborate with playwrights, the price of real estate and commercial producing interests have made an experimental playground more of a professional sports stadium. An older actor told me he didn't know how young people were able to get started in this business now without serious financial support. When he was my age, he said, you could find a place to live in New York for about forty dollars a week, and support yourself by bartending. Plus, you didn't need to have an agent to audition for Off-Broadway shows. Now, because Broadway has become a musical- and star-driven place, great actors are turning to work Off-Broadway at an alarming rate. Increasingly, offers are being made to celebrities for these shows as well. This amounts to fewer chances for the struggling actor to find paying work in New York City.

Off-Off-Broadway

Which is why Off-Off-Broadway has blossomed—artistically more than economically—in recent years. It is partly what Off-Broadway once was: a safe harbor for new artists, mixed with a mishmash of anyone and everyone trying to do a play to get noticed. It's a safe bet that for Off-Off-Broadway, the actors are not getting paid. Because New York is a cultural mecca, there is no shortage of work being performed downtown.

Downtown theater is another term for Off-Off-Broadway, as most of the venues are located there. Following the lead of the sixties avant-garde movement, theater companies took over storefronts across the Lower East Side and turned them into black-box theaters, lit by clip lights from the corner hardware store. In the late nineties, several downtown artistic directors fashioned the First

New York International Fringe Festival. Modeled on the famed theater festivals of Edinburgh and Avignon, New York was past due for such an event. The festival has now moved from the fringes of the public consciousness to full-page-featureland in the *New York Times*.

The Fringe and the Off-Off-Broadway scenes have produced some commercial successes. Occasionally a show will move from one of these venues to an Off-Broadway or Broadway house. *Urinetown*, now closed on Broadway but touring, originated in the Fringe Festival.

Looking at this literally—one out of hundreds of Fringe Festival shows made it to Broadway—helps debunk one myth of New York theater success and rationale: The show in that little space with no heat and forty seats filled by twelve audience members will transfer and make you a big star.

Rarely.

The Regional Theater

Because New York is the epicenter of theatrical performance, it has become the epicenter for all theatrical casting as well. Every major regional theater in the country casts out of New York City. This means that actors performing in Houston, Chicago, and Minneapolis are living in a strange room in a strange town, performing eight shows a week and probably eating a lot of takeout. They just met the people they are working with a month ago, and may never see them again once the show closes. Their friends, family, spouses, or girlfriends are all back in New York.

As a rule, the regional circuit pays actors very well. Yet the contracts are often short (two to three months). There are several tiers of contract: LORT A through D. LORT stands for League of Resident Theatres. On top of this, housing is provided, so overhead while away is mainly food and bar costs. Most actors will sublet their apartment or room in New York when they get a regional job.

LORT rankings are determined by the box office of a theater over its past three seasons. Actors are paid as follows:

AEA LORT Agreement

LORT A:	$800 per week	LORT C:	$650 per week
LORT B+	$754 per week	LORT D:	$531 per week
LORT B:	$700 per week		

Working regionally has benefits and drawbacks. Though the actor out of town on a gig is making money, no one in the New York industry is going to see their performance. Staying in New York is important because you can, truth be told, consistently remind people of your existence. In a flooded market, presence counts.

Major Regional Theaters You Should Know and Be Happy to Work At

Chicago: Steppenwolf, Goodman

California: Old Globe, La Jolla, Cal Shakes, American Conservatory Theater

Connecticut: Yale Rep, Long Wharf

Kentucky: Actors Theatre of Louisville (and the Humana Festival of New American Plays)

Los Angeles: Mark Taper Forum

Maine: Portland Stage

Massachusetts: American Repertory Theatre, Huntington Theatre Company, Williamstown Theatre Festival

Minneapolis: Guthrie

New Jersey: McCarter

Ohio: Cincinnati Rep

Oregon: Portland Stage

Rhode Island: Trinity Rep

Seattle: Intiman, Seattle Rep

Texas: Alley, Dallas Theater Center

Washington, D.C.: Shakespeare Theatre, Arena Stage, Studio
Theatre

But here's the flip side. Young actors must build resume credits, and this usually occurs out of town. The roles offered are usually much richer—you could play Romeo in St. Louis, whereas you never would in New York, because Jake Gyllenhaal would be offered the role. Indeed, with more and more stars being offered, and taking, theater jobs in New York, many veteran theater actors are being forced back onto the regional circuit, making the competition for these jobs even fiercer.

Understanding the regional world is a great way to begin to understand the way in which this industry makes no sense at all. There are very talented actors living in all of the major regional cities. Yet the practice of casting means that you must move to New York to get a job in Cleveland. This practice has built up over time. The acting business is about as amenable to change as the U.S. Postal System.

This also means that an actor is constantly competing against the best in the business on a national scale. Here's a substantial difference from almost any other industry. Your son or daughter, when he or she gets that job in Dallas, has gone up against thousands of actors for that one role. There really is no comparison for this kind of competition, except in the sports world. There, when you make it, you get a lot more money and a much longer contract.

An actor who does regional theater must be willing to move and travel on short notice. In other professions, this is thought of as a big career adjustment. In acting, it's a common part of the business. It's also why there comes a time in most actors' careers when they begin to rule out regional work altogether. Separation from loved ones is one reason, but there is also a stigma that some agents and casting directors put on the regional scene, as if the work being done is less professional or less worthy. Being typed by a casting director as a "regional theater actor" could be a career death sentence.

The Touring Landscape

The last subdivision of the theater, touring, is different from regional theater in every way save the out-of-town part. A tour brings a show that has had success on Broadway to the rest of the country. You know how you read that *Les Miz* was a huge hit in New York, and now it's coming to Boston? That's a tour, and I've got some bad news for you. There are probably no actors from the original Broadway cast in the show you are going to see. Everyone has been hired expressly for this touring production. They move from city to city, sleeping in hotels for a year, getting paid very well but moving like traveling salesmen. It is grueling work.

Not only are the actors not the same, but the director is most likely a stage manager or assistant director who has been hired to plug actors into the staging and choreography the real director crafted with his original cast. It's cookie-cutter theater.

Increasingly, producers are weaseling around the unions and using non-union actors and stage managers on these tours. Actors' Equity Association would have you believe that there are no talented actors out there who are not in the union. I wouldn't go this far. However, the union does validate a certain amount of professional experience. You have to work to get into the union, and once you are union, you can only take union jobs. Because the majority of reputable theaters work under union contracts, union actors are presumably more professional. The main problem is that producers are union-busting and presenting shows under the guise of Broadway. A successful Broadway show will always tour to make money. But basically, a Xerox copy of the Tony Award winner is being shipped out to the rest of the country.

The Unions

Yes. We have unions. Three of them.

The proud ranks of Actors' Equity Association (AEA), the Screen Actors Guild (SAG), and the American Federation of Television and Radio Artists (AFTRA) number well into the hundreds of thousands. Of course, there is much overlap within that figure. Most actors are members of more than one union, each of which controls a different domain of this business. There are basic rules and constructs that the unions regulate, and regulate well, but I must say, we're a long way from protected. We need the unions, don't get me wrong, but what we need even more are unions that don't operate as if it were still 1973—unions that get their demands met.

AEA is the professional association for the theater, and covers what it can within the theater all across the country. SAG is a film and television union, covering all scripted programming in film and television, with some exceptions. AFTRA covers these exceptions, which include soap operas and a few half-hour comedies (a SAG representative explained that this had to do with an obscure agreement about studio involvement in shooting), as well as radio and newscasts. *American Idol*, for example, falls under AFTRA's jurisdiction because it is unscripted.

Strange? Yes, especially considering that as an actor in NYC, you're going to work under all three unions' jurisdictions in order to eke out a living. Which means you're paying membership dues to three separate unions to pursue one career. And where the carpenter and the plumber and the electrician each have their own union protecting them as they toil in their separate tasks while building a house, the actor is some weird combination of all three. If the metaphor follows, you are a homebuilder, doing the carpentry, plumbing, and electric wiring on your own. It's an asinine proposition, and it would never work out in any other industry, yet it's a way of life in ours. There is no one actors' union. Even though what you're doing on the stage, on video, and in front of the Panavision camera is all the same thing—acting—you need three unions to take care of you. And within this morass lies my basic frustration with the unions.

Here's what they do . . .

- Provide health insurance for members who qualify
- Negotiate minimum rates for contracts
- Organize strikes when necessary

. . . but not very well.

See, it's great that they're there, but you need to make about $10,000 under the separate auspices of SAG and AFTRA to qualify for insurance, or work twenty weeks under Equity to qualify for a year's coverage (twelve weeks gets you six months). Meaning you could be a working actor for a year, make $25,000, and still have no health insurance because you made $8,000 under SAG, $9,000 under AFTRA, and $8,000 under Equity, but only worked ten weeks. It's highly possible.

Getting a union card is an equally difficult task. One must work under the union's jurisdiction to get in the union, but one must be union to work in the jurisdiction. Impossible, right? Except that because this is a business based mainly upon taste, there is a little provision in the law that allows one to get hired without a union card.

The Taft-Hartley Act made it illegal, in essence, to discriminate against union and nonunion members alike, and thus allows for a non-union person to work under union jurisdiction if he meets a requirement that cannot be filled by another member of the union. Needing a brunette instead of a blonde is probably not what Congress had in mind when they dreamt up this little provision, but it's the one that means you can get your union card. It also means that because the producer's taste is protected by law, being a union member doesn't really get you anywhere in the casting world that being a non-union member doesn't.

People harp on union membership all the time, but I have never heard of an actor losing a job because she was non-union. It's a simple piece of paper that needs to be filed. It's also incredibly expensive, well over $1,000 up front to join either SAG or AFTRA, and nearing that with AEA. So don't sweat getting into the unions until you need to. No agent will turn you down for not being in the union, nor will *Law & Order*. Once you do work under the union's jurisdiction, however, you are required to join in order to work again. This one they hold you to. And that's how you get your card.

All union members are not created equal. When SAG went on strike in 2000 to get a better commercial contract, its membership was barred, by union law, from working on commercials. Yet somehow, Liz Hurley went ahead and finished up her Estée Lauder campaign. While we little SAG actors were threatened with being banned from the union for life if we worked without a contract, or even auditioned, Liz Hurley only ended up with a fine of $500,000. More than I could pay, for sure, but not more than she made on the campaign deal, I'd venture to guess. With the union only being as strong as its membership, and some of its membership's highest-profile members not obeying union rules, well, how seriously can one take the unions?

Union Yes!

Have I been too hard on the union? Here's a little pro-labor history timeline of AEA.

- 1913—112 New York actors found Actors Equity Association to collectively bargain with theater owners, producers, and bookers. The original proposed contract included seven points addressing issues of pay, firing notice, and reimbursement for costumes. At the time, actors were paid only for performances, not rehearsals, paid for their own transportation (out of town), had no legal recourse if a producer skipped town with the receipts, could be fired without notice, and worked for half pay during holiday weeks.

- 1919—AEA receives its charter from the American Federation of Labor, as in AFL-CIO. Actors aren't exactly who you think of when that endorsement comes out in political seasons.

- 1924—AEA shuts down seven theaters for refusing to accept the shop principle (later made law by the Taft-Hartley Act) whereby non-union actors are *turned* union when appearing in an Equity-contracted show.

- 1927—The union declares that "the actor is not responsible for the content of the play" after police raid three plays, including Mae West's *Sex*, and haul actors to jail.

- 1948—Fistfights break out during contract negotiations with the League of New York Theatres.

- 1968—Three days into a Broadway strike, Mayor John V. Lindsay brokers a deal that wins Equity its largest increase to date in salary minimums, bringing the Great White Way back to life.

- 1970—Off-Broadway strikes for a month. Equity is forced into binding arbitration.

- 1987—Equity wins restrictions on casting foreign actors, challenging British thesp Sarah Brightman's starworthiness for *The Phantom of the Opera*.

- 2001—AEA calls for a boycott of the non-union tour of the Broadway hit *The Sound of Music*.

- 2003—Actors honor picket lines during the Broadway musicians' strike, closing eighteen musicals for four days, at the cost of about $10 million.

The Balancing Act: Plays, Musicals, and Celebrities

Broadway, Off-Broadway, Off-Off-Broadway, regional, and touring. That is the basic outline of the theater scene. Returning then to the original question of "What kind of actor are you?" leaves us mired in definitions that cross-pollinate and differ in terms of prestige and income, but not necessarily in terms of quality. You'd be hard-pressed to find an actor who will only do theater and nothing else. Artistic principles tend to roll over and die when they cross the stark realities of this business. Of course, who's to say that some of the work being done on HBO isn't more artistically valuable than a show in New York? *Mamma Mia!* versus *The Sopranos*—I'll take the tube.

If you do perform solely in the theater and make a living at it, chances are you sing. Musicals tend to have much longer runs on Broadway and, as a result, they can sustain an actor for a longer period of time than a straight play can. Being a Broadway belter is a special kind of skill, one that I do not have. It is a very specific ability that requires training, power, and vocal cords that inevitably take a beating. There is a danger to this as well. Nodes forming on the vocal cords make a person's voice raspy, that kind of deeper, sexy, phone-voice quality.

They also get in the way of a singer's natural ability. Removing them can be hazardous as well. Julie Andrews had surgery to remove nodes from her vocal chords. The surgeon took more than just the nodes, and as a result, she can no longer sing professionally. All this is to say that just because you, or your child, sang in a school play or likes to pick up the mike on karaoke night does not mean that either of you is ready for Broadway. To take this one step further into the advice category, don't claim you can sing on your resume unless you are a Broadway belter.

Like anything else, the theater is a business and is driven by the needs of the consumer. The top ten grossing shows on Broadway are consistently musicals. The consumer—read: tourists—likes a grand show. Singin' and dancin' usually do very well; throw in a little plot line and you've got yourself a real doozy. This is not to disparage Broadway musicals, as many are excellent and as compelling as any straight play. But the new breed of jukebox musicals are nothing but a double CD set with a plot line thinner than a Calvin Klein model.

Then there's the celebrity factor, which continually haunts actors in this profession. Theater producers have discovered that audiences will flock to see certain stars, and they take advantage of it. Even though many have had relatively little stage experience, an actor you recognize from television, live and in person on the stage, sells tickets at $100 a seat.

What kind of actor are you? A theater actor. Okay. The kinds of jobs you could accept vary greatly, and the economic hardship is unforgiving. Rule number one, then, is that all theater actors will support themselves in another way.

An actor who works, or tries to work, on stage will often refer to the theater as his first love. But it is far less lucrative than acting in front of the camera. Common wisdom in the industry suggests that a theater actor will support himself in television and commercials, and try to get a film career started. Film, television, and commercials are where the money is, and where your great-aunt will see you and think you've made it.

Easier said than done. Are you even in town to go to these auditions? Are they casting shows in New York, where all theater work is?

Welcome to the world of TV and film.

3

THE LAY OF THE LAND, PART TWO

Hurry Up and Wait: The Film and Television Business

"It's actually gotten to the point where if I go to the theater and open the *Playbill* and the actor doesn't have one of the *Law & Orders* in his or her credits, I figure they either just got off the bus or they are really bad."

—Dick Wolf, executive producer, *Law & Order*

New York was born a theater town and New York will die a theater town. Much as we New York actors might like to pretend that we will find a lucrative acting job in this city, chances are we won't.

The common misconception about film and television in New York is that there is film and television in New York, or enough of it to keep the New York members of the Screen Actors Guild working. Pick up your *TV Guide* and count the number of shows that take place in New York, or even cite New York in their title, and one would be led to believe that New York City is *the* place, or at least *a* place, to be for television.

It's not. The high cost of filming on location, despite tax breaks and an entire government agency devoted to the task (the Mayor's Office of Film, Theatre & Broadcasting), most of New York as it appears on screen is filmed in Los Angeles and Canada. Productions will land in the city for a week or two in order to film locations that cannot be substituted for by a sound stage or crafted by a scenic designer.

There is, however, one savior in the New York television world: the *Law & Order* franchise. We'll use it as our guide through the television landscape.

Television, Translated, Means *Law & Order*

Television in New York is defined by one man and his empire: Dick Wolf and the *Law & Order* franchise. *The Law & Order* credit is a mark of arrival:

You're not a New York actor until you have one. And it is a wonderful thing to have happened for the city, because we need all the production we can get. Except that as far as hour-long episodic drama goes, *Law & Order* is just about all the production we get.

There ain't that many shows, and therefore there ain't that many jobs, and so there are very few chances to make a living off episodic television. Episodics are hour-long dramas, one of the subdivisions of television, which really breaks down into three categories. Sitcoms are half-hour shows, shot almost exclusively in a studio (*Sex and the City* was an exception to this rule). Soaps, or daytime, are *daytime* dramas shot entirely on a set, one episode a day.

Hour-long episodics, if they are successful, will have twenty-two new episodes a year. That's, at best, twenty-two chances for you to book a role on the show. The list of roles goes as follows: There are the Series Regulars (also known as Series Leads), followed by Guest Stars (also known as Guest Leads) followed by Co-stars, Under 5s, and Extras. These are divided into different pay categories—a union regulated on a system of lines, as in, how many you have.

These are their stories:

Series Leads were cast long ago, when a show was first produced. Sometimes these roles are recast, and very occasionally, a new regular character will be added to the show. *Law & Order* is particularly good at filling its roster, including the leads, with New York actors. Sam Waterston, Jesse L. Martin, Annie Parisse, and Jerry Orbach, who recently passed away, are all New York–based actors. Series Leads are the ones the people tune in for, the men and women they want to see week after week in that time slot.

Aside from regulars, then, there are probably fifteen to twenty roles available per episode. A handful of these are Guest Leads. A Guest Lead—also known as Top of Show, or TOS, because your name flashes on the screen at the top of the show—pays $5,831. These roles offer the most in acting time and remuneration. Landing a Guest Lead means that you've made your mark in the television world. Some say that you cannot even venture out to Los Angeles without having at least one on your resume.

From the Guest Lead on down come a wide variety of co-starring roles, numbering one to two scenes of, more likely than not, one to two minutes each. The Co-star, which really refers to anyone who is not a Guest Star but has more than five lines of dialogue, makes a day player rate of either $678 a day or $2,352 a week, whichever is less. If both scenes are shot in one day, then you get one day's pay. If you're lucky enough to be interviewed by Detectives Green and Fontana, and then have to testify on the stand later on, then you've lucked out with two days' worth of work. Though a scale rate is paid, your final check will have more to do with how many locations you shoot than anything else.

Should your character make a return appearance on the series, your role turns from Co-star or Guest Star to a recurring role. Recurring roles are rather prized possessions, as they guarantee a certain amount of work. In fact, many well-loved characters on television shows fall under this category. There's one main difference that separates them from Series Regulars: the paycheck. Series Regulars are contracted to the show and make a set amount per episode. Recurring characters, let's say, the medical examiner, or the wife of the lead cop on *The Wire*, might have several scenes in any one episode, and may return for several more episodes, but they will not be paid as a Series Regular. If all their scenes shoot in one day, that's what they're getting paid for: a scale day rate.

The bottom category, excluding extra work, are Under 5s. This covers anyone who speaks under five lines of dialogue. Stanislavski's manifesto ("no small parts") is not hanging in the offices of the Screen Actors Guild.

The common wisdom on *Law & Order* is that once you get in the casting door, if you're any good, you'll eventually wind up on set. I can attest that this is true, to a degree. It definitely helps to have a midtier agent behind you, pressing you on the casting director week after week. A lesser agent, or an agent with a lesser relationship, might have a harder time getting you back in the room. When I was with my first agent in New York, I auditioned for *Law & Order* twice within a three-month span. I went to producers both times, blowing it originally and landing a smaller role than the one I had auditioned for the second time around. Five years later, with a smaller agent, I went to producers for a Guest Lead, and have not been back since.

Coincidence? The problem is not so much in getting the *Law & Order* as it is, "Then what?" Believe me, I was not this cynical before I began acting in the city. *Law & Order* was on my checklist, the thing that would signal my arrival in New York. Book that scene on *Law & Order* and you will be taken seriously by everyone. But I booked *Law & Order* and got dropped by my agent.

So the cynicism isn't really mine, it's the industry's. It's the agents who see four *Law & Order* breakdowns every week, who book clients on the show every week. You see, to them, it's no big deal. It's their bread and butter. They expect to have someone on every week, so they don't even watch it anymore; they just assume someone they represent is on the show. This kind of complacency undermines the true accomplishment of landing a role on a TV show. No longer is it a mark of success. Rather, it is a requisite part of being an actor in New York.

Match that with the fact that each *Law & Order* spinoff has its own, separate, casting director, which means that a good audition for one show might not translate to a job on another show. I have yet to hear a story of an actor who auditioned for one *Law & Order* getting a part on a different spinoff because of the original audition. Guest Leads are different, as usually bigger names in the business are considered for all of these roles. But appearing on one show doesn't get you in with the other. Indeed, it might work against you. These are realistic dramas. You can't appear twice, in different roles, in the same season on any one show. In different years, it's possible. You will see many of the same actors in varying roles in different seasons—indeed, most of the regulars have done a stint as a Co-star prior to landing their Series Regular role. Consider this in real time, though, and it means years between jobs, years between paychecks . . . years where you have to find other work.

What other work is there? As far as episodics go in New York, at the time of this writing, there are only three shows outside the *Law & Order* franchise. Sadly, I cannot even devote a section to New York sitcoms because there just isn't that much I have to say about *Hope & Faith*, which is the only half-hour comedy currently shooting in New York. Got that? There is one sitcom. One.

Most television is filmed in Los Angeles, which is why the New York/Los Angeles question lurks in the back of the actor's mind like a crush on a cute girl in your lit lecture. Because so many actors flock to Los Angeles for the start of pilot season in January (more on this later in the chapter), you might want to consider heading out earlier if you are an unknown actor. Episodic casting begins in August, and it's a great time to let casting directors get a feel for you before the rush begins.

The decision to venture West is one that will never be easy to make. It's one of those "trust your gut" calls. Going out to L.A. because things are not going well in New York is not a great reason. Going out because you want to get more exposure to film and television, well, at least that's honest. Agents laud New York actors and tell them that the Big Apple gives them street cred, but the fact is that any actor making a regular living in film or television lives, part or most of the time, in Los Angeles. The business simply moves too fast. How is a New York actor going to compete with an Angeleno when they both go on tape on

Wednesday and the role shoots Monday? Answer: He can't. Like real estate, television and film casting is also a matter of location, location, location.

Soaps

Soaps are not just for beautiful people. The contract roles are, but there are plenty of other day player jobs available on soaps. And if they like you, they will have you back again and again.

Soaps, or *daytime*, as those who work in it would have it be known, move fast. They shoot an episode a day. An entire script every day means there is work to be found in this area. So how does one get in the door?

Once again, there is a division of labor contractually outlined by the union, in this case, AFTRA. The rates differ slightly from SAG's, but the categories are the same. New contract players on soaps are brought in maybe once or twice a year. They go through an arduous testing process that includes a full work session before they are offered a job. Once they get it, they become some of the hardest-working actors in show business, and are paid mightily for it. However, daytime insists that its regulars sign long contracts, usually three years at the minimum. During that time, any other work you want must be cleared with the show.

AFTRA TV Pay Rates
Day Player - - - - - - - -$ 695
3 Days - - - - - - - - - -$1,757
Week - - - - - - - - - -$2,411
Major Role - - - - - - -$5,977 (minimum per episode)

Characters who appear over several episodes are a much more frequent occurrence in daytime than in episodic television. Many day player roles will appear at the end of one episode and the beginning of another. Or they may become involved in an entire plot line. Day and/or weekly rates are paid for this work.

The Under 5 world is the way into daytime. And truly, there is no guarantee that the Under 5 will advance you to a day player or a contract role. At *Guiding Light*, casting is divided into two categories. Rob Decina, the casting director for the show, casts the day player, recurring, and contract roles, while his associate casts Under 5s and extras.

Rob invited me into his office one afternoon for a chat about soap opera casting. Once a director himself, Rob began casting at Warner Bros. before taking the job as head of casting for *Guiding Light*. The afternoon I interviewed Rob, he called out to his associate while pointing at the monitor, which showed the live feed from the studio. There was a young woman who had caught his eye, and he wanted to know her name. All she did was give a flirting glance to one of the leads, but he saw something.

I took this as my invitation to discuss the many small parts available on a show that shoots every day. I thought Rob would be a good person to ask about how to handle the one-line role, especially in the audition. It's one of those things all actors hate: the one-line audition. We want Hamlet, or at least Laertes. We don't want, to use Rob's example, "I'm here to fix the pipes."

"The one-line audition is the hardest audition," Rob says. "You have to have the understanding that the scene is not about you, that you are a part of the other person's world for a moment. You are a moment in the other person's life." He uses my trip upstairs to see him as an example. "You came to see me today, so you probably walked past a security guard downstairs. He was a moment in your life. . . . In the movie of your life, there he is, he's just a moment. If he tried to make a bigger deal about that moment than it is, then it stands out as, 'This guy doesn't understand his place "in your life."'"

"Scene stealer," I say jokingly.

"I'm not going to cast him," Rob says.

There you have it. The one-liner is the art of doing less. And less is a hard thing to do as a hungry actor trying to make his mark on the industry. I pose this conundrum to Rob. What about that guy who definitely is a great actor, who's just starting out in New York and who knows he can do better than this one line if you'd just give him a shot?

"That's an actor who doesn't understand his place at that moment."

Again, this is an argument against the idea that you have one shot at making it happen. One chance at getting the attention of the people who hire you. Just play the role, do the part. You can't do anything but.

Contract roles on soaps are reserved for pretty spectacular-looking people. Soaps have been a stepping stone for actors to move on to film. Julianne Moore and Robin Wright Penn both started out in soap operas before moving on to major film careers. But soaps can also be a brand against you. Soap-opera acting is a very specific thing. The plot lines are truly unbelievable at times, yet the acting is naturalistic. If an actor is seen to be doing that over and over for three years, it can be a tough mold to break out of.

Sketch, Late Night, and Cable

Sketch comedy has made a recent resurgence. Improv troupes like Second City, the decades-old institution, and Upright Citizens Brigade, a more recent addition, have gained visibility within the industry, and several sketch-comedy cable shows have sprouted on cable networks like Comedy Central and MTV. They're the type of shows that offer a lot of day player and Under 5 work for actors, but are usually entirely one-shot deals without the chance for a recurring role.

Still, that guy who pops up in the Letterman audience and says something funny, or who plays the fourth student from the left on *Chappelle's Show*, is making a paycheck. He auditioned, got the role, and performed it. This work is usually, in career terms, dead-end stuff, although a popular character on a sketch-comedy show may make a return appearance if the producers are happy.

The comedy end of this industry, however, is becoming an increasingly crowded arena. As a trained actor, comedy included, I am at the bottom of the list when it comes to consideration for comic roles. This is due to a combined lack of imagination from those doing the hiring, and the fact that there is a growing crowd of people specializing in the field. The standup comic has become an actor. Jay Mohr, Denis Leary, Eddie Murphy, Chris Rock, Jamie Foxx—all of these guys began their careers doing standup. Look at them now. They've taken over a considerable section of the acting business. New shows are often developed around standup comics. Ray Romano, Seinfeld, Drew Carey, Roseanne . . . the list goes on and on. Add to that the popularity of brilliant sketch comedians—the Will Ferrells and Steve Carells of the world—and suddenly, casting directors who must fill roles on sitcoms and in spoofy Bud Light ads are looking for specialists.

When there are that many specialists from which to choose, you as an actor are less likely to be considered for such roles. Alternately, if you take up improv or standup, you run the risk of being typed in the opposite corner, as someone who can only do comic roles, thus losing that shot at playing Hamlet. Recognizing this means you can pull it towards your advantage. Want to be taken more seriously for comedies? Take an improv class.

Film

The film world is comprised of two basic types of movies: the studio film and the independent film. The studio film is, literally, funded and distributed by one of the major film studios: Warner Bros., Paramount, Sony, and FOX are the big ones. Oftentimes smaller producers will package a project with actors and directors and bring it to the studios for financing.

Studio films do come to New York, but cost often prohibits their staying for very long. Many films come to New York to shoot exteriors, but do the remainder of their filming in Los Angeles or Canada. For actors, this translates to the following formula: Casting for smaller roles will only happen in the city where that specific scene will shoot.

Almost any movie that takes place in New York can be used as an example. Interiors, which usually comprise the majority of a film, shoot in Los Angeles. Exteriors are in New York. Any scene where a character appears for that, and only that, scene—walking out of a deli, say, or hailing a taxi—would then be cast in New York. Any role that shot only in Los Angeles would be cast in L.A. Because the cost of filming in New York is so high, most films limit the amount of time they shoot here, and thus limit the roles available for New York actors.

Therefore, the bulk of the film work in New York is in independent film. By definition, these are films produced without the financial backing of one of the major film studios—thus, *independently*. Smaller producers find financing, sometimes teaming with other producers, and get a film made without big studio money. This once led to more artistic freedom. Miramax was the first company to make independent films that were financially competitive with studio films. Soon, however, studios began to capitalize on independent films as a brand. Since that time, the indie film has become trendy, and is more susceptible to the "filmmaking by committee" approach once relegated to the world of studio films.

Indie films are generally small-budget, intimate ventures that shoot in and around the city. Between budget and location, producers will cast these films out of New York, wanting actors with a certain regional authenticity. However, along with small budgets come small paychecks for actors. Often, these films are done under SAG low-budget or experimental agreements, which offer deferred payment depending on the amount a film makes at the box office. To get to the box office, one needs distribution, something many of these smaller films never see.

Low Budget

SAG offers a variety of agreements to producers with low budgets. This provides a way for union members to act in films for less than the normal SAG scale rate. In addition to those listed below, SAG offers an affirmative-action low-budget contract to encourage the use of persons of color in major motion pictures.

SAG Low-Budget Contracts

Contract	Film Budget Limit	Length of Film	Exhibition	Salary
Experimental	$75,000	No limit	• Film festivals only • Performers control further exhibition rights	• Entirely deferred
Limited Exhibition	$200,000	No limit	• Film festivals • PBS and basic cable • Art houses	• $100 per day for 1 to 2 days of work or $75 per day for 3 or more days of work
Modified Low Budget	$500,000	Not less than 80 minutes	• Must have initial theatrical exhibition	• $248 per day • $864 per week
Low Budget	$2,000,000	Not less than 80 minutes	• Must have initial theatrical exhibition	• $466 per day • $1,620 per week

Actors hoping to become film stars are going to have a difficult time of it in New York. That's because if there's one thing Los Angeles does well, it's make movies. L.A. is the epicenter of the film world. All of the big agents, producers, and executives have congregated there, and they are a close-knit group. These people put movies together, and therefore their clients—the writers and actors and directors—flock to them. People like to stay close to home, and close to their own. Los Angeles may be more crowded, but it's because that's where the work is.

Do some actors book films out of New York? Of course. Do you have a better shot at working in film if you move to Los Angeles? Yes.

The Windfalls: Commercials and Pilots

Ads

Where the actor is concerned, commercials provide, in a word, survival. I know you're TiVoing past them whenever you can, but last year they accounted for nearly 75 percent of my income. Because so many advertisers headquarter in New York, the commercial industry thrives here. With commercials, the actor is introduced to one of the more beautiful words in the English language.

Residuals.

Feel it roll around the tongue. The reason everyone wants to book a commercial is because of residuals. Commercial casting is untenable, even more so than TV and film casting, because there are a lot of chefs in the kitchen. Should you be lucky enough to book a commercial, you will enter a strange type of lottery. You've got money coming your way, but how much? Session fees for commercials are $535 for an eight-hour day, with overtime if you go over on a day— a common occurrence. One arrives at the shoot with a principal session fee guaranteed. Then, it's up in the air.

Commercials pay based on their usage, and based on your visibility. One can be cast as a principal in a spot and not make a dime. Or one can be cast as an extra and end up with residuals for a year. The going rule is, "A face a mother can recognize." In commercials, it doesn't matter if you speak; it matters if we see you. If we can, you are now identified with that product, and you will be paid based on how many times the spot is shown. That's why a national spot is the most prized possession a commercial actor can have. It means that the spot is being shown across the country, put out on the network feed rather than by each individual region. This means you will make, well, a ton of money if it runs. A friend of mine made $100,000 off one spot last year alone.

Commercials can also run regionally, as wild spots, or as cable-only. Cable-only means you ain't making the big dough. The recent commercial contract negotiation sought an increase in residual payments for commercials, as shows like *The Shield* and stations like ESPN and CNN are as watched as many networks, but SAG was unable to win a concession on this point. So, for a flat buyout per thirteen-week cycle, your ad can run on cable as much as the advertiser chooses.

Still, over the course of a year, this can net you a few thousand dollars. Nice money to have. But commercials are an incredibly saturated industry, which means that in some ways it's easier to both get in the room and get tossed out of it. A fresh face is a great thing for an advertiser. Find the right one—the Dell Guy, the Verizon Guy, the Subway Guy—and you could be cashing in. However, stick around too long without booking a spot, and casting directors and agents will tire of you. Each casting director has his own select group of actors that he continues to see. There's no need to continue to see people who haven't booked in an allotted time, so there's a window of opportunity that the agents and casting directors tend to allow as a grace period. If you don't book and bring in money, then they lose interest.

Pilot Season

... And on the eighth day, God created pilot season.

It rolls around once a year, to great anticipation. Come late January, postings for N.Y./L.A. apartment swaps rise in volume. Actors begin whitening their teeth and spraying on their tans. Managers pile up the pictures and arrange general meetings with the networks, hoping to get you in the door first and make an early impression. People start talking about going to network and test deals. A thirteen-episode guarantee is enough to make an agent cry.

Pilot season traditionally runs from February to early April. During that time, the networks and a host of other producers cast the several hundred shows, on which all hope for the future of television rests. The pilot episode of a series, simply put, is the first episode of any television show. Of these hundreds of pilots, only a smattering make it to air. And of those that make it to air, even fewer flourish.

Yet the faint hope of Darwinian survival rings with the *cha-ching* of the world's largest cash register. At $30,000 an episode (on the low end), plus back-end syndication deals, a pilot holds the potential for an actor to support himself for the rest of his life. An agent can rest easy on a nice 10 percent chunk of that rolling into the office door every few weeks. With a pilot, everyone is happy.

The insanity of it all is the time frame. In the past several years, producers have begun to break the rules slightly, casting pilots at different times of the year. But for the most part, tradition stands, and pilots are cast in a whirlwind two-month spell that leads to the up-fronts, where networks announce their season to advertisers and get them to purchase airtime. December and January are thus particularly good times to try to get an agent if you are unrepresented, as agents tend to bulk up their client lists during this time, then drop the dead weight once they've seen who booked.

It's also the time of year when actors, like birds, migrate to the warmer climate of Los Angeles. Just as there are only eight or so network shows shot in New York on a regular basis, the percentage of pilots produced here is also small. The going logic is that one has a better shot at booking a pilot in Los Angeles than in New York. So that's where actors go.

This argument holds a lot of weight. For an actor to book a pilot, several things must happen. First, the actor must reach the point where the casting director puts him on tape, which follows one to two auditions. The tape is then sent out to Los Angeles, where it will be viewed by producers. Should producers like someone, they will fly him out to L.A. to test, in one or two sessions, for both the producers and the network. After a total of four to five auditions, an actor will be cast.

Simultaneously, this process happens in Los Angeles for every single pilot. Agents and casting directors generally swear that what I am about to state is patently untrue, but more L.A. actors get to network than New York actors. They don't have to be flown out to test at cost to the production. Why would a producer take on the cost unless he's quite certain about an actor? In L.A., an actor is just a short drive away. If the actor looks wrong but gives a great audition, or looks right and gives a shoddy one, his chance at another shot is far better than the New York actor's.

So, following this logic, actors begin a vast two-month exodus to L.A., leading to what environmentalists commonly term *overcrowding*. Thus the flip side: There are already a ton of actors in L.A. whom the casting directors know well, so they will not see every one of these fresh arrivals from New York. Along these lines, New York actors who are known to casting directors in their hometown have a better shot at auditioning for pilots on their home turf then they do in L.A. Some advise going out to L.A. well before pilot season to meet casting directors while auditioning for episodics. The gamble inevitably exists, but here are some determining factors to consider:

Agent relationship. When your agent thinks you should go to Los Angeles, she'll tell you. One of the things agents do is select the handful of New York actors whom they want the L.A. office to sell. "Here is the cream of the crop," they are saying. Even though actors generally sign bicoastal representation agreements, L.A. branches will not just take any client who wants to go from N.Y. to L.A. Also, the size of your agency matters here when it comes to getting the auditions, especially as an unknown.

Casting director relationship. If the network casting directors love you in New York, one of two things might happen. They will encourage you to stay here because they'll bring you in on everything and highlight you when they send out the tape. Or, they'll send word to L.A. that you are coming out and that L.A. should pay attention. However, if they don't know you, L.A. casting directors are more apt to ask, "What is this actor doing out in L.A. if our N.Y. casting director has never heard of him?" Of course, there are myriad reasons this could be true. Maybe that casting director won't see people from your agency. Maybe the casting director is just lazy. Or, maybe you're just not a known entity and therefore not ready for primetime, so to speak.

Heat. A great review in a big New York show that people are hearing about in L.A. may be enough to get you out there. New York does carry a certain workhorse mystique out in L.A. The carpenters versus the interior decorators, as it were. Some great New York theater credits and a Guest Lead or two and you could be good meat for the MGM lion. No credits and no heat mean that you're going up against other actors who have it, and you might be better off sticking to the home court and keeping on building where you've laid the foundation.

This year, two of the actors I interviewed booked pilots, one out of New York and one out of L.A., so if you take those statistics, the odds seem even.

Until this moment, I feel I've been rather gentle with you. Time to meet Jon, an actor, and hear the story of his pilot season.

Jon's First Screen Test

"Once I went out there, I had to start all over."

The move from New York to Los Angeles is not easy. Jon had worked in New York, on *Law & Order*, on a cancelled show called *Queens Supreme*, and on all the soap operas. He was having a good year, and told his agents that he wanted to go to Los Angeles for pilot season. As it happened, someone from the L.A. office happened to be in New York that week. Jon took the upper hand, tracked her down, and performed a monologue for her. It went extremely well. "You come out to L.A.," she said, "and I will sell you to the rest of the office."

The next day, Jon booked a play in Portland, Maine. He accepted the offer and moved out of his New York apartment. He would finish in Maine just in time for pilot season, and take off for L.A.

Two months later, he called his agent in New York to set up the Los Angeles meeting. "They really don't have time to meet with you," he was told. Funny, considering that he had secured their support in New York—support from an agency of which he's a signed client.

Then, a pilot he had auditioned for in New York wanted him to test. "The very next day, I had a meeting with the full L.A. office, where they apologized profusely for not seeing me. They said they had confused me with another client. Of course, I was ready. They couldn't wait to represent me and get things going in L.A."

A year later, a few guest appearances under his belt, Jon was ready for his first full pilot season. His agents were working for him, his manager was working for him. "I started going out on a couple of pilots," Jon says. "Everything I was going out on, I was getting called back on, which is good." He tested for a show called *Wild Life*, a UPN pilot, and *Barbershop*, a bought series for Showtime. (A bought series has a commitment from the network, meaning that they have purchased a certain number of episodes.) For *Barbershop*, he was told he was the writer's and director's number-one choice. "They put me on something called 'watch and hold,'" Jon says, "where they needed to be informed of every audition I was going in on."

"Out of the two projects, the UPN project and the Showtime project, I desperately wanted to do the Showtime project for a whole host of reasons. One, of course, because it was a bought series. You get that part, you're being paid for a complete series of work, you're guaranteed to go on the air. It was a very big deal for me, and I really wanted that."

All this interest certainly got Jon's representation in gear. "Before I tested for the UPN series, my manager was all of a sudden back in business, talking to me every day, and my agents were constantly on conference calls with me and trying to get the Showtime people to do something called a direct offer, which says, 'Don't go to your screen test for *Wild Life*, we'll just offer you the part.' Which is just kind of an unheard of thing in Hollywood."

What is now happening to Jon is the kind of thing that rarely happens. He's getting that kind of one-in-a-million heat that we all want. At this point, however, no one will accede to making a direct offer. "Those network executives weren't going to give up their rights for some kid named Jon, whom nobody knows."

So Jon will test for UPN. "There's a studio and there's a network," Jon says, defining the testing process. In this case, the studio is Paramount and the network is UPN. "There can be anywhere from ten to fifty people in the room. All the characters from every regular part are there. Then you go in by character. At this point in the studio, there were four of us, and we all went in. For some weird reason, we only did one of the three scenes that we had auditioned with. You would think that because it is a really important audition, they'd want to see a lot."

"We did one really short scene. I got a call that afternoon, which said they wanted to bring me back for network, said they'd dropped two out of the four, that it was me and Jake that were going back to network." Jake is Jake Busey, Gary Busey's son and an actor who's got more on his resume than Jon does.

Jon describes the network test as a giant room of fear. "More times than not, you're in a room with almost all people you recognize, whose names you know. You're sitting around in a room, and everybody gets contracts thrown in front of them, and before you go into an audition, you sign a contract that your agents have worked out for you based on your rate. You basically sign for six years. So, I signed a contract that was going to pay me $60,000 to do a pilot and then $35,000 an episode for the next six years of my life. *Before* I auditioned, I signed that contract. Pretty strange."

"So, every character went in, everybody went in to do it, and Jake and I were last. Jake went in and did his audition. Jake is a standup comedian, and I heard Jake working the room of about a hundred suits. And I was waiting in the waiting room outside the door, so I could completely hear everything that was going on. There was about five minutes of uproarious laughter before he even began. I had a sinking feeling in my stomach, and I went, 'Well, I lost this part, this guy just fuckin' worked the room.' I go in, I do mine. I was shaking, I was nervous."

"We all go back in the boardroom. We sit. The casting director comes back into the boardroom where all the actors are sitting and she says, 'Everybody can leave except for Jake and Jon.' All the actors left, wished us good luck. We bid our farewells, and me and Jake are sitting there. The directors, the producers, the writers, they all came out and they sat down with Jake and they gave him about ten minutes of notes, while I just sat there by myself, twiddling my thumbs. After that, they bring Jake in, and Jake comes out completely red-faced."

Now it's Jon's turn, and he takes no prisoners with his second chance. "I absolutely nailed it—did all my scenes. It was one of the best auditions I ever did. After I was done, the entire room got up in applause."

Imagine the joy, the feeling of really grabbing hold of your future. Jon was elated, except for one problem:

"The head of CBS, he doesn't make the network test"—CBS owns UPN, you see—"so you're auditioning for everybody there, and you're auditioning for a camera in the middle of the room which Les [Moonves] sees because he can't make the network test. I was walking out of the room, people were shaking my hand, telling me how great I was, and then I heard the fatal 'Oh no,' a scream from the camera operator."

He had forgotten to roll sound.

"I just delivered the best audition I could have; however, they forgot to turn on the microphone on the camera, so my audition was worthless. . . . Everybody came out and these suits came out and they all gave me their tidbits of acting advice. 'Do exactly what you did.' 'Your focus was great.' 'Do it again, every moment the exact same. . . .' And I had to go back in and audition—alone, for myself and the camera and the casting director—and try to repeat what I had just done."

"I got a call the next day saying that both me and Jake did not get the part, and they wanted to go in a completely different direction. That was my first screen test."

Yes, it's a horror story, but so often they are. Every actor I interviewed had one to tell me. Jon's is a rough introduction to the peaks and valleys of this industry. It took him seven auditions to be told he wasn't the type. In fact, they cast an African American. Jon's an Italian Catholic.

Try explaining this logic at the Christmas gathering to the hapless crowd.

What kind of actor are you?

The kind who wants to work.

What do you do to get there?

"The job is auditioning," says Mandy, another working actor. "You are a professional auditioner. That is what you're gonna be doing five days a week. And when you're lucky and you're in a show that you love, that's the *fun* part."

CHAPTER THREE

That's the real work."

What's my job, what's my work, and what's my love? The equation balances out differently for every single actor. But it never balances out the way it does for those people at the Christmas party.

TO TRAIN OR NOT TO TRAIN

"Part of the requirement of a life in the theater is to stay out of school. The old joke has the young woman in her bedroom as a visitor at the castle in Transylvania when a vampire appears in the middle of the night. The young lady grabs two wooden spoons off the night table, forms them into a cross, and thrusts them at the vampire, who responds, '*Vil gurnisht Helfin*,' which is Yiddish for 'It ain't gonna help.' And the same is true of school."

—From *True and False,* by David Mamet, founder of the Atlantic Theater and the accompanying Atlantic Theater Company Acting School

The great question faced by young actors everywhere is whether or not to train. Then: where, how, for how long, and how much will it cost me?

When this moment occurs is different for every actor. Some get it all out of the way by the time they're twenty-two—moving at a clip through an undergraduate conservatory. Some go right from high school to college to graduate school. Some never train, then begin taking classes, and find themselves wanting to learn more, until they finally enroll in an MFA program on their thirtieth birthday.

There is an abundance of options for actors wanting to study their craft, and deciding between alternatives can be a frustrating experience. Just as there is no shortage of actors, there is no shortage of institutions and acting studios that want to take their money.

That's the cynical, more Mamet-esque view. The more encouraging view is that there are a number of dedicated professionals who want to pass along the craft of acting to a new generation of actors; who believe in the power of theatrical storytelling. There are brilliant, devoted teachers and institutions that do this for the love of acting.

Training is also one pathway toward being discovered. A trained actor sets himself above the rest of the flock and has been given a mark of approval by a credible institution. A trained actor will have a showcase, a coming-out party that can launch or destroy a career in four minutes flat. A trained actor has a leg up.

A trained actor also has a mountain of debt.

Learning new aspects of your craft is important. But staying out of Everest-like debt is also important. Eating more than peanut butter and jelly all week would also be nice. These are the factors that need to be balanced alongside the need for training. Too many actors will throw themselves into school or a program without fully thinking through the financial repercussions. That's because we're all thinking we're going to strike it rich. But chances are you're not going to strike it rich. In fact, chances are you will be unemployed and not making any money. Rather than take an overly optimistic (three-picture deal with Sony) or overly pessimistic (waiting tables for the rest of your life) point of view, why not envision your future a little more soberly? Let's say you have a good year as a working, professional actor: You might make $30,000. Instead of viewing your professional life as a romantic or tragic drama, let's look at what it really is: a job.

Study for the love of the art? Choose a graduate school for its connections instead of its credentials? Take classes in the city with a reputable teacher, or take them with a casting director who might give you an audition? Shuffling through these choices is difficult. What follows is an attempt to hack through the bramble and give some highlights and personal accounts that might make your decision easier.

Graduate School

Coming out of a liberal arts college and straight into New York City, I thought I was ready to pop. I had spent four years studying acting, performing in at least three shows a year. I went abroad to London to study. My resume was stacked with great roles in classic plays. I was, clearly, a catch.

I hit the ground running. Headshots were mailed to every agent. I worked with a theater company downtown. I sent postcards inviting everyone to my shows. I went to open calls for everything I could find in *Backstage*. Months of the same passed. I remailed. I updated. And not a single meeting with an agent or casting director came of any of this.

I couldn't understand why. I trained, didn't I? I did my time, didn't I? I was ready to be a professional actor, wasn't I?

Maybe not. Unlike those coming out of a graduate program, who are given a debut showcase, I had no formal introduction to these people. And so in the mire of twenty-two-year-old men joining this business, I was a nobody. Think of it. Each graduate program has approximately sixteen to twenty students, all in relatively the same age range. And they've all been studying theater in a conservatory setting for the past two to four years. Then add the undergraduate conservatory programs to the list, and their graduates. Soon, you are looking at several hundred actors hitting the city at the same time, all of them in the same age range. There are not enough agents, and not enough jobs, to go around.

That's one reason to go to graduate school. You immediately separate yourself from the herd. There are a select number of programs that have continuous reputations for producing great actors. Of course, when it comes down to it, the best actors coming into the class are usually still the best when they come out. That's not to say they weren't better than when they arrived, just that, well, there's only so much you can learn.

The Mark of a Trained Actor

There's a reason large regional theaters like to work with graduates of select MFA programs. The training that one gets in these programs is undoubtedly necessary for anyone who wants to work in a major regional theater. When Scott Zigler, now the co-head of the American Repertory Theatre/Moscow Art Theatre's Institute for Advanced Theatre Training at Harvard (my alma mater, and the longest-named program in the history of time), spoke to my MFA class for the first time, he said that the primary reason to attend a graduate program was for the voice and movement training. Acting was less something you could learn, he seemed to be hinting; you either have it or you don't. The mark of professionals, he told us, was their ability to use their voice and body on stage.

This is why regional theaters want trained actors: You can tell an untrained actor from a trained one in a professional production. It's as clear in the audition room as it is in the rehearsal room. While some like the rough quality, the lack of polish, of the untrained, others prefer the gloss of an MFA graduate. There is a presence, a poise, a timbre, and a gravitas to the trained actor.

One of the dangers of training is in becoming a product. Some say you can tell which program an actor went to after watching him on the stage for a few minutes. And it's true. Juilliard grads have the best speech of any actors—perfect consonants. ART grads are all physicality, while Yale grads, it has been said, are talking heads—intellectual actors who work from the shoulders up. This assessment might be true to varying degrees. Mainly, however, it emphasizes where the industry thinks these programs place the weight of their training.

Marin, who went to an undergraduate conservatory program as an idealist, arrived in the world a realist four years later. "I kind of naïvely thought that the best school to go to was the place where I responded the most to the people in the room," she said. "I was all about the training. I didn't know much about the business side at all."

Training for the Business of Acting

The business side of graduate school is where it gets complicated, because however much we would like to make our world one that exists solely on craft and talent, the fact of the matter is that being a working actor requires a certain amount of business savvy. Most training programs will not acknowledge this, leaving their graduates to confront a harsh reality when they begin their careers. In the business climate of today, you need an agent to get an audition for a LORT D production of *A Doll's House*. It simply is not the same world it was for our predecessors. Where they could bartend a few days a week, audition for an Off-Broadway show without an agent, and afford to live in Hell's Kitchen, we have to wake up at 5:00 a.m. just to get a time slot for an open call, taking the subway in from East Williamsburg in order to afford the same rent—and that's a privilege granted to those in the union.

Those who train actors and run these programs are absolutely right to want to focus on craft and craft alone. There's no way an actor could maintain three years of training, and get his ego up to the size required to compete, if he was constantly being reminded of the impossibility of the world he was entering. Still, before making the choice to go to grad school, one must evaluate this premise carefully. Am I here to learn to act, or am I here to get a career? Because I guarantee you, three years out, you're going to be asking yourself why you didn't weigh both sides as equal factors before.

Graduate school is a test. It is meant to thin the herd, and it does. Actors who come out of these programs have been so intensely trained that they are instinctive acting machines. That's what I didn't realize when I came out of my undergraduate program. MFA grads truly are a step ahead. It's not that they're necessarily better actors, they just know how to *give it*—and fast. After medical school, a doctor should be able to make a diagnosis without returning to her lab notes. The same is true for actors. If you walk into an audition room, give an interesting read, and the director wants something else, you'd better be ready to give it to him on the spot.

On the benefits of training, and its value in the audition room, Patch, a Juilliard graduate, had this to say. (Juilliard is actually a BFA, not an MFA, program, but it ranks as one of the premiere conservatories in the country, at the level of a graduate training program.) "You can make some choices very quickly, go with your gut. I think poise in those situations is the poise of having been yelled at in front of, and humiliated in front of, your friends." Indeed, most trained actors will tell you there is nothing they cannot handle when it comes to making an adjustment or taking the criticism. "Getting up and having to do a monologue ten times, and having the queen of voice and speech in this country (the Juilliard voice instructor) tell you you're the worst student she's had in her entire career . . . that'll give you a little bit of foundation," Patch said. Indeed, those who come out of grad school have tougher skin to show for it.

And when you are released into the purgatory of your professional acting career, you will need tough skin. You also need to be prepared for the fact that just because you went to graduate school, landing an agent is not any more of a guarantee than it was before. The only guarantee you have, if you attend the right program, is that some smattering of agents and casting directors will see your work in a showcase. This event, the showcase, is certainly beneficial, but is it economically wise?

If you are in it solely for the showcase, you may meet with sore disappointment come that fateful May day. "I definitely felt entitled to something when I left Juilliard," Michael, an actor who's been out in the real world for about seven years now, tells me, "because it is so much work. . . . It's like, if you make it to the top twelve on *American Idol*, you expect you're gonna get a record contract. But that way of thinking is a bit ignorant. Out of a showcase of sixteen actors, not all sixteen of you are going to get big agents. The industry only wants to find the diamond in the rough. . . . I think the deadly thing is saying, 'I was owed this. I've worked so hard for four years, I've worked so hard my whole life, someone hand me a fucking job.'"

Patch echoes this sentiment. "I think if you went to a major business school for four years, and you barely slept for four years, and you were in school from nine in the morning to ten at night six days a week, of course you'd feel like you were owed something."

But that is a dangerous way for an MFA graduate to think, because it's not like business school; there are jobs after business school. It's why in the end, it must come down to the training. If you can look back at the overall experience and say to yourself, "I may be unemployed, but I am a finer actor than I was," then you will be able to sleep at night. If you can't say that, and your reason for going to school was to get an agent where all else had failed before, then you're going to need a few more refills on that Ambien prescription.

The Regional Theater/Graduate School Partnership

In the world of theater, training is important. Graduate school matters far less when it comes to careers in television and film. If you want a career in the theater, an MFA will launch you faster than anything else will.

Some graduate schools attach themselves to a working regional theater. There are both advantages and disadvantages to this arrangement. An advantage is that there is a chance you will have real experience working in a LORT theater alongside professional actors. You will gain practical experience and a resume credit. The disadvantage is that this practical experience may involve carrying a lot of furniture around in addition to speaking your two lines. Graduate schools inevitably use their student populations to save money, by not having to pay union rates to performers in smaller roles and as understudies. They can use you instead. So while you are Country Woman #3, you're missing out on your chance to play Medea in a student production.

Of course, there are some larger parts to be had on the mainstage. Often, landing these roles is a source of pride. Students in my class who had them began to walk the halls with a bit more of a swagger. But the truth of the matter is, their work on the mainstage in no way guaranteed them any more stage work when they graduated. In fact, those from my class who worked the most in the professional arena while at school have worked the least since graduating from the program.

One must be very wary about living in the grad school bubble. Inside it, you become the only eighteen actors in the world, the best of the best. Until you arrive in New York, that is, and discover the eighteen other bests from every top graduate school in the country. Sure, you'll need poise and ego if you are to fly in this world. Just make sure you glued those wings on with something stronger than false pride.

The final and perhaps most important benefit graduate school brings you is a community. This community translates, further down the road, to connections. Most graduates of MFA programs end up knowing and working together. When I ask him about pros and cons, Michael counts this as among the best reasons to attend graduate school. "A pro is the community of people I have. And it's on a much more organic level than, 'Oh, you're going to *know* so many people. You're going to have so many contacts.' It's not so much, 'I know so many casting directors and agents,' it's, 'I know so many actors and directors.' Not necessarily people who went to school with me, but people who worked with people I went to school with."

With graduate school under your belt, once you graduate and nestle into New York, agent or no agent, you are in a community of actors who appreciate the theater. You will all do readings together and meet over beers at a bar near where your friends are working. You will, as Patch said, "have a home here."

And on that—a feeling of camaraderie and artistry—one cannot put a price.

Civilians Make Good

The Civilians, one of the top new theater companies in New York right now, was founded by a group of University of California, San Diego (UCSD) graduates who wanted to create work for themselves. In 2004, they made such a strong impression on the New York theater scene that David Cote, chief theater critic for *Time Out New York*, listed their production of *Gone Missing* as the third best thing in the New York theater. That's third place behind the Vanessa Redgrave, Robert Sean Leonard, Brian Dennehy, Philip Seymour Hoffman revival of *Long Day's Journey into Night* and the long-running hit musical *Avenue Q*. In 2005, the Civilians toured on their first Equity contract, and they continue to produce new work.

The Top Graduate Programs in the Country

Certainly, there are other programs, but these are—between the training they give and the industry recognition they receive—the top programs in the country. You may find better acting training somewhere else, but these schools guarantee that, upon graduation, you will be seen by those who will be hiring you in the future. For the money they charge, consider this a requirement in your consideration for graduate school. I would go so far as to say that if you want to go the grad school route, and are not accepted to one of these programs, wait until next year and try again.

Almost all of these programs offer an MFA, which can come in handy later in life, when you may be looking for a teaching career to bolster your income. However, don't go to these programs to learn how to teach. Go to become a professional actor.

Here are the industry favorites:

- *American Conservatory Theater (ACT)*: Three-year MFA program. Tuition: $14,207*

- *American Repertory Theatre/Moscow Art Theatre Institute for Advanced Theatre Training:* Two-year MFA program. Tuition: $26,800 (first year), $20,500 (second year)

- *The Juilliard School:* Four-year BFA program. Tuition: $22,850

- *National Theatre Conservatory (Denver)*: Three-year MFA program. Tuition: free

- *New York University:* Three-year MFA program. Tuition: $34,780

- *North Carolina School of the Arts:* Four-year BFA program. Tuition: $2,755 (in-state), $14,035 (nonresident)

- *Old Globe (USD)*: Two-year MFA program. Tuition: free

- *Rutgers:* Three-year MFA program. Tuition: $10,440 (in-state), $15,520 (nonresident)

- *University of California, San Diego (UCSD—La Jolla)*: Three-year MFA program. Tuition: $8,611.50 (in-state) $23,572 (nonresident)

- *Yale School of Drama:* Three-year MFA program. Tuition: $19,795

---

*Tuition costs accurate at time of writing. Of course, you should check with each program for yearly tuition increases.

The Showcase

"I think that showcase is a dog show."

That's what Fiona, an actor, said when I asked her about it. Fiona attended one of the MFA programs I've listed, and in the spring of her third year, she, along with hundreds of other graduates from other schools, underwent what may be the most trying time in any actor's life. It's the showcase: the moment where actors, with a pair of two-minute scenes, try to show the industry that they are the next big thing in acting.

For those of you unfamiliar with the concept, here's how it works: Sometime around January, graduating students begin reading hundreds of plays, looking for scenes that they think will best show them off to agents, managers, and casting directors. Once they find scenes that they like, they must find a scene partner who also likes that scene and thinks that it will show them in good light to the industry as well. Once a compatible match for a pair is found, it's back to the drawing board for another contrasting scene, with which, in the next two minutes, you will wow agents and casting directors with your incredible range and talent, making you the most wanted actor in New York. This must happen for every actor in the class.

These scenes are then rehearsed more than any two minutes of performance ever should be. Then, one day in April or May, the class descends on New York (and in some cases, Los Angeles) for one day. At 1:00 p.m., 3:00 p.m., and 6:00 p.m., you will perform your scenes for the entire invited industry. Then you will get a piece of paper listing all of the people who want to meet with you. And then you will drink yourself into a stupor.

That list is very important, because you do need an agent. And you do need people to think you're good. And you don't get a lot of second chances in this industry. Needless to say, it can be the most terror-filled day of a young actor's life. I managed two hours of sleep before my showcase. It's a wonder I got an agent.

Once the list arrives, and the copious amount of drinking subsides, then come the meetings. I'll detail the agent meeting at greater length in chapter 7, but for the matriculating graduate of an MFA program, know that you hold one competitive advantage. Though you may be in a buyer's market, you have entered it at the precise time when the buyers are definitely looking to buy. Plus, as the seller, you know how many people are interested in you. With the help of your list, you can create a competitive edge for yourself, a bidding process of sorts. By virtue of the fact that you are trained, are new to this world, and have some meetings, you have something more important: heat. So use it to your advantage.

"I went into every meeting saying I've been offered representation by all these people," Jon says, "and I'm not going to continue this meeting unless you tell me you are actually interested in representing me. . . . In grad school they don't teach you any of that, but you are a business, you are a corporation."

When it comes to choosing scenes, most actors make one of two mistakes. The first is that they immediately go to the type route, picking a famous actor whom they think they resemble in some way, shape, form, or temperament, and picking a scene that this actor either has acted in or could easily be cast in. They then cut the scene to give it a shape that best shows this side of themselves. This actor is now doing a performance based on type and marketability, which can in no way reveal those individual qualities for which a new talent is discovered.

Mistake number two is the exact opposite. Rather than going the overtly commercial route, actors go to the far artistic extreme, choosing material that ignores all factors of marketability and type. They end up with two great acting scenes that, though they may be great roles of the modern theater, also do nothing to showcase their individuality. Agents don't want to find the next Torvald in *A Doll's House*, they want the next unique, individual actor.

See, the mistake is to mask yourself in any way. While you may spend graduate school plumbing the depths of character, when it comes to showcase, you want to strip it all away and show the best version of yourself you can.

In my showcase scene selections, the Neil Simon scene that I thought would be a hit barely got off the ground, while the Donald Margulies scene about which I was ambivalent proved to be the one that got me the most attention. This was because I was simple, straightforward, and closer to myself than I was in *Barefoot in the Park*, my surefire shot at an NBC half-hour comedy. In showcase, it's easy to lose sight of what's important.

"You do not have to suddenly get a militaristic control over your body and over your look," Fiona said, "which is what most people do because you're so scared and you're so nervous. Everybody starts to go to the gym. Everybody dyes their hair. Everybody panics. And really, the only thing that you need to do is craft *one fucking alive moment*." She stops and laughs a little. "Just one. I don't even think you need to do two. One moment where you actually appear to be spontaneous and living and have something to share."

It's a novel concept for the showcase. Don't be the next Maggie Gyllenhaal or Zach Braff; be yourself, be truthful. "That's the thing that makes your face bright and makes you exciting and makes your cheeks flush and makes you look beautiful—or makes you look scary, or dynamic," Fiona says, "That's the thing that impacts your physicality that makes other people interested in you. And that's what I think people should focus on. . . . Everyone has seen beautiful people. . . . Don't worry about what you wear. Worry about if you know the circumstances, if you like your scene. Don't pick the scene other people think you should do; do the thing you want." It's so easy to forget all this, because the dog-show mentality takes over. "You don't even know what you want to do," Fiona says, "because what you want to do is you want to get hired. And that's what makes it so confusing."

Getting hired is not a thought you want to have in your head when you're acting. You shouldn't have it when you're auditioning, so why have it now, at the World's Fair of auditions?

Should you be lucky enough to leave your graduate program with an agent, the road ahead is by no means cleared. Should you not have an agent, things may be a little trickier at first, but all is not lost. In one of those tales of grad school lore, it's a known fact that John Turturro and Paul Giamatti both left the Yale graduate program without landing an agent. Needless to say, they've found themselves fine careers.

Training is an asset, and will continue to be one to you for the rest of your acting life, in terms of both technique and connections. Make sure you continue to mold it to your advantage.

Other Options

The alternative, training-wise, to attending a graduate program is taking classes in New York City. As with graduate schools, the approach should take consideration of both training and industry potential. Be wary when finding acting teachers in New York. Any out-of-work actor looking to make some extra money might deem himself a teacher.

Most pure training classes in New York require an audition or a referral. This guarantees a certain caliber of actor in the class. William Esper, Wynn

Handman, and Michael Howard, each of whom teaches out of his own studio, are well known and respected. You may not have these individuals as teachers, but the techniques of acting will be consistent among other faculty members. The Actors' Center is a more recent addition to the New York studio scene, and also has an excellent reputation.

There are classes for everything. On-camera work, commercials, voiceovers, sitcom technique, improvisation technique, standup comedy, auditioning, auditioning for television, auditioning for commercials, auditioning for voiceovers . . . the list is endless. Find some molecule of acting and auditioning, and there's a class about it. As a general rule, I wouldn't recommend any of these classes for their training value. However, for connection value, some may be worth your while. TVI Actors Studio offers some good options. Television casting directors teach on-camera classes, and that's a surefire way to create a contact—someone you can follow up with as you begin to work in the business. But don't expect that contact to be suddenly hiring you as a contract player on *All My Children*. Expect her to (maybe) open mail you send her.

Below these classes are the seminars that are billed as classes, which don't really teach anything. There is no screening process, and anyone can walk in the door to these studios in the hope of landing an acting career. Actors Connection is the most known of this group, where actors pay to meet agents and casting directors. Their slogan is "We open doors," and they charge $32 a pop to open them. Occasionally, these meetings result in further meetings for one- to two-line roles. However, they never result in careers. Most of the agents and casting directors who attend these seminars are assistants and/or lower-tiered people in the profession. They are getting paid to be there, an important fact to remember. This is a way for them to make a little extra cash. Sure, they might meet an actor or two in the process. But let's be honest—they've got a lot of actors to choose from here. Approach these seminars with a wary eye, and read the fine print.

You must train in some way. "It is important," Stephanie Klapper, a casting director who handles a ton of theater, tells me. "I'm not going to rule out an actor because they don't have an MFA. But I do think, depending on the project, that it can be quite useful." Or, as Kat, another actor, put it in layman's terms: "I think it's bullshit that you can walk in off the street. Only with training do you find the skills you need to be versatile enough to have a career with any kind of longevity."

5

BEAUTY OR BEAST:
Typecasting

"When asked what sustained her confidence for more than thirty years, she merely tossed her head back and brayed her big Martha laugh, just as she had done when courting Edward Albee. The play's producer, Elizabeth I. McCann, remembers hearing Ms. [Kathleen] Turner emit that overscaled roar at a meeting with the playwright and thinking, 'I don't know if that was calculated or not, but she just got the part.'"

—*New York Times*

Forget talent; let's talk type.

It is the arbiter of casting in this industry, the one thing that you must fully comprehend, own, and at times, manipulate if you want any shot at success. You are what you type, meaning that you must become a recognizable entity in the eyes of casting directors, directors, and producers. Type is the way this business operates. You know all those actors who talk about not wanting to be typecast, who talk about wanting to break the mold, not getting hedged into one area? Forget them. They're not you. They have careers. They've played roles that they don't want to repeat. They want growth and can get it because people know who they are. No one knows you, and at the start of your career, there is only one way people are going to get to know you.

As a single thing.

"Pigeonhole yourself as much as possible as a type so that people think of you as this one thing," Patch tells me when I ask him for the advice he'd give to someone just starting out. "Then, if you're a good enough actor, you'll break out of it, and you'll surprise people, and then they'll think you're even more amazing. . . . You have to be like, I'm *this guy* and I play *these parts*."

Get used to it. You will be typed. No one said it's fair. The sooner you embrace it, the better. The sooner you own it, the sooner you will work.

Some people have natural ownership over type. It's those who start with a more rudimentary understanding of what it is to be an actor who fare better earlier in their careers. That's because they are not trying to stretch the limits of their character acting ability; they are just being themselves. "There's just certain people who glow," Rob Decina says. "It's why young actors get a lot of opportunities—because some kids, they may not understand craft, but they have an understanding of themselves that's personable."

One of the great debates in acting classes is along these lines: Would you rather be a *transformational* actor or a *personality* actor—a Robert Duvall, say, or a Christopher Walken? The guy who shifts from role to role, or the guy who walks on stage or on screen and shows you what you already knew you were gonna get? Both are equally magnificent.

Leave this debate in the classroom. The greatest mistake young actors make in this industry is thinking that they can do anything. It's one that haunts almost every single performer in meetings and audition situations at the beginning of his career. When I sat down with Rob for our chat, we started talking about type and the way in which this hinders actors in the audition room.

"What if," I offer as a hypothetical question, "I come to audition for a prison guard. It's a small role, and I'm a good actor, and I feel like I could play it any way you wanted me to. So I hedge my choices, finish the audition, and then say, 'So what do you think? Is he a nice guard or a mean guard?'"

"I would rather you just play it," Rob says. "I don't even want you to say, 'Hey, I was *thinking*, he's gonna be a nice guard.'"

Do it—don't talk about doing it.

"Do you have a lot of those conversations?" I ask.

"Completely," Rob says. "I think it's one of the biggest mistakes actors make. . . . Actors have a need to collaborate on an audition. You should not collaborate on an audition. . . . If we're talking about the first time you're auditioning for a role, there shouldn't be any of that. It should be, 'Let's just get to it.'"

I press him further on the issue, because I have been in these situations, and my feeling was always, "I can do anything. Tell me how to do it and I'll do it that way."

"I feel like that's what actors are doing," I say. "When they say 'Tell me, do you think it should be more this way or that way,' what they're saying is, 'I made one choice, but I can make another.'"

"But, see," Rob counters, "I get that you can make another one because *you're an actor*. But you've already made a choice. And I'd much rather you make the choice to do the nice guard if that's what you believe in. But don't do it with this ulterior motive that it's going to get you another note or get you another shot or get you the work session or whatever the case may be. You have to read that scene and go, 'I think that guy's nice. I think this guy would be interesting to play him as a nice guard. I might just go, 'Hey, thanks for coming' and I might go, 'Wow, he didn't see that the way we all see that.' Or, I might go, 'This guy is believable, I see he's a good actor, do it again.' There's no answer to that, in a way. A lot of casting is what happens in your gut, a vibe you get in the room."

Which, put simply, means that it's out of your control. So stop worrying about it. Time to get stoic about it all.

I made the *I can do anything* mistake for a very long time. Because, like most actors, I once did everything. In high school I did Commedia dell'Arte, Shakespeare, and Miller. In college I did it all over again, and better. I came to New York City, and I think, "Why change now? *I can do anything*. I should be in the audition room for leading roles, because I played them in college."

Now, of course I'm right. I can play all those roles. But at my core I am a character actor, an actor who gets parts as best friends, as cops without names, prison guards and weirdos. I look average for a white man in this industry. I'm nothing special. My jawline is not chiseled, my skin does not glow, my eyes are not cobalt and enigmatic. I'm Jewish but not Jewish enough, pale but not Midwestern enough. I'm strictly run-of-the-mill. I am not a leading man—or at least I wasn't in my twenties.

Type is, perplexingly, both highly specific and completely general at the same time. For example, when casting a leading man for a major role in a television show, the details of facial structure, eye color, hair color, physique, etc., will be parsed to the most minuscule detail. That's the specific part. The general part is that, when it comes to formal casting, none of that matters because what they want is a leading man. The same way they might want a plumber, or a prison guard, or a nanny, or a nurse. And so what it comes down to is, in essence, the same thing that it always comes down to in acting. Are you that guy, that girl, that thing?

Are you that type?

First Impressions

The moment you walk in the room can comprise anywhere from 10 to 90 percent of the audition. Mark Saks called me in to audition for the part of a white-trash Philadelphia pimp after seeing me play a white-trash Massachusetts alcoholic on stage (aha, type!). I had grown a mullet and a handlebar moustache for the part, but had since shaved it, as the show had closed and I wanted to try to get another job instead of continuing my scumbag look. Boy, was that a mistake. Upon greeting me in the waiting room, the first thing Mark said was, "I was hoping you still had the moustache." He had already made up his mind—I just didn't look the part anymore.

Looks vs. Type

You know who really needs to figure out their type? Ugly people.

Ugly in the broadest sense of the word. Ugly as in "not a model," because the fact of the matter is that truly stunning, truly beautiful people do not need to worry about what type they are. They have other worries—acting lessons, perhaps. But more likely than not, or more likely than you, they will get the audition because they're hot.

I imagine my readership to be predominantly nonmodels. Call me a cynic, but I wrote this book for people like myself, with the same hurdles ahead of them. So unless you are used to constant head-turning when you walk by an outdoor café, unless someone other than family members, preferably someone in the industry, has told you that you were hot, or beautiful, or godlike, assume you're not.

I digress further. I don't just mean that you turn heads, I mean that you give people whiplash on a regular basis; chiropractors are paying you commission. I mean constant attention devoted to your looks. If you want to put yourself in the good-looking category, you need to be extraordinary looking. There's one moment that happens to every actor in New York. It's the one when they walk into a casting session and find themselves standing in a room full of models. Not good-looking people. Models. And let me tell you something: Models are better looking than anyone I ever see on the subway or walking on the street.

They are in a different class—the girls make me giddy and the boys make me jealous.

Why do I stress this point? Because your mother and father and aunts and uncles and cousins and friends who tell you that you should be on a soap opera know absolutely zilch. They think that they do, because everyone's got an opinion when it comes to this business. My dentist has given me lectures on the acting trade. "You know what you should do is try to get into some of those *Law & Order* shows." My friggin' dentist! Nod, smile, and let them all talk as much as they want. They're not in it for a living. You are.

Skin Deep

At one of my first meetings with the commercial agents who now represent me, the agent I was speaking with pointed to a corner of the room where several other younger, skinnier, trendier agents were busy working. A slew of composite cards, all bikinis and smiles and flesh, lined the walls. "That is the beauty department," she said to me. "And you won't be meeting them."

Casting is about finding the right person. Casting directors who do this for a living think this way: "Are you that guy?" Sure, I could *do* the role, but would I be more believable in the role than the other guy? Chances are the answer is never going to be, "That actor is better than I am," because it's not about talent.

"You have to look yourself in the mirror and ask yourself, 'What kind of actor am I?'" Rob says. "And I mean the external mirror and the internal mirror. . . . When you can figure that out, you're going to be on your way to understanding your career."

What is this internal mirror of which Rob speaks? It's incredibly complex—one of those things that you will find simpler to place a finger on the longer you've been at this. But simply stated, it's *personality*: a blend of the psychology and personal history that makes you a unique individual. Its results become the coined phrases we label people with constantly. "She's funny, and weird," or "He's awkward," or "She's so poised under pressure," or "He's got a temper." Translated, those become archetypes: quirky, wacky, collected, and fiery. Being more open to the way in which others perceive you makes identifying this internal type much easier.

Some Type Categories and Buzzwords
Ingénue (young leading lady)
Leading Man
Leading Lady
Comedic (Quirky, Wry, Zany, Wacky)
Straight Man
Character (Older or Younger)
Nerd
Young, Hip
Best Friend
Boss
Neighbor

Turning the internal understanding into an external look becomes less difficult the longer you're at this, because you'll see the people who show up at auditions to compete against you. Pegging a stranger is easier than pegging yourself. It's one of the reasons agents ask actors to compare themselves to known stars. But type, at its most basic, is truly a matter of being honest with yourself, and your look is a part of this. It is the immediate image you present— the first impression. Look is one element of type, and because it's the first thing people see, it's the most important element.

The first thing to do, in order to identify your look, is watch a ton of television. All different genres of television: soap operas, sitcoms, hour dramas. (You can skip the reality shows unless you want to be the next Jeff Probst.) Once you start to pay attention you'll notice that there are indeed plenty of other roles for you to fill—and they're probably the thankless ones. They're probably the characters who give the good-looking people the exposition, who find dead bodies, who get interviewed about the whereabouts of their friend, who is, of course, better looking than they are. That's your bread and butter as an actor.

Then, be the best-looking version of that you can be. Wear clothes that fit and highlight your good features. Shave if you don't look good with stubble, even if you are playing a homeless guy. Put on makeup even if you're playing a Plain Jane. Looks matter, far too much, so spend some time now figuring out how to put on your pretty face so that you can forget about it later. The last thing you want to be stressing about in that waiting room is how you look. Get a grip on it, then think about the scene.

Your Fighting Weight

It's no joke. Skinny matters. The camera really does add fifteen pounds. And though I would never state that the standards in this realm are equal for men and women, pressures exist for both.

My first meeting with a now-former manager went something like this. I walk into her office on a referral from a friend who knew her from her days at the William Morris Agency. I stand in her waiting area, water bottle in pocket, two different headshots in hand. She calls from her office around the corner that she's so sorry but, what else, we're going to have to reschedule. Of course, I act as if this is no problem, even though I was pretty sure we had confirmed earlier that morning so as to accommodate my nine-to-five job.

But as she comes out of her office to say hello, there is a dramatic shift in her body language. She rounds the corner, still explaining how there has been some seismic event in L.A. that has changed her day. Then, as she lays eyes on me for the first time, she stops dead in her tracks, and looks me over like a new model in the Jaguar dealership. This has never happened to me before.

I was being scoped.

It took her 2.5 seconds, tops. She knew nothing about me, save that I was an actor who knew someone she knew. Yet she stopped. Dead in her tracks.

"Do you have a picture?" she asked.

"I have two," I said, and I handed her both. One was a studly headshot that I thought made me look like Russell Crowe, the other a waist-up shot of me smiling. I thought it was lame and strictly for commercial use.

"Do you do comedy?" she asked, handing the studly picture back to me after taking a cursory glance.

"Of course I do comedy," I said. "I do everything." Alarm bells should be going off for you right now, dear reader.

"That other shot's no good," she said, referring to Mr. Studly, rapidly shaving inches off my ego. "Reschedule for Monday. We'll talk."

I did, and we did, for about half an hour. We covered type, me saying I was a John Cusack, she noting that he was pasty and I was more ethnic. And then she said something in that meeting that stuck with me. She told me I needed to lose some weight. About ten pounds. The baby fat.

Until that point, I thought this was an issue that only affected women. I was surprised. Certainly I wasn't fat, but as she was a manager with interest in me,

I took her word as scripture. In fact, she was correct. Even to be the third best friend from the left, the comic guy, I needed to trim down. "Unless," she said, "you want to be the fat guy. In which case, you need to gain a lot."

In some strange way this was a comforting thought. She wasn't actually judging me. She wasn't actually calling me fat. She was telling me what she knew from her years and years of experience in this business. *You are this type.* This is the thing you are, the thing that I will sell. In that type, people look one of two ways, and weigh one of two weights. I was lounging precariously in the middle.

It's kind of like boxing: You have to fight within your class.

The fact is, the struggle with weight is constantly present in this business. Agents turn down clients—talented, beautiful people—because they pack a few too many pounds. This industry is filled with people, some ruthless, some kind, all trying to make money off actors. They work in a field that makes 80 percent of its determinations about people in 2.5 seconds, the same way you do when you sit down on the sofa and start flipping through the TV channels. Agents are not bad people—they are only doing their job. If you pretend this prejudice does not exist, you've got a shock to the system waiting for you. But if you recognize it as one of the mainstays of the career you have chosen, then you may be able to approach it in a healthy frame of mind.

I did work out, I did lose weight. Many years later I did the same when I came out of grad school. Why be skinny? Because you get two days' notice before an audition, and you might have to take off your shirt. Because actors need to be better versions of real people. Have you ever seen a celebrity in person? Many of them are tiny and frail, yet on screen they look ideal. It's all a strange lie, one that can lead to terrible problems. Young women face an unparalleled struggle when it comes to image awareness, blasted from the covers of *Seventeen*, on shows like *The O.C.* There's an entire feminist graduate thesis here, and I am in no way qualified to make these more profound arguments, but some facts remain. Many, many actors struggle with eating disorders and weight gain and loss. Maintaining your fighting weight is a completely unnatural thing. Yet it is something that, unless you are the fat guy or girl, you are going to have to do. Finding a way to do it healthily is imperative. It can be a way of maintaining discipline in an undisciplined world.

No one said it was a kind business. You are being judged constantly. But that, need I remind you, comes with the job.

The Ponytail

Kat, an actress I interviewed, told me an audition story that highlights just how important fixing yourself up can be. She had just signed with a new manager and with a top-tier agency, and the first person they wanted her to see was a hairdresser.

"We want you red," they told her. End of discussion.

Kat is no dummy. She didn't show up to meet her new manager with bedhead. "Right before this conversation I had gotten what I thought was the best haircut of my life," she says, adding that it was also the most expensive. But she had new people in charge of her career promising to get her better auditions than she'd ever had, so she heeded their advice and returned to the salon.

Two days later she has an audition for a pilot for FOX called *The Untitled Prison Break Project.* No, seriously, that's what it was called, and at this point in the interview Kat and I break out into hysterical laughter at just how clichéd this story is becoming. The part is for Dr. Sarah, the prison doctor—more laughter— apparently a redheaded one. (This show made it to air, as *Prison Break.*)

So Kat, now replete with a fresh hairdo, readies herself for the audition. Only she has new hair and, in one of those problems that men will never be able to understand, she hasn't figured out what to do with it yet. So she does what most actresses do in such a situation. "I put my hair back in a ponytail, which fits because she's a doctor, and"—more to the point—"it fucking looked good in a ponytail." This all seems very logical to her, as it does to me as well. She's made a character choice that keeps her looking hot.

The audition seems to go well, and later, she receives feedback from the casting director. "A great actress, she's really talented, we're sending her tape out to L.A., but . . . *those bangs were so harsh.*"

Nothing on her acting; it was all about the hair. A big lecture from her agents and managers followed. Her gaffe was criminal. Apparently, one should never, ever, under any circumstance, wear her hair in a ponytail. "I heard no end of the fact that I was wearing my hair in a ponytail."

Got that? *No ponytails.*

This, ladies and gents, is a trained actor, a good actor, a good-looking actor, who made a cardinal error. The ponytail. Even more ironic is that in the theater— that old hound dog from which so many of us hail—women are incessantly told to get their hair out of their face, by putting it back in—what else?—a ponytail.

But wait. Kat's story doesn't end there. In an incredible twist only Hollywood could write, the network wants to test her. Of the ten pilot auditions she had, of the ten tapes that got sent West, Dr. Sarah, the redhead with the ponytail, is the role for which she tested. Barely able to control our laughter, Kat and I attempt to find an appropriate moral for the story. We manage two.

One: "There's no fucking rule. These people don't know anything." Well, maybe that's too harsh. "They know things," Kat clarifies. "They know from years and years of experience, but people break rules all the time and it pays off." It makes me think of something Charlie Parker once said: "Practice, practice, practice. And then, when you finally get up there on the bandstand, forget all that and just wail."

But perhaps everyone would be happier with moral number two: "A good haircut," Kat tells me, "stays off your face without having to be pulled back."

The Best Version of Me

Kat's point about hair was, well . . . profound, but her grasp of the fact that it's the unexpected choice, the risk, the original person who gets the test deal, is key. Your battle with type lies within this simple paradox: find a way to fit in, then find a way to be different. Landing the role is about your individuality, the choices you made that no one else made. Once you've gotten past the original hurdle of getting the agent, of looking the part to get the audition, of maintaining that look when you walk into the casting director's office, then you have to be original.

It's so hard. You've probably spent a few years trying to get the agent. You may have been thinking about your type all that time. Descriptions from breakdowns litter your brain. And now, to get the role, you have to get down to your core, find the truth in yourself that enables you to bring this character to life, and get the part.

So indeed, once you have found your type, the next step is to forget it. Knowing that you will be going out for certain types of roles can be a way to make your work more specific. You can focus on the little things, the minor details rather than the broad strokes.

One must find a way to bring it full circle, because if you walk into a room thinking about your hair, your face, your clothes, your height, your weight, the pallor of your skin . . . if you walk in thinking that, you're never going to get the part. So once you understand the Neanderthalic way in which everyone else views type, redefine it for yourself.

The closer you are to that truth, the more honest you are in your approach to your work, the more exceptional you will be. Exceptional—that is, the *exception* to the rule; the *exception* to the type. "In general," Mandy, another actor I spoke with, told me, "when we're truthful, when we read a part or a play that speaks to us, we're going to perform that part in that play in a way that people are most likely going to respond to." And that gets jobs.

But here's the best advice I've heard yet. When I spoke with Fiona, she was reluctant to define her type. She argued that type was beside the point:

"People really want to see something exciting. It's when they don't see something exciting that they start to get all mathematical. . . . That's when they start to get all into the five pounds, seven pounds, red hair, blond hair, because they don't have anything else to go on."

Bottom line is, be good, be new, be yourself. Because that is the only thing that no other actor can do: be you.

ONE IN A MILLION:
Starting Out

"It's like starting a walkathon. . . . You're like, okay, I'm an actor
now. Didn't everyone get the memo? I'm an actor. . . .
It's hard to figure out when you started."

—Fiona

You are not alone.

There are two ways to think about this.

The reassuring way: I'm an actor now. I'm in a community of other actors—
a core group of people like me with the bond of shared experience and knowledge, facing the same struggles, ready to lend their support, give a helping hand,
share the burden of rejection and laugh off a bad day at the temp job over two-
for-one cocktails at the Sidewalk Café.

Or the other way: I'm an actor now. I'm in a community of other actors—
a core group of people like me who make this industry a crowded place, who
make audition lines long, who make the headshot piles in agents' offices deep,
and who are my competition, my nemesis, my enemy.

Every actor will, at different times, think in both these ways, and will not
be wrong. You need both the compassion and the drive. You need scene partners to work with on auditions and you need a competitive sensibility. I can sit
in the waiting room for an audition chatting with an actor as amicably as if we
were groomsmen at a wedding party, but only one of us is getting the part. This
is the world you are entering, one where you are competing against your friends
constantly; one where the actor who gives the best audition loses the part to an

actor who looks older or younger or more Jewish. One where you lose more often than you win. If you want to persevere, here's the first step:

Be a fucking human being.

"I always say," Rob Decina says, "if you're not prepared for your audition and your audition stinks, if you don't have technique and your craft isn't where it should be, then you had better at least be charming and personable."

Hopefully it doesn't get that bad, but the fact of the matter is that most successful actors are also amazingly charismatic people, people who know how to turn it on, and when to turn it on.

Rob agrees with my theory, now coined as *Be a fucking human being*. "I go out to the waiting room and I say, 'How you doing?' And you say, 'I'm great, how are you?' Oh, okay, great, *this is a person*. Let's talk. Come on in. I'm inviting you into my space here. Look how close we are. We are two feet away from each other, the doors are closed. It becomes an intimate environment. I want people I trust, people I like."

This is a cutthroat industry without the normal rules and regulations, one where personality affects performance, and it is incredibly difficult to balance drive with compassion. The simple gesture of treating people nicely, be it in the audition room, at a general meeting, at an acting class, or after a particularly bad audition, will leave a lasting impression. Cooler heads prevail. And by nice, I don't mean "proactively nice." Don't try to get anything out of it. You'd be surprised at how many directors would rather have a simple conversation with you about the Yankees pitching staff than they would hear you launch a tempest of flattery at them about their most recent show, which you may or may not have seen. Be nice by being a person, not by being an actor.

If we assume you've come to New York, we assume that you have the drive, at least to start. Let's assume that you have talent, too. Now, try to be a human being again.

Tools of the Trade: Pictures and Resumes

You've been saving, right?

As with any business, there are startup costs, and you are now in charge of your own business. The government sees it this way when it comes tax time, so you should start thinking it too. You are selling yourself, in a crowded market, to a group of hardened, unaccepting people. You need to stand out from the crowd. You need to capture their attention.

This is done with the time-honored tradition of the picture and resume. Your picture and resume are your calling card, your way of introducing yourself and all that you are in an 8" x 10" format to a complete stranger, who will hold you in his hand for five seconds, then return you to one of two stacks: audition, or no audition.

You need headshots, and they'll cost you (see chapter 11). There is a directory of headshot photographers that one can find at any of the reproduction houses or at The Drama Book Shop in Times Square. It lists the photographers, shows some sample shots, and gives you an idea of what their style is.

But what's *your* style? This is one of those endless, evolving questions, but one that you should begin deciphering right away. Whom do you look like in those headshot photographer books? Whom do you look like in your bathroom mirror? The correlation between the two might give you some idea of which photographers to interview.

The headshot must look like you. This we know. Agents and casting directors repeat this as if it were a yoga mantra. But what does that really mean? After all, it's my face on camera, of course it looks like me.

What it means isn't so much how it looks, but how it feels. The headshot must *feel* like you. I should show my picture to my best friend and he should say, oh, yeah, that's the Jason I know, the one I had a beer with after rehearsal. It should feel like you on a good day. It should have a secret, a smile, and texture— all terms that I use in the nonliteral sense. It should convey, in photographic language, something about you: your sense of humor or lack thereof, your shyness or your overbearing personality. It should come from the heart, and a good photographer will be able to capture this in you.

In terms of sheer look, the picture should be you on your best day: you on a film set after they've done final touches. Show some potential, but don't take it too far. If you don't have a chiseled jaw line and coal-black eyes, don't try to be a leading man. Don't pick a photographer who's going to overexpose and lighten you out, giving you a real man's chin with clever use of shadow. Because that's not you and you will never be cast that way.

I made this mistake in my first headshot session. I was a leading man in college, I thought, so clearly I will be competing for leading roles in New York. The photographer flattered me about being handsome, because that's her job. I ended up with the two pictures I showed the manager in chapter 5: a close-up of my face that made me look like I could be an action hero, and a waist-up shot of me smiling, which I though showed me happy, but somewhat goofy, and so

I never used it. Remember the manager's reaction? She looked at the headshot and tossed it back at me as if I had peed on it.

She was right, of course. I'm not a leading man, but I had been selling myself as one. And was not getting hired. The waist-up shot, the one that prompted her to ask me if I did comedy—that felt like me. That's the guy I was when I walked into her office. That's the guy she could sell.

Listen, a Toyota salesman doesn't sell the Camry as if it's a Ferrari or a Lexus. He knows what he's got. A sturdy car. A family car. It's not sporty, but it's got some original features. And it lasts longer, with fewer repairs. If you're a Toyota, sell a Toyota. We all want to be a Lexus, but we can't. Get over it. Get used to it.

Interview your photographer. Do you feel comfortable with her? Does she make you laugh, relaxed? Does she see you the way you see yourself? Does she use natural light or studio light, and which is better for you? If you don't know, ask her to explain it. At any given moment, a certain photographer will be hot in New York. That may or may not be a good thing for you. Several years ago, one photographer began shooting horizontal headshots—the 8" x 10" held length-wise—so that the face appeared as if it was a still in a movie frame. Inventive? Yes. Good if you're only going out for theater and television? Maybe not.

Once you've gotten the photographer and a headshot to your liking, you may or may not need retouching, which all headshot photo labs provide for a fee. I vote for makeup on the shoot instead of retouching later. It cuts on cost and makes a better photo. Once you've selected a shot, you'll need to order reproductions, which will continue to cost you.

Reproducing

The most popular places for headshot reproduction are Reproductions (New York and Los Angeles) and Taranto Labs (New York). Reproductions is slightly cheaper because they digitize the original. Links to many NYC headshot photographers can be found at: *http://reproductions.com/NYC/Directory_Index.html*

Then it's time to get the resume together. Starting out, this is a tough one, because you can't lie, so you don't have much that's going to carry any weight. We all know what we do here: Take the college show and make it sound like it happened at a nice regional theater in Bronxville, New York. The *Workshop Theater*. Ooooh, fancy, never heard of that one.

You should be honest on your resume. If you're listing a college show, say so. Don't lie and call it a regional production. But don't stress out. Try to build up your resume. And start trying yesterday.

One of my greatest career regrets is my own pride. I've always had a by-the-bootstraps approach to this business. *I'm not paying a dime more than I need to in order to have this career.* Therefore, I never applied to apprentice at the Williamstown Theatre Festival, or any other summer stock theater. I spent my summers in college waiting tables and trying to land auditions out of *Backstage*, which probably cost me just as much in bar tabs as paying my housing in western Massachusetts would have. Remember, you're not alone, and each year hundreds of college students do what I didn't. As a result, their Spear Carrier happened under the direction of Daniel Sullivan, while yours happened under the direction of a senior drama major named Bart. Maybe Bart even let you play Coriolanus. Sadly, where the resume is concerned, better to spear-carry for Daniel Sullivan than play Coriolanus for Bart.

The resume should, at its best, not only detail your career but also be a spark for conversation. "Oh, you know Daniel?" or "Oh, how is the artistic director at Shakespeare and Company? I had a client there last year."

"What's your client's name?" you ask, and now you're having a conversation. Now you're showing your personality. The resume must open avenues to something more.

I asked Stephanie Klapper what she looks for in an actor's resume. "The size of roles they've played, the types of roles," she says, before adding, "I think it's also very telling, if they don't have a lot of professional experience, to see the kinds of roles they played in school."

Because of the small-minded nature of the business, try to, at the outset of your career, craft a resume that types you. If you don't have good names to put on under "Director," but you have done a ton of comedy, make this stick out. Comic role after comic role, plus improv training, then a class at Upright Citizens Brigade when you hit the city, and you are marketable. You're not if you crowd that skill inside a list of *everything you've done since high school.* It's not all important. Craft your image in your working background.

Another thing I loathe, and I'm not alone, is the *extra* resume: that one filled up with extra roles on film and television. Listen: No one has that many film credits, and if you do, I should be able to look you up on IMDb. Extra work is for pocketing some change and getting used to film sets and the way they work, but having five studio features on your resume with parts like "Joe" and "Passerby" doesn't fool anyone. That's what they call a bad lie. A good lie might be taking the best one of those, maybe one where you had an interaction with a lead but didn't speak, one where you have an interesting story to tell about your experience, and crafting that into a line on the resume. I have been at this for a long time and, sadly, I don't have every TV show shot in New York on my resume. How could you?

Your resume should make you into an identifiable thing. Emphasize your training if you have it. And don't be afraid of being new. People like new.

Promotion

I don't buy it.

"The self-promotion kills you," Kat, of ponytail fame, tells me. "That is a full-time job."

Every other book out there is going to tell you about the value of self-promotion, but to me it seems like a lot of added stress and money for something that so rarely produces results. The reason being, you must have something to promote. Invite people to shows, but be careful. Make sure this is the one that shows you best. Just the other day, I sat in my agent's office as he laughed at a postcard for a musical version of *Lysistrata.* Then he put it in the trash. As an actor, I truly believe that a good show is one where the entire company comes together. I believe in *no small parts;* in the ensemble that converges to make up a show. But the industry thinks differently. "The play, direction, and cast all have to be *great,*" Teresa Wolf, of Schiowitz, Connor, Ankrum, Wolf, Inc., told me. "I'm at my office ten to twelve hours a day. If I go to see a show at night after ten hours of work, it had better be *really* good." She doesn't just mean unsigned potential actors. "I tell my clients that I'll see anything they're in if they want me to, but they should judge carefully and honestly. A wasted night in the theater or at a film screening is not beneficial for anyone's career if I hate it."

So make sure you're a standout, and that the show's a standout. If it's not, do the show, focus on the work, but don't invite the agents. There'll be another one. You will endure. If you can't stomach that, get out now.

What is there to promote at the beginning of a career? I agree with Brian O'Neil's *Acting as a Business* in one regard. Callbacks for good roles in major shows, big roles Off-Off-Broadway, or roles in small regional theaters are all worth notifying people about. But even if that does get you in the room, or delivers the agent meeting, then what? I've yet to meet one person to whom I sent a postcard promoting a show who, upon meeting me later in my career, remembered that I had ever contacted them.

Kat was once devoted to relentless self-promotion, but upon signing with a personal management firm, things changed.

"I walked in and I showed them my little postcards and business cards and my little Web site and they're like, 'Get rid of the Web site, no more sending post cards, never go to any audition with a headshot and resume, it looks unprofessional.'"

But how is that possible? That's what we're taught over and over by these actors' guides.

"Because if I'm supposed to be [at the audition]," Kat explains, "then [the casting directors] have my headshot and resume, and if not, the logic is, my manager can create a relationship with the casting director." See, in a business where headshots pile up five feet high, sending yours around doesn't separate you from the flock. "Managers want to create a mystique. Even though I'm not a name and a high-profile person, they want me to appear that way."

Following up, however, is different from aimlessly promoting yourself. Contacting someone with whom you have a relationship is a worthwhile expenditure of time or money. Casting directors I have auditioned for will call me directly to ask for tickets when I send a postcard for a show, because they know me. Instead of spending all of your time and money mailing headshots and postcards and cover letters to people you don't know, focus on something else: building relationships and making contacts.

Making Connections

Whom do you need to meet? That's the first question.

At the beginning, do not concern yourself with agents. Concern yourself with actors, playwrights, directors, and, to a degree, casting directors. Focus on the craft first, and the work will follow. So where are these people?

Actors should be easy to meet. In classes, at open calls, at bars. If you can't find an actor in New York, you don't get out enough.

Directors will attend preview performances—the time between the first public performance and opening night—of their show. Now, I'm not advising you to start stalking directors, but there might possibly be a small window of time where they're shaking some hands, and you might be able to say hello, mention something about the show, and tell them who you are. Or you might just be able to get a look at them, so you know who they are, so that the next time you audition, or run into them after another show, you could make an introduction. I refer back to rule number one here: *Be a fucking human being.* Do not say, "Hi, I'm an actor I really loved your show and I'd love to work for you sometime." Instead, say hello, maybe add something positive about the show. Make the connection and leave. You will see this person again. That much is a guarantee as long as you stick around this industry. You might audition for them one day, or see them at a bar after a show, when one of your friends knows someone in the cast. Worry less about making a lasting impression, about thinking this is your only shot to get this director to hire you. Instead, make contact.

Readings

The number-one way to meet people, to create a network, and to work is to do readings. You will meet other artists and have people see your work. Places like New Dramatists, Naked Angels, the Lark, the New York Theatre Workshop, Manhattan Class Company (MCC) and Manhattan Theatre Club (MTC) are doing readings of new plays all the time. Most new plays remain in development for years. Plays need actors. Playwrights need them too. Chekhov wrote parts for the Moscow Art Theatre company members. Emerging writers do the same for the actors they love.

No reading is too small. "Say yes to everything," Kat says. "If you do good work, then it's a way for you to hone your abilities. . . . You need a community. You need a network. You need a support system. You need people who know you. It's about your name. It's about street cred. . . . You do eight readings in a week, you come into contact with seventy-five people. If you do well in those readings, then seventy-five more people know you as a good actor."

Make all of these venues know you are available and interested in doing readings. When it comes to finding actors, "any theater we're associated with can be a resource," Brooke Berman, a New York playwright with several Off-Broadway and regional productions to her name, says. Become involved in a show, and you can become integral to it. "Once someone nails the tone of a play or brings something to a character that I feel is invaluable, I will fight to keep that person involved."

Playwrights in the New York and the regional theater world have a lot of pull. They have a voice in casting and they have their people. If you find a writer you click with, consider it a blessed opportunity. Though film and television writers are notoriously unsung by directors and producers, life is different for the playwright having his or her work produced. While they don't get the status or remuneration they might deserve, they do get to have their say more often than one might think.

Sometimes this involvement reaches the final production. It is by no means a given, but it is certainly better to have the playwright behind you going into the audition. "I have final approval of all casting," Brooke says. "But it's more than that. I can ask to see specific actors in the early audition process. I can veto them from getting called back. I can ask to see them again. I try to be as involved as I can."

Being a Reader

Actors love to blame a failed audition on the reader. It's either "He didn't give me anything" or "She took over the scene." But it is your job as an actor to avoid these traps and take over the audition. For a better taste, and as a way of breaking into a casting director's office, you may want to try doing it yourself.

Being the reader for auditions can be an enlightening experience, and is yet another way to meet people while getting a sense of the casting process. Every casting director needs readers, and so one way to contact casting directors is to offer your services in this capacity. As a reader you will not only gain the benefit of meeting the casting director, director, and any of the artistic staff for the theater they are casting for, you will also watch a full day of auditions. This experience is invaluable.

Mandy told me that she worked as a reader soon after coming to New York. At one point the director asked her whom she would call back. She told him what she thought. He responded that she was right, those were some of the best auditions, but they weren't right for the part. "It was a really fascinating experience," Mandy says, "to be like, 'Wow, you can give the best audition and still not be right for the part for whatever reason.'"

Being a reader will not only help you make contact with people you need to know, it will give you a jump on the experience of auditioning. And auditioning is fast going to become your job.

Finding a Money Job

Finding a money job can be difficult enough. Finding a money job that allows you the freedom to work your real job, acting and auditioning, is an entirely different story.

Start by making a commitment to days or nights. Much of this depends on where you are in your career. If you are finding your own auditions, i.e., an agent is not submitting you, then you should probably aim for a day job. This will free up your nights for rehearsals, classes, and other resume- and skill-building work. Much of the work done Off-Off-Broadway is rehearsed nights and weekends. You'll work for the same rate as your cell phone plan charges for usage during that time: free. But you'll be acting, building a resume, and meeting people. These people will become your network, your friends, and your future employers. If you did not come out of a well-known graduate program, or even if you did, this is your training ground.

You will not have that many auditions at first as a newcomer to New York. Temp jobs and other day-shift jobs usually are very reasonable about allowing an actor to take lunch a little early or late in order to make an audition. If you have only one audition a week, this should work out fine. The minute you get a commercial agent, however, your life will change, and it will be time to shift to nights. Auditions for commercials come far more frequently and with far less notice. Bosses are also far less understanding when you're clocking out three times a day, not three times a week.

Night jobs mean waiting tables or bartending, which is why they're such popular employment for actors. It's not that we like standing up and performing for customers; it's just the best gig for the money at that time of the day. Still, it can be tough. "I think being a bartender and an actor is really hard." Mandy says. "You're the last person to leave, at five in the morning. If you have an audition at ten. . . . " She lets out a small sigh. "Some people can do that. I knew that I couldn't." So she opted to wait tables and found a restaurant that only served dinner. That way she never had to worry about switching out of a lunch shift for a daytime audition, but knew she wasn't going to be serving food until 4:00 a.m.

Some Money Jobs for Actors ─────────────────────────
    Catering
    Waiting Tables
    Bartending
    Temping
    Real Estate Broker
    Private Detective
    Freelance Editing and Writing
    Script Reader
    Set Painter

It's a crapshoot, really. More than one actor told me that he fears getting attached to his day job. And it's a reasonable fear. The work provides money, benefits (on occasion), and, perhaps most importantly, a stable, consistent schedule. But it is not without its own stresses. Actors are generally good, hard workers who don't want to let people down and don't want to lose their stable form of income. Still, they must balance the time pressure between auditions, which constantly run late, and the job, which operates based on punctuality and a nine-to-five schedule. "Just because it says you're gonna audition at two doesn't mean they'll see you at two," Fiona tells me, recalling an experience she had. "And they didn't. And I sat there and it was getting later and later and I was getting stressed out."

It's a frustration that does not go away. No matter how big your agent or how often you work, most actors in New York continually face this problem. "Acting is a full-time job," Kat says. "You have to have a very high level of availability. You have to be available to do all the readings you're asked to do. You have to be available to go to all those voiceover auditions and commercial auditions."

These are the choices you will be making, which means someone will inevitably be disappointed in you. Sorry, but there is actually no way to please them all, to keep all the jobs, and to always balance your financial and career needs. Get used to it.

Get Validated

You need validation.

Any actor who is working on a regular basis has, in one form or another, been given a stamp of approval. It's the kind of mark that tells agents you won't embarrass them when you meet casting directors; it tells casting directors you won't make fools of them when you meet directors; directors that you won't let down the artistic director, or the producers, or, most importantly, the viewing public that will be paying to watch your work. "A lot of theater is trust," Patch tells me about his auditioning experiences. "Can we trust this person not to freak out on opening night? Can we trust this person to show up on time?"

So how are you going to earn this trust? How will you get this mark?

Most actors think, *I need an agent.* And they're right. Because without an agent you will have a very difficult time being a working actor in New York. Did I say *difficult?* I meant *impossible.* Agents thin the herd. That's one of their main jobs. Some do better trimming than others, but their role in this insane world is to give you a mark of approval. *Trust me,* they are saying when they submit you, *this kid can act.*

You need a reason for people to pay attention to you in a sea of others just like you. Yes, you're an individual, I know, but who's going to take the time to find that out? Get a mark of approval. You've been to grad school—you've been validated. You have a regional theater credit at a major theater—you've been validated. You've worked with this director or that playwright—wear it like a tattoo. You had drinks the other night with a director who knows the woman you're auditioning for tomorrow and he wants to put in a good word for you before you walk into the room? Great. Something, anything to make them *want* to watch you, make them *want* to listen, make them *want* to see a little more. You never know where this will come from. Ninety-five percent of the time, it doesn't come at all.

It will take so much time, you'd better stop worrying about it. Just start doing it.

Yes, have objectives. Set out a game plan. But realize that careers happen over a very, very long period of time. I like to play a game when I read an actor's bio in a *Playbill.* I take the number of roles he's listed and divide it by my approximation of his age. Great actors with twenty credits on their resume, if they are forty years old and started acting professionally in their twenties, are averaging just two shows a year.

That's not a living. But over time, it builds. You're just starting out. Of course you're in a hurry. But no one does it overnight.

An Actor with Drive

I do think, of all the people I know, that Marin was truly born to be an actor. I've both worked with her and seen her perform. The 2005 "Hot 25" issue of *Time Out New York* named her one of the actors of note that year, and she's had a spate of success Off-Broadway alongside actors like Kathleen Chalfant and Frances McDormand. Marin has a certain mystique about her; her presence pitches forward, as if she is always in motion, always heading toward the next success. I asked her how she started out.

She had drive. Literally.

"What I decided to do that summer," she told me at a bookstore one day, "was go on my own audition tour." She had recently completed her BFA at The Hartt School in Hartford, Connecticut. Throughout her schooling, she spent summers doing stock theater in western Massachusetts, paying her dues. The first year she made $20 a week. In her final summer, they offered her mainstage roles that would make her eligible for her Equity card. While she performed at night, she used her days to explore theaters around the region in her car. So she drove.

"I had all my stuff in my car. I had my days free. I had the regional theater directory . . . and I would go through and I would call every single theater that I ever wanted to work at on the East Coast that was within driving distance— that means up to like nine hours, okay—and I would go, 'Hi, I'm an Equity member and I would like to audition for your theater. When is your open call?'"

And, much to her, and my, astonishment, this actually worked. "You'd be surprised," she tells me. "If you say you're gonna come to them, and they're a regional theater," then they'll see you. It beats having to come to New York. But, she warns, there's a danger to this. Theaters will know you as a local hire, which can mean something altogether different come contract time. Keep this in mind as her story continues.

Over the next several weeks, Marin pulled out her directory, made phone calls, and hopped in her car. Sometimes the artistic director of the theater would watch her audition. Sometimes she'd talk to him on the phone. And sometimes, she'd get jobs.

These were not the most prestigious of theaters, at least at first. They were places in Worcester, Massachusetts. Places in Philadelphia where you had to find your own housing. But it was work. She was building a resume. There was an added bonus as well. "You get to know friends all over the country that you thought forgot you. 'Hey,'" she says, reenacting some of the awkward phone calls she had to make, "'I can pay you $100 a week if you guys will let me sleep on your couch.' And you do it," she says, "because the only other thing I learned was to say yes to every single thing on earth, even if it seems like a bad idea financially."

Say yes. To *everything.* When you first start acting in New York, or anywhere in the country, say yes to it all. Find your own reasons. If the material isn't quite what you'd hoped, do it for the director. If the director is terrible, do it for the other actors. If the other actors are no fun, do it for the resume credit. Find a reason to do everything. Yes, you will sleep on couches, and it will be rough. You will work, between your money job and your acting job that pays no money, at least twelve hours a day.

Another benefit Marin shared of going to each of these individual regional theaters is that you get to meet the staff and see the space. You get a feel for what the people, those same people you may see for two minutes in an audition studio in New York, are truly like. You can tell a theater's taste from the posters of past shows in its hallways. You can see if the people who run the theater prefer intimate productions, or if they play to large crowds. "It makes the whole idea less scary, and a little more real," Marin says.

The faster you make this business real to you the better. Drop the illusions; do the work. It will save you a great deal of pain and bitterness later.

One of the theaters Marin dropped in on during her road tour was the American Repertory Theatre in Cambridge, Massachusetts. She thought it was a long shot. It is, after all, one of the premier regional theaters in the country. A week after her audition, which consisted of a pair of one-minute monologues, she got a phone call asking her to come audition for a new play the ART was doing. It was originally written as a one-man show, they told her, but that might change. There were a couple other things too. *You might have lines,* the ART casting director told her, *and you might not. Also, you need to know that you might be nude. All of those things are possibilities. In fact,* they said, *you should come to this audition assuming the worst: that you'll be nude, and that you won't have any lines.*

"In theory," Marin tells me, "I'm like, ART? I'll do whatever you say."

So she goes. And then gets a callback. And then two days after that, she gets a phone call. She got the job.

Meanwhile, another summer stock company that Marin had auditioned for during her travels has offered her a non-Equity lead role. There's a little window of time that Equity gives you after you become eligible for the union when, technically, you can do nonunion work, which was what she intended to take advantage of.

Then the ART calls her back the next day. They *just* noticed that she's Equity. Marin gives me a reenactment of the skeptical look she wore when she heard that news. "I went to the Equity call," she says slowly, "and my phone number is directly above where it says 'AEA' [on my resume], so this is hard to believe."

But the ART management is adamant in their position that they cannot afford to hire her at union rates. So Marin was faced with the kind of choice that actors must make all the time. "Take this job where I actually get to fucking act, and they're going to pay me weekly, or . . . take the no-liner because its ART," where she would have to agree to find her own housing and only get paid a stipend.

The basics are always the same: *Someone is going to be pissed, someone is going to get screwed, and you will take all of the blame.*

Never mind that ART knew she was Equity from the get-go. They know the system, and they know what they can get away with. Theaters are struggling to stay in the black (the ART actually does an exceptionally good job at this, and this kind of hiring practice can't hurt) and actors are struggling to find work.

"And I said, much to my dismay, 'Well, the thing is, I was planning on doing a non-Equity job in this time frame anyway.'" Marin had met the director of the ART show, auditioned for him twice, and heard him talk about the show. She made her decision based on the same thing that actors get paid for: instinct.

"My gut was like, *You have to be in that room.*"

So she started telemarketing at the ART, literally selling subscriptions for the very show in which she would be silent and naked, while she was doing nude modeling for Boston-area art schools. She recommends this highly to any actor who has to be nude on stage as a way of getting comfortable with your body. She sat in on every rehearsal, watching as the director and playwright and actor collaborated. She felt a certain magic happening in that room. "I began telling everyone I met that these guys are going to be huge."

The show, *Nocturne,* a new play by Adam Rapp, received critical acclaim in Boston and ended up transferring to New York. Adam Rapp has since had several more plays Off-Broadway, and wrote and directed a movie starring Will Farrell in his first ever noncomedic feature-film role. The lead actor in the show, Dallas Roberts, appeared alongside Ed Norton in *Burn This* and with Colin Farrell and Robin Wright Penn in the film *A Home at the End of the World.* Marin was correct in her assessment.

A year later, Marin was back in New York, appearing in *Nocturne* at the New York Theatre Workshop, in her first Off-Broadway show. NYTW would grow to love her, but that too would take time. She had no agent, but she had a show. All because she hopped in her car one summer. That was her start.

It takes a little while to learn the ropes, because everyone has a different set of ropes. The first step is becoming immersed in the world.

"If there were a young person coming to me who wanted to move to New York to be an actor," Mandy advises, "one of the things I would have to really express to them is that what your job really is, is to be a professional auditioner. That's what we should be paid for. It's not what we get paid for, but that is actually our job. Our job is to audition all the time. That's what we do. . . . That's not our work, but that's our job. And people don't tell you that."

The second step? Make the world notice you. That's when you get to know the neighbors.

7

THESE ARE THE PEOPLE IN MY NEIGHBORHOOD—

Agents and Other Necessities

"There are 39,981 members of Actors' Equity Association . . .
. . . 3,448 have agents"

—AEA 2003 Annual Report*

Agents are as vital a part of the infrastructure of this business as stethoscopes are for medicine. They are the actor's lifeline to the rest of the world.

You're in the business now; get to know your neighbors. It's their party, you're just a guest. That is, until you work, at which point they'll sell their child for you, or promise to, anyway. They're not all sharks, by any means. In fact, most of the ones I've come in contact with, and certainly those I choose to work with, support me in my artistic efforts while they struggle with the fact that I don't make them nearly enough money. They believe in me, and have a passion for acting, craft, and talent. But they still need to make a living.

It's a strange universe. The unions regulate it, sort of. There are big agencies and small agencies, and everyone can give you a reason why one is better than the other. One thing is certain: You need them more than they need you. Until you convince them otherwise.

There is an old joke about actors and agents. It goes like this:

An actor sits at a bar with a friend. He's noticeably upset, and moving onto his fifth whiskey. Finally, his friend coaxes him into telling him what the trouble is. It seems, you see, that he had arrived home that afternoon to surprise his girlfriend and found her in bed with another man.

"Man, I'm so sorry," the friend sighs.

"No, it gets worse," the actor replies, ordering up another shot. "I know the guy."

"Noooooooo."

*Statistics on agent representation of AEA members not given in 2004 report

"Yes. He's my agent."

The friend is livid. "Agents. Fucking spineless bastards."

"Yeah, no soul," the actor nods in agreement.

"We should kick his ass."

Suddenly sober, the actor looks at his friend, incredulous. "We can't," he tells him.

"Why not?" the friend replies in utter bewilderment.

"Because he's my agent."

"So?"

"Dude, I don't want to burn any bridges."

Agents are of the utmost importance in this business, and anyone who tells you otherwise doesn't have an agent. Technically, they are employment agents, licensed by the state and working on a regulated 10 percent commission. That's the law. For an actor, they're the single most important player in the game. If you want to be known, if you want to audition on a consistent basis, not to mention work with some frequency, you must have one. Actors with careers have agents.

I've already told you how to get their attention, namely by letting them come to you, so this chapter is going to assume that you have reached the point where you have their attention. By some miracle, you have landed five minutes with an agent. Now what?

First, you need to understand what good agents do, what they should do for you at the various stages of your career, and what you should expect out of the relationship.

First of all, you know that old line, *They work for you?* Don't ever tell an agent that unless you are making her a ton of money. There aren't enough agents for all the talented actors out there, and that kind of attitude will get you right on top of your agent's shit list. Technically, they get paid when you do. But this doesn't make you the CEO of the corporation. Agents vary in their artistic goals and desires, but they have a bottom line to meet. They need to make money off their roster, and though this does come down to the individual clients they represent, it also revolves around larger strategies. They are essentially playing the percentages, and have a business model based on that. That's why they can afford to wait out actors during cold streaks, because hopefully someone else is hot at the time. They are managing a roster of clients, not you alone.

You are managing you, and don't forget it. In the back of your mind, you should know that your agent works for you, but telling her that is not going to make her work any harder for you. As an entry-level actor, you can expect your agent to perform one job: getting you auditions. This doesn't really change much over time, but at some point it will hopefully transform into *Get me the offer.*

"You want them to really know what you can do," Jon tells me, recounting his first round of agent meetings. "At least, that's what I thought at the time. At this point, I know it doesn't fucking matter. I know they don't give a shit if you can act or not; they just care if you can book jobs or not. You could go turn in the most amazing performance on stage, and I don't think there are many agencies out there that will see that and say, 'Oh, I gotta represent this kid.' It's all about look and marketability."

I spoke with one agent from a higher-tiered agency, whom we'll call Dan, and he agrees that talent is not the only factor in selecting a client. "I look for good talent," he tells me, "but it's a lot more than that. I've met actors who are amazing talents, but if they have that attitude. . . . If I don't want to work with someone, I don't have to. Life's too short. So, if there are two actors and one's amazing, and then one's not as amazing but really good, but the really good one is just the greatest person and the amazing one is a pain in the ass, I'll go with the just really good one."

The first days can be rough. You've worked long and hard to get to the level where you have an agent. Now that you have one, you're yet another actor on the list. "My phone calls were getting returned but there wasn't very much time for me. I clearly wasn't a priority," Jon says.

Good agents develop solid relationships with casting directors of note, so that instead of sending a headshot, they pick up the phone and say: "You should see my client. Trust me." And the casting director does. This is a business built around relationships. "Certainly there are agencies that have more power," Rob Decina says. "They've established themselves and they have a credibility factor based on the client list." Will he see actors from other agencies? Of course. But it comes down to efficiency. "It makes my business go quicker for me to call up an agent and go, 'Hey, I'm looking for a twenty-five-year-old leading man. Who do you got?'"

At the beginning of your career, the most important thing you want from your agent is belief. After that, it's your call. Because this is a here-today, gone-tomorrow industry, belief in your ability to succeed is more important than any other factor. Endurance is paramount, and to endure, you need an agent by your side. "I didn't want to connect with somebody on the soul level, because if you connect with an agent on a soul level, there's something wrong with you," Jon tells me, only half joking. "Let me amend that," he says, noting that, as in any human relationship, respect builds over time. "I've become very close to my agent and I definitely love and respect him very much, but you know, the reason why I ended up going with my agent is because, of all the agencies I talked to, the one that I ended up with was the one that promised it would come down and see my show in D.C."

They never made it to the show.

Here follows the realist's guide to agents—from the basics of size, shape, and operation to a more detailed inquiry. This is the agent as seen from the working actor's perspective, not the agent seen from the agent's perspective. This is the way it really works.

Commercial Agents

Agents exist in two basic categories: commercial and legit. While legit agents dally in film, television, and theater, commercial agents work, as the title suggests, on commercials. Within the commercial division there are further subdivisions, the most basic being between on-camera and voiceover. On-camera is just that: performances that are seen on television, or in nonbroadcast video, called *industrials*. Most on-camera commercial divisions will divide clients between their beauty/model/print divisions and the regular-actor folk. Print work is an additional bonus that a commercial agent may offer you if you are, well, pretty.

Commercial agenting works differently from legit agenting, in that the commercial world moves so much faster. It's audition Monday, callback Wednesday, shoot on Friday. Because of the speed at which this side of the business operates, the submission process is not quite the same as it is for legit work. Much of this I've deduced on my own, but in three years, my commercial agent has only asked for ten headshots from me. This means that he is submitting me by name, and based on a relationship of trust that he has built with a casting director. It's also formulated upon my track record with certain casting directors.

How often do I get called back? Have I booked a spot out of that office? Do they remember me, and if so, do they like me?

The larger commercial offices are stocked with agents. At my agency, there are three on-camera agents, four or five voiceover agents, plus a kids' department and a beauty department, all with several agents. Then there are the assistants, with whom you will be speaking most of the time. Be nice to assistants, because they will one day be your agent. Most agencies divide their agents to work with different casting directors, as opposed to different actors. This means that all three on-camera agents are my representatives, pitching me to a certain number of casting directors.

There are five big commercial agencies in New York; some have legit divisions and some only do commercials. The bigger they are, the more respect they get from commercial casting directors. The more respect, the more trust, and the more trust, the more appointment times. An actor I know was considering signing with my commercial agency, but was worried about its size. He asked me how many clients the agency had. I didn't know precisely—something like one out of every three actors I know. But, I told him, it's not like any other commercial agency works with fewer clients. They all have a hundred other guys like you. The fact of the matter is that there is one way of guaranteeing more auditions, and that's by getting callbacks and getting work. If you're making them money, they'll keep sending you out. If you're not, they're going to give the other ninety-nine guys like you their shot.

When signing with a new commercial agent, one wants to get the most out of the relationship, but there is a danger in thinking too big. In the wooing stage of meeting a new actor, many commercial agencies promise both on-camera and voiceover representation. Once signed, however, the totality of this agreement doesn't always hold, the reason being that there are plenty of people who pursue voiceovers, and only voiceovers, for their career. Representing you, in this case, can be a threat to those clients. Plus, simply being an actor does not guarantee that you have a "commercial"-sounding voice.

Be up front with the agency. When my commercial agent asked to re-sign me, I said that I would certainly love to be represented on camera, but that since I wasn't getting any voiceover auditions, I did not want to sign in that area. In response, I was told that the agency only signs across the board. "Well," I said, "I think in all fairness that you need to give me a shot at voiceovers."

No Negotiation

The idea of an actor holding power in signing a contract is a rather ludicrous proposition as it is. "You know, when it came time to renegotiate my—" Mandy begins, then halts to correct herself. "Not renegotiate, you don't *renegotiate* your contracts, you just get them and you sign. Which is exactly the difference. In another business, you renegotiate the contract. But when it came time to re-sign, my friend who was in finance said, 'Why don't you say to your agents, *You have to get me X number of film auditions in the next year or I don't have to stay in my three-year contract.*' And I was like, 'Because that's not how it works. I mean, in your business you can say that and it's something that's done.' That is not done in this business."

"Basically," Mandy says, hitting the proverbial nail on the head, "this business doesn't work like a business."

By week's end, I had a meeting with the voiceover division. They were skeptical at first, and sent me into the studio to do a thirty-minute work session. By the end of this time, and thanks to some fabulous advice, I had three spots that actually sounded like they could be on the radio. My tape would be passed along to the agents and I would await their verdict. Of course, no promises.

This seemed to be an exceedingly fair way of managing this situation on their part. The agency offered me my shot, even gave me time to work out the kinks in my admittedly raw technique. I was coached and given tips, and my reads improved over the course of the session. It took almost three weeks, but sure enough, the voiceover department called me and said that they liked my tape, and that they would start sending me out on auditions.

So don't be complacent, but don't be a nuisance either. Your career is always in your hands, under your control. I waited until I had a moment of leverage, in the agency wanting to re-sign me, and I used it. Was it a lot of leverage? No. I hadn't made them a dime in a year. But the agents had faith, and I took advantage of a potential opportunity. I would have been extremely bitter if the voiceover department had said I wasn't cut out for voiceovers, but now that I've been through the testing and a trial period, I know that the agents stand behind me. I have faith in my representation.

This is something I cannot stress enough as we delve deeper into the world of agents: faith. It is the foremost thing we should look for in an agent. It's partly an instinctual, gut thing. Practically, it means that you are going to work with someone who knows, and believes in, your work. Good agents will only sign clients they believe in. Bad agents will sign someone they think has a pretty face, and will throw them out to the casting wolves to see who bites. I've seen both.

Legit Agents

While size is beneficial on the commercial side, things get a little trickier when it comes to the legit side. *Legit,* as in *legitimate,* refers to agencies that rep theater, film, and television. There are three basic tiers of legit agents, though some divide the lowest tier into two groups. At the top are the big guns: Creative Artists Agency (CAA), International Creative Management (ICM), William Morris, United Talent Agency (UTA), and Endeavor. They are the kind of agencies that package film and television projects, and that do not, as a rule, "develop" new clients. They wait for someone to get a big movie, or a television show, and then come calling with promises of hot cars, hotter girls, and, hottest of all, a career. When one actor I spoke with, currently signed with a midrange agency, was offered two pilots in two days, William Morris called to take him out to dinner an hour after he got the second offer. Until you have offers like that, you need not concern yourself with these agencies.

Below the big guns are the midrange agencies that do, to varying degrees, develop clients. Abrams, Gersh, Innovative Artists, Paradigm, and Don Buchwald—the kinds of agencies that can offer you opportunities beyond the smaller agent. Then, below these, are the small agencies. The small agent, in this case, refers to the bulk of the agencies left in New York. They have names like law firms: Henderson Hogan, or Kerin Goldberg. They handle a smaller, less famous, client list. As such, the opportunities they can get you are fewer, but often they are willing to chance it out with you for far longer; to endure the hard times that are most likely going to appear at one point or another during your career, supporting work that doesn't pay well but offers exposure. Because there are so many actors, talent doesn't always hit right away. Sometimes it takes a while, and sometimes patience can be the most valued commodity an agent offers an actor.

The question of big versus small agent is one that will haunt you at some point or another if you're in this business long enough. *You've got to trade up,* I've been told. And it's true. It makes good business sense. But moving up the ladder means becoming the low man at the big company. The only absolute truth is that the size and repute of an agency is an important consideration. Just as there are with actors, there are degrees of competency with agents and agencies.

Size Matters

As a general rule, I think of large agencies like a supermarket-sweep game show. You get your shot at fitting a ton in that little cart of yours, but the clock is ticking. Larger agencies will get you the auditions that you want—all of them. You will have general meetings—a type of get-to-know-you that doesn't include an audition—with everyone you ever wanted to meet. Your pilot season will consist of a hundred pilot auditions, not two. It is the equivalent of being a kid on Halloween and waking up in the Hershey's factory.

Only problem is, you don't have all day. You are in make-or-breakville: no time for warming up, no time for failure. You are expected to book jobs, big jobs, and soon. You will not be seen for smaller regional theater, for plays in NYC that pay little money, and for all those other developmental jobs that help build a resume. The clock is ticking on you from the moment you sign.

Kat ran off a checklist of things she now has with her big agent.

"As soon as I signed with these people, I was out on about ten pilot auditions, and I've had three general meetings." Kat pauses, then adds with emphasis, "I didn't even know that happens." She was getting the type of access that her smaller agent never got her. Kimberly Hope, a casting director you'll hear from at length in the next chapter, confirms this without my even asking. "I never heard Kat's name before she signed, and now [her agent] talks to me about her every day." In addition, for every audition, Kat also got neatly printed appointment sheets with all the relevant production information, and the character and story breakdown, attached. Kat can now focus on acting, not selling herself to casting directors.

But here's the inevitable downside. "It makes me more nervous because there's more direct contact," she tells me. "My agents and managers have been dealing with big casting directors for a long time. I walk into that audition and I know that they can just pick up the phone and say, 'Hey, Bonnie Finnegan [a well known New York casting director], how'd she do?'"

Which is why you should truly and honestly evaluate whether or not you are ready for the big agent. Look in the mirror the same way you did when you figured out your type and took your headshots. Are you ready to take this kind of risk? I know acting is all about risk-taking, and of course we should go head-first into everything, but this is a business sufficiently lacking in second chances. I've seen good friends of mine sign with big managers and agents and fall right off the map. The good news is, Kat just landed a pilot, so I'm fairly certain these people will stick with her. But what if they don't?

That's what happened to me. I signed with one of those midtier agents when I was twenty-four, and the honest truth is, I wasn't ready for it. Suddenly, I was going into FOX and Warner Bros. every other day. I was underprepared because I didn't know what to expect in those auditions. The first time I walked into a room for seven producers, I was so nervous, and so bad, that as soon as I finished the scene I got up and walked out without saying good-bye. For three months I auditioned for pilots, movies, and episodics. I would go out for a different *Law & Order* episode every week, and finally I landed a small role on one. This, to me, was a huge deal. A whole scene with Jerry Orbach! I'd been dreaming of this since high school. Plus I was working. I booked! My agents will love me.

When pilot season ended without me in a pilot, they didn't love me. They dropped me. Didn't even call me personally. My manager broke the news. *Don't worry,* she told me. But she was worried. I could tell.

A number of factors contributed to my demise at this agency, to be sure. For a long time I felt like they should have stuck with me, because I showed potential. Certainly, it would be difficult to argue that they weren't playing a game of throw-them-against-the-pilot-wall-and-see-who-sticks. It's common for agencies to load up for pilot season, then dump clients afterward. From the perspective of a larger agency, my one scene on *Law & Order* was not the coming-out moment they expected. And as far as pilots were going, well, I just wasn't impressive enough.

Dan confirmed much of this when I spoke with him. Indeed, there is a meeting post–pilot season where agencies decide which clients they will drop. Dropping a client, Dan tells me, is usually rationalized with, "They don't want it as much as we want it for them. We're not hurting for the money, so one actor's not going to make or break it." I put my own situation into this perspective. My

Law & Order role was not a Guest Lead, something that larger agencies place more value on. "I don't represent the guys who are going to play the cop," Dan says. "That's not a bad thing; it's just that there are other agencies for that."

This catches me slightly off guard, because though many actors refer to their agents as good at theater but not television, or vice versa, I have never heard an actor refer to his agent as someone who only handles Guest Leads. "Isn't an agent an agent," I ask Dan, "and shouldn't all of the roles be available to me?"

"Not true," he says. "And I don't care what agency you're talking about. My L.A. office doesn't work on Co-star roles at all. And it's not a snob thing. We sign the actors we want to work with. And if they're not Guest Leads on episodics, then they're not going in for one-scene roles. At this level, that's the truth."

That's the level I was supposed to be operating at that year of my acting life. And truthfully, I was unprepared for the whole goddamn thing. The ABC building! The *Law & Order* studios! These were places I had been dreaming of for a long time. In a way, I was too naïve, too innocent, and though I played it cool, I was far from it. I was a nervous little kid, a tiny fish in a really big pond.

Which is why the next time around, because I was lucky enough to have a next time, I promised myself I would go with an agent more my size. Maybe I'd have fewer auditions, for less prestigious projects, but it would all happen at a pace I could manage. I wanted someone who would stand behind me for the long term.

Which is exactly what I have now—an agent who, when I apologized because the agency wasn't making much money off me, said, "It's not about that." An agent who I go to the theater with, who comes and sees every show I do, who gets excited about my roles on *Law & Order.* An agent who understands bread and butter, and doesn't need a five-layer cake . . . for now. Because that's where I am in my career.

Small is not for everyone, and small means I have to do a lot more work on my own behalf. But the benefit is that I always feel comfortable in my choices. I have not made a deal with the devil where I'd better be paying up by the end of the year.

Think this size question over carefully and answer it for yourself. As I've illustrated, it can go both ways. Kat got a pilot; I got dumped. Sorry to say, there are no magical answers.

The Meeting

Agent meetings go according to the agent's interest in you, and according to how many other agents are interested in you. If you have a little heat—are the hot kid in your grad school class or just got a fabulous review in the *Times*—you can count on agents putting on their best face, especially if they know others are interested in you as well. For the first meeting at a midtier agency, you'll usually meet with one agent. At a smaller office, you might meet with both agents together. They will ask you fairly standard questions about yourself, your background, your career goals. They will do this in between answering phone calls and responding to e-mails. They are feeling you out, getting a sense of your personality. And that's the most important thing to bring to the meeting with you: personality.

Giving good meeting is important. Preparing a laundry list of answers to questions you think they will ask is not going to show off your personality. Knowing what you want out of your career, having interesting details to share about growing up—these are the things that capture people's attention. The first agent and manager I signed with had never seen me act before. They heard from other people that I was talented. It was my meeting with them that got me signed.

My approach to the meeting is to be a slightly amplified version of myself. You must have energy, you must be entertaining, but you can't come off sounding rehearsed. This doesn't mean that only boisterous personalities get agents. There are plenty of shy actors with agents, and plenty of quirky ones. So express this in the meeting, in the clothes you wear, in the stories you tell—in any way you can.

If other agencies are interested in you, share this with the agent. Chances are the agent will ask you, and full disclosure works to your advantage here. If he thinks someone else is about to move in on you, he'll be more apt to sign you. There's always a bit of a card game going on, and you must figure out how much bluffing you can get away with. But do not lie. These people all know each other, and they will talk. So if you're only meeting with one agent, be up front about it.

Should the first meeting go well, you will be invited back to meet with the other agents at the agency. Usually, a consensus is required to sign a client. If they haven't seen you act, they may have you bring in a monologue to do for them. Find something close to your personality, something that plays to your strengths. Don't be a great tragedian—be you. Be the guy who walks into a room and has thirty seconds to get the job. Show them one color, maybe two.

The group meeting will be more of the same as the first time around. There will be flattery, and a discussion of your headshot, the kinds of roles you may be interested in playing, and those you aren't. It's important to make sure everyone is in agreement on your type, and you should be prepared to talk about yourself in this way. If they're having you back for a second meeting, you've done something right. So relax, and do more of the same.

The longest agent meeting I ever had was forty-five minutes, and I thought for sure they were going to sign me. They had seen me act in my showcase and wanted to meet me. I was funny and charming. I talked intelligently about where I saw myself as an actor, the kinds of roles I saw myself playing, and what I wanted out of my career. I walked out of the room confident that I was going to get a phone call offering me representation ten minutes after I walked out the door.

It didn't come. And when I finally called them to say I had other offers, I was told they would be passing on me. Where on earth had I gone wrong?

For starters, forty-five minutes is a long time to spend in a room. It's a long time to be "on" without a script, and maybe my energy dropped. But I also misread the situation. There is always one agent who is going to have more say in the matter, and I had played to the wrong one. Turns out the woman who was asking the more skeptical questions was the agent who had a stronger foothold. It was also league season, the time of year when hundreds of graduate school programs release their young into the wild, and this agency wanted to see all the new young talent before the agents made decisions.

Or so they told me. But when Jon came out of his meeting with the same agency, he was offered representation immediately. Why? He had a list of people interested in him. He was in a bidding war.

Really, none of it matters. You must trust that, in the same way you can't force a girl or a boy to like you, you can't force an agent to either. Had I ended up with that particular agency at that particular point in my career, I'm confident they would have dropped me by now. Someone who wants to wait and see on you is not what you want in an agent. You want someone who is excited about you. So make him be excited about you. The meeting is a chance to do just that.

Be Wary

Here are a few things to be wary of in a first meeting.

- *Too many promises*—In general, agents shouldn't promise you anything except getting you the auditions. Getting the job, well, that's your problem.

- *Promising legit representation to get you to sign commercially*— Larger agencies that have both commercial and legit departments might lure you with the promise of signing you for legit in order to get you to sign commercially. More than any other business, the commercial world is always in need of a fresh face, so agents bring on new clients more often. Less so in the legit world. If they want you that badly commercially, they'll take you regardless. Remember, you might be better off with a smaller agent in the legit world.

- *We only have a hundred clients*—Everyone has more clients than they admit to. Get over it. A more relevant question might be, How many are in town and out of work versus those working in the regions? Because that's who you are up against.

- *The promise of submission*—When I was meeting agents after my showcase, they would call me and tell me they were submitting me for certain projects. Wow, I thought, these people are hungry. Of course, not one of those submissions turned into an audition. Remember that any agent can submit you, but not every agent can land you the audition.

- *The long contract*—Especially with managers, watch this one. A lot can happen in three years.

Managers

I've been trying to figure out the manager game for a long time. Its elusiveness is a rather central part of its definition within the industry. Managers tread upon new ground. They are not bound by union or state rules regarding commissions, and are therefore unregulated. This is often used by the unions as proof that all managers are bad and will steal your money. It's a blanket statement that is far from the truth. Like agents, there are some good managers and some bad ones.

The basic construct behind the agent/manager relationship, and the reason managers began appearing in the first place, is the idea of personal attention. Namely that agents, in order to keep in the black, must represent so many clients that they don't have the time to give each individual client's career the personal attention that can make a career. Managers were born into this world under the premise of fewer clients and more personal attention.

They do indeed provide this, and it can be—depending on your own ability to market yourself, keep yourself emotionally secure, and handle rejection—worth every penny. Every penny equals another 10 to 15 percent of your income, depending on the manager. As with agents, there are different tiers of managers. Some have star clients, some have a list of nobodies. Some develop actors, some don't. And there is no hard and fast rule about either one being better.

"What scares me," Dan says, "is that managers aren't with unions. With managers, literally, somebody can have a card made up and say, 'I'm a manager.' There's a lot of those out there. They make my life miserable because they want to be part of it and they kind of feed off the actor. So, I guess what I'm saying is, when it's a good manager, great. I think some actors sign with managers way too soon."

But again, where rules are lacking, logic exists. I've had two experiences with managers. The first, as I detailed earlier, was with the manager who tried to launch my career. She was responsible for finding me an agent, and getting me general meetings with casting directors so they would know who I was when she called to pitch me. But when things didn't pan out the way she envisioned, and I was agentless, she soon gave up on me.

Do You Need a Manager?

At the outset of a career, one of the manager's foremost responsibilities is finding an agent for her client. Oftentimes, this agent-getting is used as an argument against managers, as in: All they do is find you an agent, and then the agent takes over. Even if this were the case, finding an agent is a difficult enough task on its own. That might well be worth the extra 10 to 15 percent of your income. Ten percent of zero is still zero, you see. That, of course, is a decision for you to make. And your feelings about it will most likely change as your career progresses, depending on the money you are making. This is why people frequently drop and change managers and agents.

Also, many agents and managers have previously established working relationships. As your career develops, you might want to give greater consideration to finding an agent and manager who have worked well together in the past.

With my second manager, I was much more hesitant. I decided I would do the organizing, not leave it to him. I found a manager I liked, and an agent I liked, and decided to work with both of them. The manager's pitch to me was simple. Basically, they said, you need to get your picture out there as much as possible, and we will make sure that happens. Having twice as many people spending time on you is a plus. I agreed. I just made sure that I was selecting the other half of the team instead of letting them do the selecting.

These new managers had only been around for a couple years when I signed with them, and they had no star clients. I liked this workhorse ideal, but it leaves the potential problem that they don't get their phone calls returned as often as the manager who represents a star. Of course, relationships rule the day.

Another actor I know made the entirely opposite choice from mine. He had met with one of the larger of the small-tier agencies as well as with a manager. She boasted Marisa Tomei as one of her clients. Somewhat starstruck, and thinking he wanted to launch his career with a bang, my friend opted to sign solely with the manager, not with the agent. The agency was pissed, and they warned him: She is going to forget all about you if you don't get work immediately, while we will stick by you. But the manager was making other promises. That agency is too small. They have no access. Come to me and I'll get you with a bigger agent.

He did, and she didn't. I watched the few auditions he had. When it came to building a career, this manager had no idea what to do. She either wouldn't allow him to go out for regional theater, or didn't know the smaller casting directors who cast regional theater. He would show up for an HBO movie once in a while, but once in a while is a pretty tenuous proposition, especially when it comes to booking an HBO movie. She never did get him that meeting with the bigger agent, and if he had gotten that meeting, he probably would have needed to show the agent some tape, of which he had none. He was caught in a representation quagmire.

Were there warning signs? Sure. Might you make the same mistake? Sure. The smoke that is blown up unmentionable places at these times smells sweet. That's the job of the manager and agent who want to sign you—to make you feel invincible. In a business based on risk-taking there are always warning signs. But traveling the unmarked path is often the way to a career. The only hard and fast rule is to watch your own, er, ass.

This policy guided me through my second round of representation. The lone fact that I needed a second round was lesson enough. See, in round one, after my midtier agent dropped me, my manager called and told me not to worry. So I didn't worry. I didn't worry as the auditions suddenly stopped. *(It's just that pilot season is over.)* Then I didn't worry as the manager tried to get me with another agency, which made me do monologues for them, and then said I wasn't good enough. *(He gives great meeting, but the work didn't match his personality.* Remember what I said about showing them who you are?) Then, without an agent for a few months, I suddenly found that I had a manager who wouldn't return my calls. Knowing I was not long for the management company's world, I made one final demand and had them set me up a meeting with another commercial agent, who began freelancing me. One thing that can always be said about managers is that they get their phone calls returned by agents where actors don't. Good thing too, because soon after my managerial relationship died, I booked a commercial.

Jump ahead five years to my second round at all this, and I am determined not to fall through the cracks again. I signed with the manager who had seen me act in my showcase, and an agent who hadn't. I knew that it was possible for the relationships to sour, and I knew that because I had been out of town for two years, it might take a little while to restart my career. Having an agent who had never seen me before made me nervous ("You were a fluke," she told me the other day), and so I was glad to have the manager to back me up if the agent ever got doubtful. And she did get doubtful. I went a year without working before finally booking a show. At the time, she told me that she was starting to get nervous. Then she came and saw the show, finally saw me act, and from that moment on, knew what I could do. I worked for a year straight after that.

This time around, it has worked out perfectly. Both my manager and my agent believe in me and give me personal attention, answer my phone calls, even invite me to their birthday parties. But this is just one of the ways it can go. And the unions do have a point, especially because most managers want to tie you into a three-year or longer contract. Because there is no union regulation, one should be very careful about signing contracts with managers. It used to be that 15 percent was standard, but most managers now take 10 percent. Most will take commissions on everything you make, commercial and legit, regardless of union rules. For example, if an AEA member makes less than $500 in a show, the agent is not allowed to take a commission, but the manager is. Most managers also have little to do with commercial agenting, but they will take 10 percent of the commercial money you make, unless it is specifically detailed otherwise in the contract. A manager may go to Los Angeles for months, leaving you in New York without representation, and with no location clause in the contract (i.e., the manager has to be where you are). And while three years can be a very long time, some managers have no time frame or sunset clause in the contract. With agents, if you don't make a certain amount of money or work a certain number of days (it varies from union to union), you have the right to break contract. With a manager, it is far more difficult.

Actors, Agents, and Managers: Notes from the Underground
Why Nobody Knows Me

"This doesn't necessarily have to be off the record, especially if we don't use their names," a now-nameless actor tells me. "I mean," he continues, "you probably should use it."

And so I will.

We're midway through an interview and I was asking this actor, let's call him Jack, about what his agent thought of his working out of town. This is when he tells me that he just left his agent, and is now working solely with a manager.

"What basically happened is . . . a friend became an assistant at this manager's office six or eight months ago. She was wanting me to come in and she got one of the managers to see me, and another, and then I met with the head manager. And she was very hesitant about working with me. It was the middle of pilot season," meaning that she was busy, but that there was a lot being cast at the moment. "We just kind of really hit it off in the meeting and she said, 'Well, I'll sort of take a risk on you and send you out for a few things . . . see how you do.'"

"So I did that. Second audition I went on was for a major casting director." He shall also remain nameless for these purposes. Jack auditions, and "afterwards [the casting director] was like, 'Great! Really great audition! I'm going to send the tape to L.A. I like him a lot. Who is this guy? How come I've never heard of him? Who are his agents?'"

So Jack's manager proceeds to tell the big television casting director who the agents were.

"Oh," he says, "I won't deal with them. I hate them. I won't answer their phone calls. I don't take submissions from them."

And Jack's new temporary manager says, "You need to fire your agents."

Are you getting a sense of the hierarchy here? About the power shifts and who's in charge and how relationships matter? Good.

Now, Jack has been tiring of his agents for a long time. But Jack didn't exactly have many other options until now. He tells the manager that he agrees with her, he's been wanting to get rid of them.

"You need to fire them now," she says.

"I know. I'm ready to," Jack says.

"You need to fire them *now*," she repeats.

"Right now?" he asks, somewhat incredulous.

"You need to go *right now*."

"So, it's like five o'clock on a Wednesday," Jack tells me, "and I go up there at six-twenty and I fire them like that."

"What did they say?" I ask.

"They were surprised."

"Did you explain why?"

"Yeah," he continues. "I didn't tell them specifically what someone said. I said that some people had seen me in [a play I had just finished] and were interested and that I wanted to make a push to get more. This was in late February, early March. Pilot season was more happening, and I was like, 'You guys have been great at supporting my theater career but I want to make a push to television and I don't feel that you can offer me that.' And it's true, I would have maybe one pilot audition per year. And with the manager just sending me out, just kind of testing me, I had eight in three weeks."

Relationships matter in the representation game. Is someone not fulfilling his end of the bargain? Sure. That big TV casting director. You could be the greatest actor in the world and because he doesn't like your agent, he's not going to know you exist.

The ladder you're trying to climb is missing every other rung.

Marin's Meetings

I include this tale as proof that this can be a nasty business and that surviving the nastiness is a part of your job. The nastiness has naught to do with your talent, or your chances of success.

While I believe cold mailings to be a waste of time, they occasionally do result in a meeting. You've been plucked from a pile of headshots, which means you may have plenty more to prove. Here's how a meeting might go.

Marin mailed pictures and resumes and postcards with the industriousness of a Soviet laborer, and was granted a meeting with a smallish agency. It was the only meeting she got off cold mailings and it was, in her words, "awful and humiliating." I ask her what was so awful, and she launches into the story without hesitation.

"She behaved like—and this may be true—she had never seen my resume." As if she hadn't bothered to flip the photo over and read what Marin had been up to professionally. But then, in the meeting, "she basically just mocked everything I had done, and basically started out by saying, 'What are you doing in my office?'"

"Literally?" I ask, interrupting to make sure that this isn't one of those angry actor stories rife with embellishment.

"Yeah," Marin says, "And I said, 'Well, you called me.' And she's looking at my resume and she'd be like, 'Well, I've never heard of that play. What the hell is that play?'

"'It's a new play.'"

"'What's this thing in New York?'

"'Oh, it's a new play by Adam Rapp.'

"'Do you have a big part?'

"'Well, I don't have a big part, but it's a really strong scene.'"

And then, just to make sure Marin got the message, the agent told her exactly what she thought of her career to date.

"'I can't do anything with you.'" And then, Marin says, "she basically threw me out of her office."

This is the kind of story that brings to a rapid boil all those emotions that one feels living the life of an actor. How did this leave her?

"'Totally devastated."

Because she was doing well. She had auditioned for major casting directors, had found work Off-Broadway of her own enterprising volition. She had done all of those things they tell you to do, had landed the meeting, and was then told that she was unworthy. "I think, for no agent, I'm doing okay." Which she is. But all of this toil, years and years of Marin's life, is not good enough for this agent. "I leave, and I'm like: the end."

It's easy to feel that way after an agent meeting that does not pan out. "Getting an agent is probably the hardest thing in this business," Rob Decina told me when we met. So hard that the opportunity feels like the only one that will ever arise: *Here is my chance, my break into the business, my one shot that I've been dreaming of for years.*

Marin and I are here to tell you to never treat it that way. If you have talent, if you keep at it, there will be other chances. The big break is a myth, and a harmful one at that, because it sets expectation at an incalculable, and unachievable, level. Marin kept at it, meeting with even more nonsense. Soon, however, she met an agent who liked her, who thought she had talent, who knew that, though she wasn't always going to be the prettiest face in the room, she was an actor who should have a shot. But even this took some time. They met, there was an unclear relationship that one might call freelancing, and then, the perfect storm hit. The Vineyard Theatre in New York wanted her to audition for a show right about the time she landed another job, *Proof* in Delaware. She called the agent. Marin says it went like this:

"'Listen, they [the Vineyard] asked me if I had an agent, should I give them your number?' I said. And she was like, 'Um . . . sure.' And I said, 'So are you my agent?' And she was like, 'Ummm . . . yeah.'"

So Marin had Delaware send the contract for *Proof* to the agent, and when she showed up at the office to sign it, there was another set of contracts, for representation, waiting.

See? It's never easy. It stretches out over months and months. Money is usually the deciding factor, as in, are you making any? Other than that, you need to have your own mystique, your own heat. Work, sex appeal, talent, personality—you decide. And then sell the fuck out of it to them.

Signing vs. Freelancing

"We like to date before we get married." This is one of the more common refrains of the first agent meeting, and while it is a completely valid argument, it is one that benefits the agent far more than it does the actor. Many tout freelancing as a way for the actor to benefit: More agents working for you is the going logic. But better to have one agent working hard for you than several tossing your picture into the mix as the urge hits. Plus, with freelancing, they must clear you first for an audition, meaning that you must then tell other agents who submit you for the same project that someone beat them to the punch.

Freelancing is the agents' way of saying, *We're interested, but not interested enough.* You know when they'll be interested? When you book the job and make them some money. The more auditions, the better the odds of booking. And more auditions come as a signed client than as one who is freelancing. I once made $20,000 on a commercial while freelancing, and they still didn't sign me.

Laura, another of the actors I interviewed, tells me that she left her agent to freelance with another agency. "I knew that was a gamble. And the first year freelancing was one of the most frustrating. I was working all the time . . . and I was like, 'Oh, they'll sign me.' And then I kept working and they didn't."

So when it comes to dating, play it closer to the arranged marriage than to the traditional formula. Marry, then get to know each other. It's far easier to break a union contract for representation than it might seem. After all, commitment is what counts.

Too Big for Your Agent

One last agent/manager/career craziness story.

Kat was represented on a freelance basis by a small agent named Judy. She desperately wanted a better agent—she knew justice was not being done in the freelance department. Then, a writer who liked her called.

"God bless Theresa Rebeck—she brought me in to audition for her pilot," Kat says. It wasn't a Series Regular, but it was a good guest-starring role. She books the role. Kat then takes the tape, worth its career weight in gold, and sends it to the more reputable, larger, better agents that she was chasing. *Here I am, in a pilot.*

"They don't even respond. . . . This is a pilot with Stanley Tucci, directed by Barry Sonnenfeld, Theresa Rebeck's a big writer in the city . . . and they could give a shit. They want people who already have name.

But then, craziness of craziness, CBS calls Theresa Rebeck. They had just put the episode through audience testing. "Apparently," Kat says, "my scores were so high with test audiences that CBS was like, 'Who is this girl? You need to write her a whole episode.'"

This kind of heat gets someone attention. *Boston Legal* was starting up at the time and they want to see her for a Series Lead. And so what does her small agent do? She gets her a meeting with a manager named Toby Haggerty, who just took over the New York office of Vince Cirrincione (that's Halle Berry's manager).

"Why?" I ask Kat.

"Because Judy doesn't have any fucking pull and Toby Haggerty does."

Voilà. The agent/manager relationship swings back the other way. The next day, after meeting with Toby Haggerty, Kat is soon auditioning for ABC. "There was all this heat, all of a sudden. . . . It was just too much at once. That was my first taste of how quickly things can happen."

Then her small agent calls her.

"Kat," Judy says, "it pains me to do this, but really, you're gonna need a bigger agency. We're starting to sign people and we know you're not going to sign with us, so we're gonna let you go."

A pilot, consideration for a Series Lead, a big manager interested, and where is Kat? Completely unrepresented.

Oy, to have such problems, you say. But the truth is, it doesn't get any easier as your career develops. Perhaps you're hustling less, but decisions have more weight, and the choices you make seem to have far more dire consequences. The agent game and the manager game only increase in competitiveness as you go. And the balance between who needs whom more is under constant reevaluation. Agents and managers have meetings to decide whom to sign, whom to drop. You have to engage yourself in these meetings too, with yourself. When is your small agent too small, when is the big one too big? When to make a switch from one to the other? By the point you reach this stage of your career, you will have a more innate sense of the way the business operates. But it's still a difficult task.

In college, graduate school even, I would often think, *I can't wait to be a professional.* Then I could just act all the time. There'd be no other schoolwork to worry about, no other business to attend to. You know what? This doesn't happen, because as a working actor, you're always working on something else. Your career, a money job, the next audition, or a reading. Agents to find, keep, and maybe drop. Career choices to be made. It does not get any easier, ever. Most of your work, including negotiating the treacherous debris field of getting an agent, is done on your own time, on your own dime.

Fiona reels me back in with a reminder about agents. "They love artists," she says, "and everyone wants to be a part of that. Everyone wants to be with someone who's exciting. People don't go around saying, 'I want to be with people who have great hair and who are skinny.'"

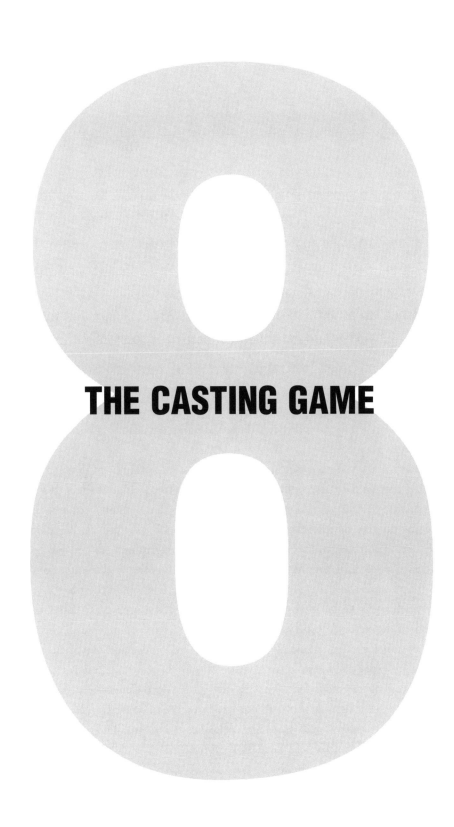

THE CASTING GAME

"Talent is a guarantee of nothing. There can be brilliant, talented actors who don't get the right breaks, who don't get the right representation— they don't have the right audition, they're not evaluated properly in the right audition, and things just didn't go their way. And then there's people who are not incredibly talented and maybe they get a few breaks— and by a few breaks, I mean they audition well at the right time for the right role—and the project becomes successful."

—Rob Decina, casting director for CBS Daytime's *Guiding Light*

The only thing more difficult than finding an agent in this business? Finding a job.

In the end, you and your agent are after the same thing: employment. The vetting process for this employment is unlike anything else out there. It's a filtration system, the world's premiere Brita, whereby a mountain stream of actors become the one purified droplet in the casting pool. This process begins with the casting director and works its way down through directors and producers and executives until, finally, all heads have gotten together and a single role has been cast. And then, they do it again. For every single role in the project.

So how to define this complicated and exhausting process? "I'm human resources for actors," Rob Decina tells me in his office, giving me the best job description I could imagine. It's so simple in its logic that I can't believe the analogy escaped me for so long. And it is the single best explanation I've heard of the casting director's job. Why mystify it? If you make casting some deep, dark secret, as it often is in the minds of actors, you're doing yourself a disservice. Putting casting in real-world terms clarifies everything. The only difference between hiring an actor and hiring a receptionist is the craft. And the craft— the art—is your job, not the job of HR.

Of course it is more complicated that that. Matters of taste and look and type mean that you will get hired not on your acting skill alone, the way that a receptionist might get hired on her faxing skills.

"I say 'human resources' in the sense that I know people who work in human resources and they say, 'This company needs someone who can type fifty words per minute,'" Rob continues, "and they think, 'Who can type fifty words per minute? Can Jason type fifty words per minute? No, Jason actually can't type fifty words per minute, so let's go to someone else.' Well, for me, it's, 'I need a bodyguard, a street thug, I need a waiter, I need a three-year contract role, I need a beautiful woman.' I think of actors who are right for those roles to fill those jobs."

Casting directors fill roles. They have a script, they talk to the director, the producers, and artistic associates. They get a sense of what people are looking for, and then they bring in a selection of actors to fill in the characters. Their job is to know actors. And they do this in two ways. They rely on agents and, to varying degrees, they scout talent. If I tell a casting director that I need to hire a girl next door, preferably a redhead because the script refers to red hair, who is at least 5'5", because I don't want the leading man to look taller than her, that casting director should be able to list ten such actors off the top of his head. It is the job of casting directors to know you. So how do you get them to do this?

There is no one answer to this question. Your end goal, however, must be to develop a relationship with as many casting directors as possible. It's something that occurs over a long period of time. "You have to get to a point where you really realize that they are your ally," Jon tells me, "because they absolutely are." Jon treats casting directors as his partners in crafting an audition. "A big thing that got me in the beginning," he says, "was that everybody would pressure you to make relationships with these people. *You have to make relationships, get fans.* I don't know about you, but for me, the whole idea of trying to get someone to be a fan is a revolting idea. It just doesn't make sense to me. At the end of the day, you don't audition for casting directors, that's not what you do. No casting director will ever give you a job. The job of a casting director and the job of an actor/casting director relationship is really . . . to become great allies and to construct an audition in the room, using their help, by drawing them in."

So how to draw them in? Inviting them to see you work, when you work, is one way. However, chances are there are enough actors they already know whose work they're not getting around to seeing. I ask Rob if actors without agents send him mail directly. "All the time," he says.

"How many do you get in a day?" I ask.

Instead of giving me a number, he holds his hands apart for a measurement. "A two-foot-high pile. An intern or an assistant opens them."

"So what would get that person in this room?" I ask.

"A short, to-the-point letter, telling me where they are in their career," he says. "I hate the letters that go, 'Hey, I would be the next great blah-blah-blah in your show. Hey, I'm a big fan of your show and I watch this and I would be perfect as this.' I don't need anybody to do my job for me. I love letters that go, 'Hey I'm new to New York and I'd love any work possible.'"

And inviting people to see your show?

"I always think it's just as valuable to know that you're actually doing something as it is for me to actually go and see it. I love getting postcards saying, 'Hey, I'm doing this here, I'm doing this there.' Maybe I won't go to see it, but it's good to know that you're sort of working. It gets back to that working thing."

Work. The sexiest four-letter word in this business.

In other words, maybe. Maybe he'll get to your show. But he'd rather know you're doing a show than actually have to see the show. You've got a better shot at getting him to see your show if he knows you first. You've got a better shot if you have established some form of relationship.

Now, I'm biting my lip as I write this, because I loathe the events I am about to promote, but one way to get a relationship is to buy one. That's why I loathe them. Actors are supposed to be protected from having to buy auditions and jobs. It's why agents work on a commission basis. But a crowded industry makes room for all sorts.

Here's how it works. You buy in. As I discussed in chapter 4, most casting professional teach *seminars* to actors through groups like TVI, One on One, and Actors Connection, among others. For a fee, you are given the privilege of meeting casting directors and agents.

The important thing to remember about these seminars is that you should not walk into the room thinking that this is your way of getting an audition for the next pilot cast at NBC. It's not. These meetings provide an introduction, an opportunity to begin a relationship with someone—to add personality to that postcard you might be sending to announce the show you're doing downtown. These meetings are not going to land you a test in L.A. They might get you a shot at a two-line part.

Even so, without an agent, you're a real shot in the dark, especially for a part of more than five lines. Rob estimates that 98 percent of the actors he meets with have agents.

It's the classic catch-22. You need the agent to meet with the casting director; you need the casting director's recommendation to meet with the agent. Some actors will have more contact with agents, some with casting directors. But if you had to focus on a target, I'd aim for the casting director. Timing and luck being such huge factors in this world, you have a better chance being right for someone who's doing the hiring than someone who is trying to get you hired, which is what agents do. A better chance at filling a slot equals work. Remember what Rob said about making his job easier.

Ideally, casting directors are your allies. "Every callback is a casting director's audition," Jon explains, "and they're just as nervous as you were when you were in the audition for the casting director. So the quicker you get over trying to impress casting directors, the better off you'll be."

Casting for a Day

And so, I decided, if you can't beat them, join them. At least for an afternoon.

That's how I landed in Adrienne Stern's office with Kimberly Hope, her casting associate at the time. The office is best known for casting independent films, among them *13 Conversations about One Thing* and the 2001 Sundance Grand Jury Prize winner *The Believer,* which introduced Ryan Gosling to the masses. When I interviewed her, Kim had been working there for nearly two years. She came from a management company, and thus has a pretty thorough understanding of both sides of the process.

It's a process that begins with submissions. Agents receive announcements of projects and roles being cast from casting directors in the form of a break-down. They then take the character descriptions and match them against their own client list. When they've decided who they think is right for a role, they pull that headshot, attach a cover letter, and send it off to the casting director in an envelope.

This is where Kimberly and I begin. She tosses a script to me.

"Here's what we get," she says. Atop the script is a cover letter detailing the project and, in this case, the fact that a well-known actress is attached to produce and star in the lead role in the film. It is Kim's job to cast the two male lead roles. In this case, that might prove slightly difficult, because not only is there nudity required for the roles, there's a violent rape that occurs in the film. Two violent rape scenes, in fact. The male character both gives and receives.

The film is an independent film, and in SAG terms this means that it is covered under one of its many low-budget agreement contracts. Most of the films that Kim and Adrienne cast are of this sort. Pulling a copied sheet off the wall, Kim points to a possible pay rate for this film.

One hundred dollars a day. Seventy-five dollars if you work more than two days. Not a lot of money. Certainly only desperation might cause an actor to work for this rate. On her computer, Kim pulls up a copy of the breakdown she has submitted to breakdown services. At the end of the character descriptions, two words pop off the screen: NAMES ONLY.

Sample Breakdown

Breakdowns are the property of Breakdown Services, so I can't show you an actual one. But I made one up that looks just the same. You get the idea.

BIG TV SHOW NAME, Episode 32
Super-Big Producer
In Association With
Super-Big Studio
In Association With
Super-Big Network
One-Hour Drama Series

Casting: Someone You Should Know
Location: New York Start Date August 26

SUBMISSIONS SHOULD BE SENT TO:
Someone You Should Know
Big TV Studio Casting Name
9999 Avenue of the Americas
New York, NY 10019
ATTN: BIG TV SHOW
PLEASE DO NOT FAX SUBMISSIONS
[Johnny] LATE 20'S—LATE 30'S: A down-on-his-luck
drifter looking for the girl of his dreams. NAMES ONLY

[Joey] TEENS: Johnny's brother. Math genius who hasn't stopped surfing. Tries to get Johnny to come home for PA's funeral. LEAD

[Pa] LATE 70s: The boy's father. Struggling with asthma. Still pines for the woman who left him forty years ago. ONE SCENE

[Carol Anne] 20s: The proverbial hooker with a heart of gold, and a penchant for sweets. LEAD

Thus begins the process of casting a film: the name game. Independent films need financing, and the way they get financing is by getting a recognizable actor in the role. From top to bottom, everyone knows this. This is how it goes.

When the breakdown hits the air, e-mails go to all the agents informing them that there's a new breakdown. Breakdown Services, which holds the monopoly on this ritual, is subscription-based. Though they are moving forward in the technical arena, offering the option for digital submissions and something called Actors Access, neither of these are really effective. Kim never releases her breakdowns on Actors Access, which would allow unrepresented actors to see what's being cast and self-submit, nor does she handle anything but paper submissions, making that digital option—a money-saving option, at least where paying for reprints of headshots is concerned—practically obsolete.

Kim's phone starts ringing. "What do you mean, *names?*" agents ask her. "Big names?" And so Kim begins a process of trying to define the name range—a Tobey Maguire versus a Steve Zahn, say. And, because of the raping, she tells people to read the script before submitting clients.

Now it's midafternoon, and with the breakdown having been sent out earlier today, Kim already has a stack of manila envelopes in front of her. They have been messengered over from agents and managers big and small. There's even a modeling agency in the pile.

Remember, names only. But, as Kim explains as she tears open the first of the stack, "Names only . . . doesn't really mean anything. Like," she says, pulling out a photo, "who's that?"

He's Adam. And he has a name. But not one you've ever heard of. What's the point of saying "names only," I ask.

"It says to the bigger people," Kim responds, "like to the William Morrises and the CAAs, that there is money to be paid, so please feel free to submit your names."

The stars have now been given permission to compete. I guess $100 a day is a celebrity-variable rate, like a prime plus on a credit card.

We move on. Wilhelmina Modeling has submitted a pack of hot men, some of whom don't even have resumes. Kim reads the credits of one who does.

"Under 5 . . . SAG Extra in a commercial." I look over her shoulder in disbelief. It really says these things. It's a resume of nothing. She moves on to special skills. "He's in the Coast Guard, he's a firefighter, and he ran the marathon in Miami . . . in three hours and one minute."

I laugh, somewhat in shock at the nerve of this, thinking of all the great actors I know with scores of great roles in regional theater on their resume. "You gonna call him in?" I ask.

"Nope," she says, and into the trash he goes. There is justice in the world.

The Don Buchwald Agency, in Los Angeles, has faxed over a list of names. Tomorrow Kim will receive their photos. There are twenty-six actors listed. For two roles. From one agent. From one office of a bicoastal agency.

Twenty-six actors from one high-tiered agent. I'm beginning to see why my auditions are fewer and farther between.

In the next envelope we meet Tony, who has a goatee, and wears his wedding ring in his headshot, giving Kim the impression that Tony is "a skateboarder and probably a really great husband." Alas, Tony goes in the trash too. His agent submitted him without so much as a cover letter, so she knows nothing more about him.

Submissions from a manager, one Kim knows well. Maybe she can tell me the difference between agents and managers.

"The difference is . . . legally, they're not allowed to *procure work.*"

What does that mean?

"I don't know."

They can't make the final deal?

"But they do."

She flips through the contents of the envelope. A terrible actor, but hot. The older brother of a pretty well-known actress, fresh out of school. And Joe, the guy Kim signed when she used to work with this management company. Kim went out to dinner with the other managers in the office. A few martinis down, the waiter flirted with her. And she said, "So, do you want to be a waiter when you grow up, or an actor?"

They signed Joe the next day, having never seen him act.

A submission from an agency that, technically, only represents children. But there's not one single kid in the breakdown for this movie. So sure enough, all are guys in their twenties.

Two women. Submitted by a well-known agent. For two male roles.

A nice thorough cover letter from an agent who notes that one of the actors "always brings an interesting read to the table." And another, for an actor who the agent says "always gets down to the final one or two." Kim likes this kind of attention. It shows that the agent cares.

I ask Kim what good agents do that bad agents don't.

They call. They pitch. They keep on her. Because, as I'm learning, even if you have an agent and get submitted, that alone is not enough. We're six agencies into the pile and already we're over fifty actors.

Next, an unknown actor who self-submitted without an agent.

"How many unknowns do you get?" I ask.

"I saved you my postcards," Kim says, handing me today's pile. There are about ten postcards, sent to Kim not for this project, but as a general "I want an audition" type of thing. "Postcards are really interesting," Kim says, stretching out the word. "Here's a classic case."

> *Dear Adrienne,*
> *I was recently sent to read for a Xenadrine commercial by*
> *Electric Talent and also met with Heather Stewart from*
> *Clear Talent. Please keep me in mind.*

Not exactly impressive. "I don't need to know that you got to audition for a commercial," Kim says. "I need to know if you booked that commercial, or if you signed with a new agent."

We find a good postcard. A pretty young woman telling Kim that she'll be on *Law & Order* next week. Perhaps most importantly, this card comes from someone Kim met at a class she taught. "She met me, she's following up, and she's telling me she's going to be on TV," Kim answers, when I ask her why this card is better than all the rest. "The people I've never met. . . . It's kind of like, 'What do you think I'm going to do with that? Do you think I keep every single postcard in categories that people send to me?' Like, okay, today I'm going to cast this movie and so I need a twenty-year-old blond girl and I'm going to pull out my folder of twenty-year-old blond girls whom I've never met?"

"Well, yes," I say. "I think that's exactly what people expect."

"We have to protect ourselves, too," she counters. "We're not going to bring in people whom we've never met or spoken to before, because then we look bad."

See, young actor, you're not the only one in this business who's watching out for himself. Everyone is accountable to someone, somewhere. Kim's job is to get the best people she can for a film. So why should she take a chance on someone she's never met? And why should you think she should? Unfortunately, you can't just ask for the audition. You need to audition for the audition.

"If anybody is volunteering to be a reader in my office, I keep them and use them, and that's really how I introduce people to my office. 'Cause that way you get a sense of who this person is."

And in that stack of postcards, not a single person made such an offer.

"But this girl did," Kim says, pulling a card from her shelf, "and I'm totally going to call her in."

There's something to this. It hearkens back to my theory of getting validated, and Kim is proving my point. She points to a pile of headshots on her top shelf. "My go-to girls"—the people she's met through classes she's taught. She uses them as readers, or calls them to audition for industrials or to be an extra in a commercial. On the floor there's an eight-inch-high pile of more actors, the ones she plans on calling in to meet with when she has time because she's either seen their work or met them at a class. We're talking hundreds of actors here. Some with agents, some without, all of whom Kim thinks are good, but who will not be auditioning for this film, or any film, in the near future.

There are simply too many actors. "These people might get a shot at a two-line role," Kim says. So why then, I said to Kim, if you've met them, and you trust them, and know they can act, wouldn't you call them in for a bigger part?

"Because there's so much pressure in indie film to get names or recognizable faces in every single role."

"Every single role?" I ask, elongating each word.

She nods. "It just goes down the ladder. Like that movie we just looked at." She had just finished screening a DVD of a movie she cast when I sat down with her, and I had caught the tail end. "Those are known people in every role. That cop guy is a very well-known soap actor who at one point had his own television show. And that's the kind of pressure it is."

Because, she says correctly, "there are so many people who need to do movies."

How many people? Kim pulls two large binders off her shelf. It's the meeting book for an independent film that, now finally cast, was one of the hot projects this winter. I open it. It contains at least a hundred of pages of meeting logs—everyone the director met with in Los Angeles for three roles in this film. As I flip through page after page, I see name after name after name. As in, *name actors only.* Donnie Wahlberg, James Badge Dale, Jerry O'Connell. Actors who have done a lot more than you or I.

This is what you're up against. This is what you're facing. Two inches thick of submission sheets, just names on paper that Kim has put in a binder. Hundreds upon hundreds of submissions for three roles. Everyone gets submitted. It doesn't matter how famous you are. Sure, some won't meet you until they get the offer. But the pictures and resumes of Kevin Bacon, Brendan Fraser, Aidan Quinn, Ashton Kutcher, and Ralph Fiennes are sitting in a pile too. Ashley Judd's headshot is a *Glamour* magazine cover.

I'm starting to get name-crazed, and depressed, and so Kim opens up IMDbPro on her computer to show me the STARmeter. The STARmeter ranks the number of hits a certain actor gets on IMDb, which translates into their popularity at the moment. (Paris Hilton was number one this particular week.) She uses this to convince directors of actors that they may be unsure of. As in, *This actor is 230 and Sarah Michelle Gellar is like a 200.* And this works.

Kim approaches all of this with a modest sense of irony. She's aware of how insane it sounds, and, indeed, how insane it is. But day in and day out she works her way down the star ladder to cast films. Because films need money, and names bring this in.

But there you are, actor, at the bottom of the ladder, faced with this conundrum. You have the small agent, the agent who doesn't have the connections, who doesn't make the phone calls. All you want is a little indie movie to call your own. But so too does Giovanni Ribisi, or Kyra Sedgwick. And yet one day, powerless as you may be right now, you might be the one who is name enough to get the movie made. Actors have all of the power and none of the power, all at once.

Names aside, casting is never a process that is advantageous to the actor. And so it is time to introduce the box theory. It came up when I asked Kim to explain what a good audition was. She should patent this theory. It's like Einstein for actors.

"What an actor needs to keep in mind when walking into a room," she begins, "is that people have a vision in their head of what they want to cast in this role. So they have, like, a body type, and they have kind of a look, and they have kind of how it's going to sound when it comes out of this person's mouth. And so, a very small box has been created. Because it was written out of the writer's head, and then somehow transformed in the director's head, and then transformed into everybody else's heads. And you're walking into the room because the casting director thinks you may *in some way* fit into this box."

See, there's nothing you can do about that. So why try? I had an acting teacher who was adamant about Stoic philosophy, the basic tenet of which is this: Do not try to control that which is outside of your control. Instead, focus on what you can control. Kim, a great modern stoic herself, continues.

"The best thing that you can do is walk into the room as the best representative of yourself. Because that's your best tool." She runs down a brief checklist, none of which, you'll note, have anything to do with acting. "Dressed well, clean, showered, happy, smiling, personable. There's a lot of these actors out there—you know, the angry brooding young guy type of actor. I think if you put on your best front and your best show, and then you give a good read, you kind of know what's going on in the scene. You're comfortable with the material. You have a rapport with the director and are able to talk about it. I think that's the best audition. Because if you're a seven-foot redheaded guy with freckles and they have in their mind a five-foot-nine blond kid with blue eyes, then it doesn't matter how good your read is."

And then she adds the most important lesson of all. It's something I will talk about at greater length in chapter 12, but while we're in the world of casting, we might as well plant the seed.

"Actors who take it all so personally are just wrong, and are headed down a path of lifelong rejection. Because it has so little to do with you personally and how good of an actor you are. It has more to do with how many people's boxes you fit in."

There is nothing you can do about the boxes. The boxes were there long before you got into the room. Don't worry about the boxes. Let them worry about the boxes. Remember when you took your headshot? Be the best version of you. Exude self. When you do that, you might even make them forget about the boxes they walked in with.

There's one more thing Kim touched on when I interviewed her, another stoic point within this industry. You can control something else when you walk into an audition that no one else can control. You can prepare.

No one can take that away from you. Preparation for an audition is yours. You know which actors casting directors love? The ones who blow you away every time they come into a room. The ones whom they have yet to cast, but whom they call in time and time again, maybe because they just like watching them act. Jon, an actor who's had a significant year of acting work, put it rather emphatically, "Any actor who doesn't work hard and takes everything for granted doesn't deserve your respect and deserves to be fucking knocked off a boat in the middle of the ocean with lead shoes on his feet, as far as I'm concerned. They're the ones who make it hard for the rest of us."

Take the room when you audition, because it's finally yours. Give the performance you want to give. Someone rushes you? Tell them not to. The reader wants to skip a part of the sides that you had planned a whole routine around? Tell them you'd like to do it. You own that room for the next few minutes, so take your space.

Pistol-Packing Actor

Kim shared a great audition story with me. In its complete absurdity, it illustrates all facets of the casting madness.

She was casting the role of a security guard, a hulking, beefy guy with tattoos. He was in a lot of scenes, but only had two or three lines total. A lot of the people she was seeing were actual cops, or retired cops.

One actor comes in. He's wearing a fleece vest over a tight white T-shirt. "I could see that he had tattoos peeking out over his T-shirt sleeves, so I said, 'Will you take off your vest and show me your tattoos and stuff for the camera?' He does, and there, strapped to his hip, is a pistol.

"Is that a gun?" Kim asks.

"Yes."

"Are you planning on shooting me with that gun?"

"No, no, no," he says. "I'm a cop. . . . Well, I was cop."

"So what are you now?"

He nods, and acknowledges his mistake. "I mean, my wife tells me I should leave the gun at home, but I got used to walking around with it and I figured, since I'm coming in to be kind of a cop, I should bring it. I mean, I can go put it outside."

That's a great idea, Kim thinks. *Stick your gun out in the waiting area.*

So the actor does the audition, gun strapped to his waist. The lesson here? "Please do not bring firearms into the audition. Please do not bring any weapons where you could kill the person you're auditioning for," Kim says.

"Did he get the part?" I ask. And of course. . . .

"He did."

And so the saying goes: It's those who break the rules, who go above and beyond, who get the part.

Even so, no guns in the audition, please.

Settling into the Neighborhood

So now you've met the neighbors, or at least you've seen them walking around ignoring you until you've proven that you'll be a worthwhile neighbor. That's okay. Keep knocking on doors.

See, this actually is a creative community, which is why it runs so poorly as a business. Most agents, casting directors, even union reps love the art and craft of acting, and want you to be damn good at it. They want to believe in you, so make them do it, even if you have to lie. And remember, a career is not a day, a week, a month, a year. A career is a lifetime. So give yourself a break. The agents and managers and casting directors and unions will come to you eventually.

Or maybe we should go with Fiona's thoughts on the subject. "My fantasy of it is that people who are in the theater know that it takes a long time for artists to cook. And that of course some people come out of the gate and they're exciting and they're young and they have a lot of ideas. . . . But there are other people who slowly build their artistic voice."

It takes time for some, a millisecond for others. There is no one way. Except to keep plugging, keep trying, keep after it. No way but to endure.

JOB HUNTING:

A Day in the Life of an Actor

9

"The reason we are depressed and take such a gloomy view
of life is that we know nothing of work."

—*Three Sisters* by Anton Chekhov

Usually, we wait.

For the phone call, for the casting session that's running behind schedule, for the audition, at Starbucks while killing time between appointments, in line at the Equity building for an open call. . . . Waiting is very important in this business.

There is no typical day in the life of an actor—the variety is part of the reason we do what we do—but there are some general guidelines that we all follow regardless of experience, type, representation, and the myriad other factors already covered up to this point. The waiting is one. Hurrying is the other.

The law of the business states that the audition comes only when plans have been made; the job you book always happens over your previously arranged summer holiday; and you never, ever know what you are doing tomorrow until 5:00 today. This lifestyle can affect the actor's temperament in some pretty horrendous ways. One is expected to drop plans if a job arrives, and may even lose money to take a job. Take the day on *Law & Order* at scale and cancel that plane trip to see the family? A rarity, maybe, but what about losing a temp job because you need the day to shoot an Under 5 on a soap opera, because if you don't take the job, the casting director will never call you again? The constant factor of not knowing what's coming next, while hoping for something brilliant, leads to a loss of mastery over one's own life.

Not that we'd have it any other way. Sure, we'll complain until there's no one left listening, and then complain some more, but it's the life we chose for the big payoff, right? Well, as the payoff starts looking smaller, the lifestyle choices loom unhealthier. And that's for the actor with both a legit and a commercial agent, a decent resume, and a network of people who know his work.

Gruntwork

Let's start by looking at the other kind of actor. The fresh-out-of-college, hitting-the-cement-sidewalks-of-New-York-without-the-benefit-of-a-top-tier-training-program-and-New-York-showcase freshman. The one I used to be. The one we all used to be. Headshots are done, a resume is crafted out of college credits and that public service announcement he did in junior high, and mailings are complete. All to no response.

Actors in this position do one thing. They buy a copy of *Backstage.*

Backstage is a weekly trade publication that has reviews and some blandly written and generally inane editorials that offer advice on making it in the business. Most importantly, it lists auditions. The auditions are divided into film and theater, and subdivided within this into categories of union and non-union. Some will have addresses where pictures and resumes can be sent: the submission. Student films and extra work comprise the bulk of this category, with a few independent films mixed in *(The Blair Witch Project* was cast through *Backstage).* Other audition notices will have a date and place for the audition. This is the *open call.* By union law, all Equity shows must hold an open call for members.

Subscribers

To get an idea of the number of actors not in unions or represented by agents, I checked *Backstage* circulation numbers for New York. There were 6,482 Fiptions and 15,365 newsstand copies sold for the second week of April 2004.

That's 21,847 actors looking for jobs.

The open call, also known as the *cattle call,* is perhaps the most dehumanizing of the multitude of humiliations the actor endures. At least cows get put out of their misery upon reaching the end of the line. When these auditions are held by union productions, at the behest of the union, Equity doesn't consider them "open calls." It calls them *Equity auditions* (the famed Eligible Performer Auditions or EPAs) or *chorus calls.* This means that only card-carrying members of the union can attend. But if it looks like a duck. . . . The actual open call, once you've scored an audition slot, goes something like this. Go upstairs, wait in the waiting room with a bunch of nervous actors, get called in, hand over your headshot and resume, take some stage, do your two-minute monologue, and leave the room. Unlike auditions arranged by agent submission, open calls are almost always of the "prepare a monologue" variety. The idea behind this is that the actors get a chance to show themselves in the best possible light by selecting their own pieces, and the auditioners get to, well, save themselves the trouble of telling the actors to prepare something specific. The fact that there is nothing specific requested for the majority of these auditions sends an immediate mixed message: We're not listening even though you're speaking, or alternately, We're listening even though you're not really auditioning.

Say you're in the union and are one of the 36,443 actors without an agent. You go to the Equity callboard or look up the casting notices online at *www.actorsequity.org*. Oh, look, a revival of *The Glass Menagerie* is being done on Broadway and you are just perfect for Laura. Auditions are Tuesday through Thursday at the Equity Building from 9:00 in the morning till 5:00 at night.

Let's also say that you are currently temping during the day, because you and some of your college friends have formed a theater company that rehearses eight stops out on the L train in Brooklyn at night and that is going to change the landscape of the American theater. This rules out waitressing because you can't pick up any decent night shifts. Work starts at 9:00 A.M. and ends at 5:00 P.M., and rehearsal begins at 7:00 P.M. But you are determined. Still, it would be best to get an audition time during lunch break so that you don't get fired from your job.

This requires showing up at the Equity Building early. Very early. The line starts forming at 6:00 A.M. Thankfully, the open call system is now organized in such a fashion as to provide an actual audition time instead of making actors wait all day for a slot. This is the advantage of being in the union. Non-union open calls require waiting all day until your name is called. Between the number of actors who need or want a specific time slot and the sheer number of actors in total, most of the slots for all three audition days will be filled by noon on the first day.

We could all help each other out a little bit here by following some of the basic guidelines by which casting directors and the rest of the industry operate. Namely, don't go to the audition unless you are right for the part. Unfortunately, theaters and producers don't always make it easy for you to know if you are right for the part or not. If it's a new play, and there is no breakdown, you're not going to know the type of any of the characters. Still, there is a lot of information out there if you know where to look. Check out the play at The Drama Book Shop or check online to see if Equity posted a breakdown.

The point is that actors, knowing the general futility of the open call, are not necessarily auditioning for the specific play that is being cast. Rather, they are auditioning for the casting director, or the artistic director, or whoever happens to be in the room, in the hope of making such a phenomenal impression that they will be remembered and called upon for future work.

This never happens. I swear. This is a crowded, hectic, busy, competitive industry. Actors who have agents sending out their pictures every day are not being remembered. Why should they remember you? Short-term memory rules. Anyone who is watching the open call is there begrudgingly. They dread the open call as much as the actor does, if not more. When one New York director was asked to describe the process, he called it "hell on wheels." But he had some targeted advice as well. "Go secure in the knowledge that 99 percent of the time it's useless. Go because you never know, but know that most of the time it's not going to get you anywhere." More likely than not, the director, the casting director, the producer, and the artistic director are not there. Nor are they required to be. This director has only been to one open call in his entire career, and he's directed far more than one show. The people who are there—casting assistants, literary managers, director's assistants—are looking for a specific thing. That's what casting is about. A specific thing. Specific to character and specific to type.

The other reason this never happens is that "good" is really a subjective construct, as is a great performance. Tastes and styles vary from place to place and person to person. No actor is brilliant all of the time, which means that given the worst possible auditioning circumstance—the open call, for my money—your chances of brilliance are slim. Someone who is completely wrong for a part is going to lose the casting director's attention from the get-go. Someone right for the part will be listened to, but has a lot to prove. The actor who walks into the open call is making a clear statement: *I'm unemployed as an actor and I don't have an agent and I don't have much of a network. In other words, I'm desperate.*

You may not be. You probably are brilliant. But circumstantially, the deck is stacked against you in this situation. And if you have the 4:50 P.M appointment on the last day of auditions, that room reeks of desperation. It has seen more bad performances than audiences of German Shakespeare. More likely than not, you're screwed before you even open your mouth.

Unless you are physically perfect for the part. Because if you walk in and you are what they are looking for in type, then they will pay attention. That casting director's assistant, still developing a brain of his own, is under precise instructions. Type is the exception that proves the open-call rule. Here's an example:

An actor I'll call Adam, who looks Middle Eastern, does his research well, only going in for parts he's right for. He's not going in to impress someone in the future, he's going in to get the job now. For the case of *Omnium Gatherum*, which enjoyed a short but well-received run Off-Broadway, the producers were looking for a young Arab man to play a terrorist. Bernard Telsey was casting the production, Will Frears was directing. Neither was at the open call, but Telsey's assistant was, and she spotted Adam. After he did his monologue, she invited him to the office for an audition.

All that for an audition. Not the part. Not a callback. Up at 6:00, in line for three hours, an appointment for lunch the next day, come back, wait while the auditions run behind, do your monologue, and, if you are completely right and good, you get an audition.

Adam not only landed an audition, he got the part. He now has an agent and has worked since. Perhaps we could even say he was *discovered*. He is the Cinderella story, the happy ending. But he is not all of us. Don't be confused. Adam isn't more talented than all of the other people who showed up at the Equity building that day. He was exactly right for exactly the right person casting exactly that part.

That's what it takes. You must be willing to get to the Equity building at 6:00 A.M. You must have a monologue prepared that suits your type. You must fight the desperation that fills the air. If we were a communist nation, we would try to help each other out by only auditioning when we're right for the part, thus trimming the fat that makes these open calls such a nightmare for everyone— but that will never happen in a system as overcrowded as the former Soviet Union. Someone please pass the kasha.

It is easy to tire of these experiences. Even though this is a business of the 1 percents, it's actually a better 1 percent when you have an agent, manager, or casting director on your side. Going to the open call is the act of trying to be the 1 percent, only to find yourself at the bottom of another 1 percent pile if successful. You're back into a new auditioning fray, and the competition only gets fiercer.

There is a nostalgia factor to the open call as well. It's the way in which Al Pacino and many of his generation got their start. Then, you didn't need an agent to audition for an Off-Broadway show, so the playing field was level. Agented and agentless actors all waited democratically for the appointment. Now, ironically, you often need to be Al Pacino, or at least some type of celebrity, to even be considered for an Off-Broadway show. Casting directors use agent submissions to cast shows that pay a minuscule stipend ($500 for two months of work), or don't pay at all. This is strictly unfair. These are the jobs that, even ten years ago, one could get through *Backstage* or its equivalent. Now, my manager calls me with auditions for Fringe Festival shows. Not that these can't be quality productions, but the division of labor that once gave younger and newer actors a shot at entering the business is no longer. There are just not enough jobs out there, and the actor with the agent is often as hard up as the actor without.

The Represented Actor

An actor with an agent has plenty more opportunity. He also has more frustration. Auditions come more often, and since this can be a real numbers game, making oneself available for as many auditions as possible is part of remaining competitive. This means being available every day, all day, often on short notice. Some weeks this means you don't do a thing, other weeks it means you audition four times a day.

So where's the money job? Most likely at night, which means that you cannot do a showcase that rehearses at night, which means you can't be "honing your craft" or "working out" or however you want to put it because you're trying to feed yourself and pay the rent, which means life can become highly frustrating because you are not working at what you love, you are making money doing something you hate, all the while auditioning and facing more rejection than a five-foot-tall point guard in the paint.

When I finally took a temp job between acting gigs for money, my commercial auditions suddenly picked up. I had three in one day, and I was unable to explain to my boss why I kept leaving for hours at a time—and it is hours. The commercial audition process is unlike all other audition processes, both because of the breakneck pace at which it operates and because of the money that goes into making commercials. It's a bad combination, involving lots of people declaring emergencies and prioritizing commercials above other types of work.

The Commercial Audition

Large commercial agencies in New York, one of which represents me, get the majority of the audition appointments. Calls go out for auditions the day before, usually in the late afternoon. The actor must then call back to confirm that she can make the appointment. People in normal workplace environments, where most actors temp, do not seem to understand this. They might want a little more notice if you are going to be ducking out at odd hours of the day. I used to try to explain to supervisors the way getting auditions worked, but it was beyond their comprehension. "Just try to schedule the audition around your lunch," they would say casually. Well, I don't do the scheduling, the casting director does. And if I can't make it then, ten others are ready to fill my slot. I took the oddest lunch breaks as a result, showing up at 9:00 only to duck out for lunch at 10:30.

And it takes forever to get anywhere in New York. It's a twenty-minute subway ride to the audition, each way, at best. That's two-thirds of the lunch hour right there. Of course the casting session is running late; the only time they ever run on time is if you are running late. You're going to spend anywhere from two to ten minutes in the room, so before you leave the temp job to get there, you already know you're not getting back on time.

If you work at night, you've bartended or waited tables until the wee hours of the morning and are not looking your best for that 10:30 appointment. You show up, sign in, have a Polaroid picture taken, fill out a size card, pick up the copy, and wait. Headshots are rarely used in commercials. The bigger agencies are trusted to submit the right clients. My commercial agent only has ten of my pictures on hand, and I often get more than that many auditions in a two-week period. Thus the Polaroid—the least-flattering form of photography ever. If you look good in your Polaroid, you are indeed a divine being.

The size card you fill out lists vital stats such as height and weight, phone numbers, social security number, and agent. The copy, which you are now seeing for the first time, is the script or the storyboard or sometimes both. It has the lines on it, and a drawing of a man or woman who looks nothing like you. One needn't memorize the lines, however, because union law dictates that for commercials, the copy must be printed on a cue card in the audition room.

Elisha Goldstein, a producer who has worked for McCann Erikson and Arnold, two of the largest advertising agencies, gave some perspective from the other side. "There are no discussions of casting until after a director is chosen and the estimate is approved and schedule set," she told me. "Then, the first thing they do is start talking casting." Actors need to realize this. By the time casting comes around, the campaign and the scripts have been approved; the director has been selected through a competitive bidding, pitching, and meeting process; locations have been scouted; budgets have been made; equipment has been rented. The only thing left to do? Cast the talent.

Which means that by this time, the creatives, who wrote the spot, the director, who will be shooting the spot, and the client, who must approve the spot, have been involved in the process for anywhere from one to three months. They've thought about the spot a lot, and they know exactly what they are looking for. Or, as Elisha puts it, "We consider talent an empty vessel."

Talent is the word the film, television, and advertising industries use to refer to actors. I asked her to elaborate. The first thing they are looking for, she said, is a look. Then, can the actor "follow direction and perform it the way they [the director and creatives] imagined it?" Unlike all acting training, which teaches an ability to create a role with imagination, where an actor's input is an integral part of the process, here you are strictly there to fill the precise outline someone has in his head. "It's like a jury process between the creative and the director. If one likes it and the other doesn't, the actor usually goes in the rubbish pile."

Paradoxically, however, because the ad folks have been working on the spot so long, there seems to be an assumption that the actors have known about the ad they are about to audition for more than, oh, ten minutes. The striking gap in familiarity with the ad lies like the giant elephant in the living room. Even though there are cue cards, you still look awkward when you are sneaking glances toward camera to read them. That casting is last-minute also means that the process, from first audition to callback to booking, all happens in a week maximum. On Monday you are poor, on Friday you could be set for the year.

Once you've looked over the copy, the casting director, or associate, or intern, will call you into the room. Never bring the script in with you. When I first learned this I thought it was amazing. All my life I had auditioned for things with the script in my hand, but now, thanks to the cue card, I leave it outside. I'm unsure how sneaking a glance at a cue card is any different from sneaking a glance at the script in your hand, but it must mean something to someone. Not to mention the fact that actors use scripts, not cue cards, in the rest of their acting life.

The first thing that happens in the room is the more detailed explanation from the casting director. I was once a reader at a commercial audition, filling in the off-camera voiceover. The spot was complicated, involving a lot of dialogue, blocking, even a costume change. The casting director seemed unaware that the actors coming into the session had just seen the copy for the first time upon arrival. She kept rolling her eyes and looking to me when an actor screwed up or asked for something to be repeated. I learned a fast lesson. One, they don't care, or don't know, how hard it can be to absorb that much information in thirty seconds. Two, that's the job. Three, what goes on camera is what the client sees—that and nothing else. No one knows how long you had to look at the script and learn lines and blocking, and no one cares.

The slate follows the explanation of the spot. This is when you look into the camera and smile and say your name. Do not blow off the slate. It's the first impression you make. A smile and a grand hello may feel silly in the room, but on camera it is your introduction to the poor creative who is fast-forwarding his way through the tape. I've contemplated doing my commercial auditions in slow motion so that I'm the only one who appears in real time. Everyone slates his name and, only if asked, the name of his agent.

Then you do it. Twice if you're lucky. Sometimes you'll get direction, sometimes not. You leave. The next day or the day after, you may get a callback. This means going in and doing the same thing on camera for the client, director, and agency—perhaps one, perhaps all. When you are called back for a commercial, you are placed on *first refusal,* also known as *being on hold,* giving over all rights for possible shoot dates. Often, people confuse the meaning of first refusal. It does not mean that I the actor have right of saying yea or nay to the job. It means that if I get another job, the *client* has the right to *refuse* to let me take another job, even if I haven't been hired yet. It's kind of like being a prime cut of marbled meat. You've got to offer it to Peter Luger Steakhouse before you show it to anyone else, but there's no guarantee that they'll take it. You could end up at Sizzler. Hold times vary from a day to two weeks. Because commercials put you on hold frequently, and have no limit as to the number of actors they can hold—everyone who gets a callback is on first refusal—conflict between industries can arise.

Crank It Up

Casting directors are not necessarily on the same page as the client. At a recent Olive Garden audition, three of us were told to "crank it up" because "the creatives are fast-forwarding through the tape." So we did it bigger, faster, and funnier. Guess what the director wanted at the callback?

Totally natural.

The way you find out you didn't get the job is by being released. The first few times this happens, your agent will put on a real apologetic voice and tell you that you'll get 'em next time, but pretty soon after that, it's the assistant calling. Getting released is the only time anyone ever tells you that you didn't get the job. It's depressing, too, like the girl who returns your call only to tell you that she doesn't think you should be dating anymore. Sometimes, not getting a phone call at all is better.

Film and Television Auditions

The television and film worlds operate in similar ways to the commercial world. Basically, the more money involved, the less notice there is for auditions. *Law & Order* shoots ten days per episode and casts anywhere from a week before up through the time shooting has actually begun. The breakdown goes out, submissions go in, and appointments are set up. Most series work in this fashion, and because the whole production moves at a breakneck pace, there is very little time for preparation. Scripts are not available for actors to read, and sides are available a day beforehand at the earliest. Distribution is now done by e-mail in addition to faxing, but if you are without a fax machine or printer, you'd better find some time to run by your agent's office to pick up the sides.

You have the night to prepare. That's it. Often the scenes are short, but in cases like pilot season or for Guest Star roles, you could have three ten-page scenes to learn. Learning is important for on-camera auditions in a way that it isn't for theater. Honestly, most actors dread learning lines, and though the frequently asked question of "How did you learn all those lines" is often greeted with actor snobbery and a "That's the least of it" attitude, the truth is that learning lines can be a time-consuming chore.

The other thing about learning is that it inherently involves a level of commitment and, in this case, you aren't committing to anything beyond the audition itself. Recognizing this is important. To audition, one must find a way to execute the scene and the character without committing to having the actual job. After not getting the job over and over and over again, it becomes increasingly difficult to commit, and your audition skill drops right along with your self-esteem. By finding a way to commit to something other than landing the role, you actually have a shot at getting the job.

There are no cue cards in television and film auditions, and because the camera catches everything, frequent glances toward the script are not helping your cause. My first manager admonished me to be off book at all times. I agree and disagree with this, depending on the situation. Often, not having a script in hand can make it look like you've settled on a performance choice. This is great if the director likes it, but you're out of luck if he doesn't. The general rule is, learn the scene but keep the script in hand. That way, if you get stuck, it's there. If you don't, you're still giving the impression that you can take direction.

After learning your ten pages and making choices, you go to the audition. If you're new to the casting director, new to the medium of television or film, blew your last audition, or are a questionable choice for the part, then this audition is going to be a prescreen. The prescreen deems you worthy or not of being put on tape. Tape stock must be very expensive, judging by the lengths casting directors will go to conserve it.

The prescreen often happens in the casting director's office. They're not going to rent studio space to tape in unless they're actually taping, and in this case they're not taping. The casting director's assistant, or perhaps another actor, will read with you. The skill of the reader varies greatly, and, too bad for you, this can never be an excuse for a poor audition. Auditioning is unlike acting. You can't sit back and react to the reader; you must take the offensive. This is antithetical to everything the actor is ever taught in acting school: "Acting is listening." "Acting is reacting." "Acting is paying attention to your partner." Variations on these themes are the actor's mantra.

Because the audition is about getting noticed by separating yourself from the hundreds of other actors up for the role, waiting for an impulse to hit is an unreliable technique. Finding a way to take control of the scene (and this need not be an aggressive choice) is imperative. Tempo is incredibly important. By mastering the rhythm of a scene, you can highlight specific moments for the casting director—the theatrical equivalent of finding your light. For some scenes this is easy, but for others it can be an immense challenge, especially if you only have two lines and do a lot of listening. In big speeches, the reader may read the first line and then, as was literally the case for me once, "blah, blah" their way through the middle and give you the cue line. No acting teacher would ever allow this in class, yet this is what you face in trying to get hired.

On more than one occasion, I have not only read *for* the casting director in these situations, but *with* the casting director. This inevitably leads to me screwing up the audition, because I spend all my time wondering how she can possibly be observing what I'm doing while she's looking at the script and, in some cases, trying to outact me. I thought casting was the process of observation—the casting director observing my performance and judging it. I brought this up with Rob Decina when I interviewed him. I told him I found it distracting.

"Why is it a distraction to the actor? What's so distracting about it?" he asked.

"I think that one might think, 'How can you read and think about—'"

He cuts me off. "Why are you worried about what I'm thinking about?"

"That's sort of my point," I say.

"That's my answer," Rob says. "You have a job to do, and that's to audition. Actors want to be actors, but the truth is, you're auditioners. You act at night, you act at the theater, you act when you're working on a play. This is an audition. It's not a perfect thing. If there was a better way to do it, somebody would have figured it out. I've actually tried. There isn't a better way to do it. Is it better if you're reading to a reader and I'm sitting and evaluating you? It might be, but . . . as you as an actor can feel connected to another actor when you're doing a scene, sometimes as a casting director reading, I can get connected with the actor. I certainly wouldn't get connected with an actor who's thinking, 'How's this guy evaluating me when he's reading with me?' 'Cause that actor's not present in the audition. You can't worry about that stuff."

It doesn't get much clearer than that. One doesn't need to watch to know if an actor is connected, is in the moment, and has an understanding of the scene. And that is what television and film are all about—being totally "real." Less is more, they say. When Jon worked on *Without a Trace* recently, he told me that the only thing the director kept asking him to do was stop acting. Basically, say the lines, don't fuck up the blocking, and we can all go home happy.

After reading, the casting director will decide if you get a callback. Often this is an on-the-spot decision, and the casting director will ask you to come back the following day so you can be put on tape. For a film, the director will most likely be at the callback, with a producer or two in tow. If it's a running network series, you may go to producers. In the case of a pilot, you might eventually go to network, which entails getting flown to L.A. (more on all of this in the next chapter). This is an approval process. You must meet the approval first of the casting director, then of the director, then of the producers, and then of the network. If all these people agree that you're the one, you get the part. Series Regulars go through the same process of approval. This may mean an additional two to four auditions for the different people.

The rest of the time, it'll just be you, the casting director, and a video camera. If I leave a prescreen without getting a callback while still in the room, I count the part as lost. Still, depending on the size of the role and the length of the day, whether you came in at 10:00 in the morning or 4:30 that afternoon, the callback may actually come to your agent by phone later that night. Again, the same hurrying and waiting. Count the job as gone to save your sense of self-worth, but be prepared to be in front of the director the next morning to land the role.

The callback happens the next day and you are put on tape. Depending on the casting director's mood, you may get a couple shots at it. Sometimes you get one. The rule for callbacks is to improve on what you did to get the callback. Don't change, don't show something new. This is a place where actors often get confused in auditioning, where the years of going to open calls to prove you're a good actor conflict with the logic of more legitimate auditions. Here's the rule: No one cares how good an actor you are. They care whether you are right for the part. Changing what you do in the callback to show that you have range as an actor will lose you the part. Get the job, not a career. Careers are built one job at a time.

Will Frears puts it this way: "Find new things at the callback, but be the same person. The reason you got called back is because they liked what you were doing. We're as desperate as you are to find you're right for the part." Casting directors care more about talent than directors do. They will have other projects to cast. Their job is to know who's good. Directors only want to know if you can do this particular part in this particular production.

The Theater Audition

The audition that requires the most amount of work will lead (if you book it) to the job that pays the least amount of money. This is the theater audition. To properly prepare an audition for a play can require hours of work. In the theater, scripts are not only available, they are required reading. Reading that, depending on the stature of your agent, will cost you out-of-pocket copying expense on top of time and transportation. Larger agencies usually have a copy of the script for you. Sometimes the script is e-mailable, but if you're not repped by Abrams, Gersh, ICM, or one of the other bigger guns, you must pick up the script with the casting director or at your tinier agent's office. Sure, you could sit in the office and read the script if you have an hour plus to spare during regular business hours, but if you don't, or if you want to be able to refer to it later, you're going to run to Kinko's and make yourself a copy.

Then you're going to read it and get on with preparing the sides for the audition. On average, I have ten to fifteen pages of sides for theater auditions. Sometimes one of the scenes is marked as a callback side, but since the callback is usually the day after the first audition, one must get a head start on preparing all the material. One thing is for certain: The scene you spend the least time prepping is the one they will want to see first.

Audition Timetable

Pick Up Script: - - - - :40
Read Script: - - - - - -1:00
Prepare Sides: - - - - -2:00
Go to Audition: - - - - :40
Wait Time: - - - - - - - :20
Audition: - - - - - - - - :10
Callback Prep: - - - - -2:00
Go to Callback: - - - - :40
Wait Time: - - - - - - - :20
Callback: - - - - - - - - :10
TOTAL - - - - - - - -8:00 hours

Overall time for preparing these auditions, if you get a callback, can be as much as six to ten hours of work. Say three sets of sides, two hours of work on each, plus reading the play at an hour minimum, and you're there. Many actors like to memorize, especially for Shakespeare. Plays generally present more complex and challenging material than film and television, and certainly do so in their breadth. Though one is usually given more notice for theater auditions— up to five days to prepare—the prep time usually occupies a two- or three-day window. If you're temping all day and have two auditions come in on Wednesday afternoon, both for Friday, finding the time to read both scripts, prepare twenty pages of sides, and keep your job in the meantime is a challenging feat.

The Room

The theater audition rarely takes place in a theater. It occurs in the same room as a film audition might, but you will have to show that you can play to the back of a large house. Most actors have a natural tendency to play to the space that they're in, so "being theatrical" in a small room can feel weird. This is not a huge concern, but it can be tricky to have a commercial audition and a theater audition back to back, sometimes in the same building. An actor is under the constant strain of making such adjustments.

Casting directors for theater also prescreen, but once they know you, you'll go straight to the director. Theater casting sessions happen over the course of several days for most regional gigs, but can drag on far past this depending on what they find and how big the theater is. After auditioning for the director once, you will either be called back or not. The theater callback is much more specific than the commercial callback. Occasionally, you will read with other actors who are up for roles opposite you, so that the director can judge chemistry. More often, you'll go back and give a more refined version of the performance you gave last time. Sometimes it's just as simple as, "Can they do it twice?"

Casting for plays happens about a month before the show opens. One of the major problems of being out of town is that when you return to New York, lining up another job, even if you get cast upon your arrival, is at least a month away.

A Fun-Filled Acting Day

Any given day could contain all or none of these audition scenarios. Recently, I had a day that was so typically atypical, it illustrated everything I've just discussed. The cast of characters involved have all been introduced by now: actors, agents, managers, unions. It's the kind of day that most actors would give their left lung to have, and it illuminates the way an actor is tugged and tossed around.

Monday, around 5:00, I get a phone call from my commercial agent. The agent—we'll call him Frank—lets me know that I've been called back for a health insurance ad. However, I am booked out for the shoot dates. This means that, due to the conflict, I shouldn't go to the callback. Okay, I say. Sounds fine.

"Where are you going?" he asks.

"The Humana Festival," I tell him.

"Kentucky?"

"That's right," I say. Fortunately, Frank is the one commercial agent who knows and cares about the theater.

"Well. I'll tell them you can't make it."

This is okay, because the reason I'm booked out is because I got a really wonderful regional theater job. *Booking out* is the commercial term for being unavailable for work and auditions, for whatever reason. My reason, in this case, the Humana Festival, is the annual new-play festival at the Actors Theatre of Louisville. More than occasionally, shows from Humana come to New York City, which means that work there is new, of high quality, and attracts industry attention. All great things for an actor.

I assumed this whole commercial availability thing had been settled, when my phone rings at 9:00 the next morning with a message from Sam, the head of the New York agency.

"Jason, it's Sam, call me," he says in his thickest Long Island accent.

Sam's voice is not the first thing you want to hear in the morning. It brings to mind thoughts of my Jewish relatives and my seventh-grade teacher. Neither are fodder for a pleasant day. I think I'm in trouble. I make some coffee and call him back.

Turns out to be just the opposite. There is a high level of interest in me for this particular commercial, and they want to know what dates, if any, I am available during the course of the shoot week. It seems I have some leverage here. What's apparently happening is that the casting director is starting to panic, because they have to answer to the client, who should, like God, get whatever he wants, whenever he wants. This God factor comes into the commercial world far too often, and is the reason why I am in this predicament in the first place. The first audition for this spot was well over two weeks ago. In commercial time, this is the equivalent of four years. It's usually audition Monday, callback Wednesday or Thursday, shoot early the next week. For some reason known only to God, this client needed two weeks to decide to call me back and couldn't let me know until *5:00 P.M. the day before the callback* that he was interested. Of course, during those eternal two weeks, during which I had totally and completely forgotten about this commercial, I had booked another job out of town.

The casting director must answer to the client, my agent must answer to the casting director. I, apparently, have to answer to all of them, and, though I thought my agent was in charge of negotiating these kinds of things, he's about to hand this off to me.

I tell Sam that the typical Equity day off is Monday, so if they really want me, they can fly me out Sunday night, shoot on Monday, then fly me back very early Tuesday. Can I guarantee this, he asks? Well, no, I say, because I'm not going to start threatening the people who have already hired me with the chance that I'm leaving to go to another job until I know that said job is in hand. Sam tells me that the casting director tells him that I must be certain about my availability.

Certain? Are you kidding me? I was called less than twenty-four hours ago about this and they want me to be certain? Why don't *you* be certain? Hire my ass, and then I'll let you know if I take the job or not. This is, after all, the way things work in the rest of the world.

But this is not the rest of the world. I now call my legit agent, who has no financial interest vested in this commercial, and has a whole lot riding on the Humana Festival. I explain the situation. She's a true sweetheart, and agrees to call Humana to find out the day off. This is an ever-changing thing, determined at the director's discretion, and depends on how things are going with the rehearsal process. Meanwhile, the commercial agent is calling me every ten minutes to see if I have an answer for them. In the span of three hours, I'm supposed to find the director of the play and negotiate a timetable with him for another job I have not yet been offered.

I get back a 90 percent assurance that Monday is the day off, which I parlay into a guarantee to my commercial agent, which means I should indeed go to this callback. My legit agent reminds me that this isn't worth the hassle if it's not a national spot. Translated, this means: *Don't fuck up the job that you already have that's giving me commission.*

All this just to attend the callback. I'm nowhere near booking the job.

I show up at the casting director's office. I'm greeted with an, "Oh, good, so you can do it."

"Well, here's the deal," I say, and I describe the deal, my availability situation, and all my conversations with my agent. This deal must then meet with the approval of the head of the casting agency, who, having begged me to come to the callback (at least according to my agent) is now throwing me all kinds of attitude.

"I can't put you on tape and have the client approve you without knowing for sure if you can make the shoot dates," she tells me.

"Well," I tell her, "I can't negotiate with the job I already have until I know I have another one for sure."

This basic conflict in the division of acting between commercial and legit, and between the different unions' areas of responsibility, has left me, the actor, screwed in this situation. Basically, someone is going to be pissed. I want the audition because I want both jobs. that's the inherent idea: Support your theater career by doing commercials. I figure I should try to make this work, but if it doesn't, I'm going to take the fall for it. Not my agent who pressed me to go to the callback; not the casting director who apparently pressed my agent but then greeted me with a snarl. Me.

She and I settle on saying that I am available for one day. I figure that if they want me badly enough, we'll all figure out a way to make this work. So I sit down and wait. And wait. And wait.

For an hour.

I finally go in and do the audition. The direction I am given is, "Do the same thing you did last time." I, of course, remember precisely what I did two weeks ago in a commercial audition. This is a lie. I have some idea of what I did, but it's pretty vague, considering that commercial auditions are all about making choices on the spot. The even more egregious offense in this whole situation is the fact that though the client and the director are *always* at callbacks, they have decided not to come to this one. I'm left wondering why I have been asked to come back and do the "same thing" on tape if they already decided they liked it the first time around. Did they lose that copy?

I finish the audition, make nice with the casting assistant who ran the session, and leave. One should always make nice with casting assistants, because one day casting assistants will grow up to be casting directors. Moreover, there aren't enough nice people in this business, and though it doesn't pay off karmically, it's nice to be nice.

I get on the train, go buy some groceries. Twenty minutes later, my phone rings.

"Jason, it's Hannah," Sam's assistant. "They want you back because the girl you were supposed to read with was late and just showed up. But it's not a callback. They just want you back."

Funny, no one mentioned this during *the hour* I was waiting to audition.

"Okay. Tell them I'll be there in fifteen minutes."

By the way, this is highly against union laws. It's also why Hannah made it clear that this was not a *callback* even though they literally just *called* to get me *back* in the office. After an hour of waiting, union guidelines state that I'm supposed to get paid. After two callbacks, I'm also supposed to get paid. Both would be true in this case, but I won't see a check. If the casting director has to pay me, it's coming out of the client's pocket, and the client is going to be none too happy about an avoidable overage. Therefore, I'm not getting a make-or-break third audition—with the girl they really want me to be seen with—if I demand payment. I am again forced to grin and bear it and somehow find a way to be back at their office in fifteen, no, now make that ten, minutes.

I do. I catch my breath, make small talk with the girl who's supposed to be my wife in the ad. Her agent, who is also my agent, just called in a state of panic about being needed elsewhere for another audition and she's late. "I know it's a business," she says to me, "but it's not like I'm a heart surgeon and the patient is bleeding on the operating table. This is not dire. It's a fucking Swiffer commercial."

We do it again. I'm trying to keep a straight face about having my blood pressure checked and being told it's too high. She's acting like I'm dying of lupus. We're having a great time.

I leave. The end.

Abrupt? That's how these things always end—suddenly and anticlimactically. If there's a lesson here it's this: Don't take it all too seriously. You are the one in charge when it comes to your career. The agents don't know what to say, and the casting directors don't know either. Everyone's answering to a higher power and they're making the rules up as they go along.

Sure, it would be nice if the union did a better job regulating the audition process. That way I wouldn't have to risk my own hide to report one of the biggest commercial casting directors in the city. I won't report them, though, because I want to keep auditioning there and of course they'd find out it was I who ratted. It would be nice if there was direct communication—if I could talk to the directors of both the show and the commercial and try to work it out. But because there are so many actors, because everyone is in a rush and operating at the last minute, these kinds of accommodations are never made.

Sudden bursts of activity followed by weeks of nothing. If you're lucky enough to audition, it can be like starting a car in the cold after being out of town for the week. Simply getting to the place in your career where you're getting these auditions is an accomplishment, though no one will treat it that way. But you should. And those around you must recognize that it's an incredible feat simply to get seen by some of these people. Unfortunately, you cannot stop to pat yourself of the back for too long, because while you're doing that, someone else is getting your job.

It's true. The glass can be half full. "Someone is booking those jobs," my agent once counseled me. And she's right. Every part that's auditioned is cast. And as a career gains momentum, as the auditions come with more frequency, if you've trained, if you spend your heart, the jobs will come too. Sooner or later there will be work.

Work. Once again, the sexiest word in the acting trade.

10

ON SET, ON STAGE:
On the Job

"O God, send me some good actors . . . cheap."

—Lilian Baylis, English theatrical manager

Then one day, as you sit at home watching *Judge Judy*, or *Oprah*, or the good *Dr. Phil*, or one of the many other shows for housewives and unemployed actors, the phone rings. Caller ID shows one of the extensions at your agent's office.

It's early for them to be calling—usually you don't get appointments until the afternoon. And there was that callback yesterday. . . .

"Hello?" You pick up.

"It's Diane. *Law & Order* wants to know your availability Wednesday."

Your heart picks up. This is step one. Checking if I'm available. Of course I'm available. I'm watching a hair braider get sued for bad cornrows on *The People's Court. I'm available!*

"Hold on, let me check." You play it cool. "Yeah, no conflicts."

"Great, call you back."

And suddenly time slows to the speed of an F train on the weekend. Seconds tick by as you walk from your kitchen to the bedroom to the kitchen again before finally getting to the gym to work off the energy. And as you're walking home, the phone rings again.

"Hello?"

It's Diane. "You're booked for Wednesday, role is Dr. Solomon. Scale plus ten. Production will call you the night before with your call time."

"Great."

"Congrats," Diane says, then hangs up the phone.

You stop where you stand on the street, savoring the moment before you speed-dial mom, dad, brother, and boyfriend to tell them the good news. Dr. Solomon on *Law & Order*.

And then, the panic sets in. Four years of undergrad. Three in grad school. And you've never set foot on a film set.

Well, let's get acquainted, shall we?

Working in Episodic Television and Film

Most likely, if it's your first time on television, you're a day player or an Under 5. You are delivering a baby, or delivering a pizza, or delivering exposition. You are integral to the story only in that you are, as Rob Decina pointed out earlier, a moment in the main character's life.

Location shoots are mainly the same in episodic television and film, the major difference being the amount shot in a day, and therefore, the pace at which things move. But the general tenets remain—they both shoot on film stock, and therefore light the same and use vaguely the same number of ADs, grips, and teamsters.

Before you arrive on set, several things will happen. You will have gotten a call from production telling you when and where to pick up the script. I always loved seeing the pretty colored pages, reds and greens and yellows, signaling rewrites, which are done right up until cameras roll. Make sure you do not use the sides you were given in the audition. Rather, use the new script—things might have changed, and they may change several more times. Get ready, because being on a set is about being on your toes.

The second thing that will happen prior to shooting is the call from wardrobe, where they will, depending on their schedule and the size of the shoot, either tell you to bring some things to set with you and/or schedule a fitting. You get paid for the fitting, which is nice. You will find out your costume at this point, and so if you're one of those actors who really takes costuming seriously where your character is concerned, this will be a plus. However, you may not get to see your outfit until the day of, so be prepared.

On Hold

In television and film, no holds or first refusals are put on actors until they have actually booked the job. Once you are booked, you are guaranteed payment. If your scene is cut, you get paid, regardless of whether you work or not.

Your call time will be early. If you are shooting anywhere in the main areas of Manhattan, Brooklyn, or Queens, you will be expected to get there yourself. Shoots in New Jersey or faraway places in the boroughs will use van pickups. You will be given a street corner where you wait at 6:00 A.M. for the van. It's steered by a low-ranking production assistant (PA), who will then drive you to the location.

Once at the location, grab anyone with a walkie-talkie and tell him you need to check in with the AD. The first assistant director is your lifeline while on the set. She will check you in, check you out, and sometimes direct you, if your role is small enough. First ADs usually choreograph background action for the director and deal with all those little things the director doesn't have time for.

Someone will show you to your trailer. Don't get too excited. The trailer is divided into several cubby-sized rooms, nothing like the ones the Series Regulars get. No matter how big your role as a guest on the show, you will all be given the same size trailer. There is a little bed for you to fit on, maybe a TV that doesn't get reception, a sink, and a bathroom that's really a glammed-up Porta Potty. You will begin to notice that the glamour of showbiz is fast waning.

The AD will give you the day's pages. They are probably shooting five or six scenes that day, ten to fifteen pages of script. This is *a lot.* The pages are about 4" x 6" in size, shrunk down and small enough to fit in, say, the pocket of your costume to carry to the set. On movies they will shoot far less in a day, which translates into more waiting time for you, and also more chances to get it right. In television, budget is king, as is the shoot week. Everything is on the tightest of schedules. The pages will be in the order of shooting, so you'll have some idea where in the day you fall. Under no circumstances should you ask what time you'll be up. There is no time on a set. There is only getting through one thing and to the next, and so many things that affect the timing of the day can go wrong, or right, that it's impossible to tell. So don't be the irritating person who keeps asking.

You will be given some vague idea of *when*, however, and your call time has been structured around this. After checking in, you will go to hair and makeup, where you will be prepped and shorn and made ready for market.

And then you will wait for hours.

Really, the waiting is the worst. You know your lines, but you have no idea of what the set looks like, maybe even what the other actors look like. And so you sit in your little cubby, maybe running out to craft services, too amped to read a book or magazine but tired as hell of running through your four lines over and over again. You wait and wait, and then the knock comes.

A PA is going to walk you to the set for blocking.

Now it's showtime. You're about to meet everyone—the whole gang. The director, the other actors; grips and cameramen and DPs (Director of Photography) will be swirling around, measuring things, putting down spike tape at your feet as you hit marks. It's time to focus up and chill out.

You arrive, and see the scene for the first time. This is now your reality. Whatever you had pictured in your imagination, change it. The director introduces himself, as do the other actors—hopefully. They may not. They may completely ignore you. Now you realize that these people do this every day of their lives. You do this one day a year. You are on totally uneven footing. Namely, theirs is solid, yours more closely resembles a California mudslide.

You begin to make your way through the script. You know your lines. The other actors probably don't. They are probably holding the pages in their hand, and barely speaking them. There is no acting happening. This is strictly a rehearsal for blocking so that the camera knows where to aim, so the lighting guys know how to light, so the sound guy knows where to place the mike. It all happens very fast. You may not even say all the lines; you may skip over some. "Then you point at the body, say the line, and hold up the golf club. Camera pans left and we go off Jerry. Great."

And with that, it's done. Back to your trailer.

That's about all the information you're going to get until you shoot. There will be one more rehearsal, but by then, it's time to rock and roll. As they continue to light the set, stand-ins will be used for you and for the Series Regulars. You might appreciate a chance to walk through your blocking once or twice, but this will not happen.

More waiting, and then, time to shoot. It's so extraordinarily different from everything you might have trained for in the theater. One of the more unsettling parts is the lack of notice. You're the last to know when you're going to go back to the set, and therefore it is difficult to know when to prepare. You must find a way to keep a state of relaxed focus all day long. "For an entire day," Kat told me, "you need to be in the mental and body space that you are in on stage."

This is extraordinarily tough to do, seeing as you don't do it every day. Did I say every day? This is your first day. You've never done this before. And that's another of the funny, sometimes wonderful, sometimes terrifying things about acting. Every job is like your first day at a new office. You never know what to expect.

You're back on the set now, and it feels a lot different. The lights are brighter. The props have all been put in place. The sound guy puts a wireless mike on you and asks you to test it out. You stand around waiting for someone to tell you what to do. The other actors appear. And then, for the first time, you will act the scene.

This is your one and only dress rehearsal. Depending on the type of scene, and what the star actor wants, it may be your turn on camera, it may be his, or it may be both. You have to be ready for both. Television shows are using the one-camera format to cover a lot more now than they used to. And you're about to learn an important lesson about TV acting, which is that the only time it matters is when the camera is on you.

When I interviewed Marin, I asked her about her first experience in television, on a pilot that never made it to air. "Save up your shit till it's your turn, till it's your shot," she advised. "Also, when you're not the star of the scene, your angle is when the star says it is. So even though you have to save it up, you have to be ready, because you don't know who they're gonna do first. And if the star wants to get his over with, then they'll do his first. But if he has a particularly demanding scene, then they'll do yours first."

It's your job to be ready for every eventuality. Here are some possibilities.

The star will not really act with you if he's not in the shot. He may be reading his lines off the page or, as was once the case with me, off the prop notebook. He has a much greater awareness of playing to the camera than you, and will use this to his advantage. Like an actor who upstages you in the theater, stars in television may do the same.

The star may give you direction other than what the director told you. Stars have a lot of power on TV, and they know it. They are the consistent element of a show, the reason people tune in week after week. In episodic television, there are several producers and a team of writers who oversee the show, and who are responsible for week-to-week story and other continuity. There are also many different directors, which means that this week's episode is being directed by someone different from last week's. This directly affects the amount of respect directors are given, as they are jobbing in and out.

Lots of chitchat. Staying focused in between takes can be difficult. I've heard stories from actors about starting a dramatic crying scene while the star was finishing up a cell phone call, just as the director called background action. You may find yourself very alone on a set.

The rehearsal has concluded and cameras are about to roll. The nerves kick up. This may be the first time you've ever heard action called on a set. They call action depending on when camera and director are ready. You may not be ready, but you've gotta hit it when they say it. There may be a call for camera action, if the director wants the camera moving before you speak. There may be a call for background action, if the extras are filtering through the scene, and then there will be a call for the scene.

And suddenly, it's quiet. Funereal. Fifty people are watching you. There's a camera in your face, your voice sounds strange because all day you've been talking in the noise of the real world. Now it's utterly silent.

There will be screwups, just hopefully not yours. The basic objective in filming is getting that *one good take*, where all the factors that entail a good shot have come together in some sort of harmonious existence. Think about it—there are so many things that can go wrong. There's lighting, sound, camera operators, boom operators, and actors. The dead body may blink his eyes (yes, I saw this on a set). The camera guy may trip. The other actor might go up on a line and you might have done your best work that take. Too bad. You're going to do it again and again and again.

The Series Regular's performance counts more than yours. He will get more shots at doing it right than you, more chances to be happy. In television, you basically shoot until it's good enough, not until it's great. This means, was the camera in the right place? Did everyone get their lines out, or at least an approximation of the lines? So we have the shot we can use? Yes? Good—we move on.

Certainly, I've just presented the most cynical of descriptions, but it's what you should be prepared for. It's what my first experience was like. People are stressed on location; they need to *make the day*, meaning get everything done on schedule. I've actually heard many actors talk about the joys of working in New York television, where each and every actor is respected, where directors consult you on a scene, give you the freedom to have fun. You should be ready, willing, and able for that anyway, because that's the job of the actor. If it turns scary, though—if they're running overtime and over budget, and you're up last on a fifteen-hour day, and everyone really just wants to go home as soon as possible—don't keep them waiting. It's another reason why casting directors look for training. "I want to know actors have training because I feel like they are going to fall back on that training when times get tough," Rob says. "Certainly, [in daytime] when you're doing that much work, it gets hard, and you need to have that to rely on."

Kat tells me about her first television job. "It was *The Education of Max Bickford*, and I had one line. It was, 'Excuse me, Professor Bickford, how could you say that JFK wasn't a great president?' I didn't realize that there's no room to fuck up your line. All those tee-hee-hee bloopers they do on sitcoms—*that doesn't really happen.* You can't fuck up your line. There're *seventy-five people* standing there on a schedule needing you to not fuck up your line. Unless you're a big star."

Marin's story echoes Kat's. "I was playing a bartender. We were in this huge bar in the Meatpacking District, and we rehearsed it with nobody else there. And then suddenly I come back five hours later to shoot it, and there's about a hundred extras. I go behind the bar. I'm told I can't touch anything, I have a rag I can use. . . . I'm freaking out."

She got more accustomed to it eventually, but it amazes me how many actors have the same experience in New York. That's because in all that work to get the job, after all those auditions, no one tells you what to expect when you show up. Lines change during rehearsal. Roll with it. Big shiny metallic thing in your face? Pretend it's not there.

"Sometimes the person you're talking to isn't actually there," Marin says. "Sometimes they left to get coffee while they shoot your angle. I had to say lines like 'Get in the car' to a tree."

Still, at $200 a word, not bad for a day's work.

Working in Commercials

Forget the economics of it: Commercials are fun.

Auditioning for them is hell. Booking one is even harder. Theater actors are somehow expected to support themselves through commercials, but, as Mandy succinctly put it, "It's not any easier to get a commercial than it is to get any other job." Once you get one, however, it's rock and roll.

You know why? You're the star. Or you and a girl or another guy are the star. At most, a group of you. And you will be treated as such. There are people devoting themselves to tracking whether your facial hair is growing too fast. You're the guy they're shooting. You're the gal who's going to represent and sell this product to the world. And it's fun to be treated that way. It's like being king for a day, regardless of the money. If they're shooting out of town, they'll fly you there and give you a union-regulated per diem. They'll put you up in a hotel, pick you up, and drive you to the set.

As an actor, it's a blast too, because they shoot miles and miles of film. Tens of thousands of dollars are being spent on thirty seconds of airtime. Shooting this much can be frustrating, because the reason you're doing it over and over and over again is that there are too many cooks on the soundstage. You've got the creatives, or writers. Then you've got the client, the marketing people representing the company whose ad you are making. Then there's the director, who has to translate all of their different opinions to you.

Plus, all that smiling can literally cause cramping in your jaw muscles. But do not get frustrated or think that you're screwing it up. Instead, realize that you have been given an amazing amount of acting freedom with which to play. Also realize that it's finally about you, not the other actors as it was in that episode of *Law & Order*, or *CSI*. You're the focus of every shot. This can be a tremendous learning experience about the way filmmaking works. You'll discover what to do in a close-up versus a master shot. Suddenly you'll find out that you're stuck with a choice you made because of the way they're planning on cutting from one shot to the next. All the while, you're getting touchups and watched like a hawk by makeup and wardrobe.

The rest of it is the same as film and episodic television work. Except that in one day, you'll get more experience than the combined total of everything else you've ever shot.

Working in Daytime

You think the plot lines are far-fetched? Wait till you hear how they try to shoot this stuff.

An episode a day. Let me clarify that. In a single workday, they shoot every single page of the script for one episode. An hour of television. Sixty-some pages of script. One day.

A primetime show? Ten days. A movie? Maybe ninety days. A soap opera? *One day.*

Glad that's clear. It's important to understand because it dictates the entire process of working in daytime. The following description is based on my work on *Guiding Light*, a show that has been kind to me, to say the least. I have appeared as a priest who looked just like one of the main characters who was fleeing from the law, or at least the back of my head looked this way (imagine that audition). I've also played a dock worker who lied about seeing someone jump in the lake, an FBI agent who caused the villain he was arresting to have a heart attack and die, and, most recently, a morgue attendant. Death and reincarnation is very important in this line of work.

The day for a soap opera begins at 7:00 A.M. in the rehearsal room, and is broken into two sections, depending upon the soundstage they are shooting on. Before lunch, the hope is to finish all shots on Stage A. After lunch, the same applies for Stage B, or vice versa. Shooting revolves, as it does in film and TV, around location. The scenes for the day are therefore ordered from first to last, location by location. They are shot one to the next, so chances are that you, as a day player, let's say, will shoot all your scenes back-to-back, because you probably only appear in one location. Later, in editing, they will be dispersed throughout the episode.

Upon arrival, you will be given a dressing room. Nothing glamorous—in that way of New York City democracy, yours will be the same size as the stars'. You'll wait for a few minutes, and then you'll be called for dry blocking. This occurs in the rehearsal room, not on set, and you will be pretty confused about what is where. Regulars on the show have been working on these sets for weeks, months, and years, and so when the director points to the hallway, marked only by two metal folding chairs, it will make all the sense in the world to them and no sense to you. Don't worry, it only gets crazier.

When you walk into the rehearsal room you may be noticed, and you may not be noticed. The other actors will be milling around, and they probably will not introduce themselves to you. The director will be the one walking around, telling them what to do, and will soon call you to tell you what to do.

Bring your script up with you to blocking in the rehearsal room. There will be changes. Rewrites, often at the other actors' behest, happen regularly. Mark your blocking down as you get it, remembering that there will be references to you both in relation to the other actors and in relation to the camera. Most scenes are shot with three to four cameras: a close-up for each actor, a two-shot, and then entrances and exits for the fourth, if there is a fourth.

There will be no acting in rehearsal, so don't expect to get much of an idea of what the other actor is planning to do. Soaps are, benignly put, improvisational in their nature. The company of actors on a soap are a tight-knit bunch, in that they work together every day. In some strange way, they are the closest we have to a bona fide company of actors in this country—an ensemble. Day after day they work together. They know each others' rhythms and temperaments. They are also an incredibly hard-working bunch, and they know their characters to a tee. Since they know what they're doing, they often save it for the cameras. This is a wonderful thing for them, but it will make you feel like something of an outsider.

Dry blocking moves quickly—once and you're done. Then it's back to the dressing room to wait. Always waiting. Once the entire morning session has been blocked upstairs, the team will move down to the studio, and dress rehearsal and shooting will begin. On your way back to the dressing room, check in with hair and makeup and find out what time they would like to see you. If you do not find them, they will not find you. And, sorry to say, makeup helps. It's necessary under those lights, with other actors who are made up too. You want your makeup.

The waiting now can be killer. Working in television, it's important to figure out how to wait. Some people read, some watch movies, some listen to music, some run their scene over and over. Just be aware that you will need to occupy some time and then, suddenly, you will be called on to perform.

It comes as a warning call. This means that your set is up next on the soundstage. The warning call means to get into costume if you haven't already, for soon you will be called to the set. I always bring my script to pocket and keep it until the cameras roll. One never knows when something might change, or if I'll forget a piece of blocking or dialogue. It's nice to have it there. However, you may feel entirely differently, so do what makes you comfortable.

Showing up on set is a whirlwind experience. It's the first time the camera operators will see your blocking, so they're planning shots as you're negotiating your way around a set that is entirely new to you. Those folding chairs in the rehearsal hall are suddenly real walls and doors and gurneys and desks. You'll need to take a moment to familiarize yourself.

Then, on to rehearsal. The director is still on the soundstage floor, and will lead the rehearsal. You will work the same way as you did upstairs, in the order of scenes at this location. You will, most likely, rehearse a few scenes back-to-back, and then go on to tape those few scenes one right after the other. This saves time on their end. Once rehearsal on set has concluded, you will go to tape.

That's when everyone pulls it together. Makeup steps in and fixes your hair. Props might affix a badge to your shirt. All the final touches are put on while the director disappears into the booth. In soaps, they cut as they go. The director is calling camera angles while you're acting. The underscoring music is running underneath as well, as are most sound effects. The entire operation moves at a breakneck pace.

And then, quiet. The stage manager, whom you've never met, is running the show. She's got a little earpiece, and the director is talking to her. Anything you need to know, the stage manager will convey. For a while, you will feel like you are in Oz, as the man behind the curtain wields his mighty directorial hand. Should a piece of information become imperative, you may hear a booming voice over the *god mike*. The aptly named mike is what it says, the voice of the director telling you, or someone else, what to do.

You're going to be acting the scene for the first time. Energy levels have risen and adrenaline is pumping. You've never heard your voice in the scene before with sheer silence, never heard the volume with which your scene partner is approaching the scene. You must act from your character, from your circumstance, within the situation. You suddenly realize how prepared you must be. And you are prepared, because you had to be to get the job. Right?

Tape is rolling, and you will get a countdown. In daytime, they never actually say "Action"; rather, they count down from five. Only five through three are audible, so it goes, "5 . . . 4 . . . 3. . . ." You wait a beat, then begin. No one told me this the first time I did a soap, and though many times they'll do a mock count in rehearsal, they hadn't for me.

Entrances and exits will be cued by the stage manager if they do not come off a line cue. Again, this probably won't happen until you actually shoot. Just look to them and they'll drop an arm, letting you know it's time to make your move. Keep on acting until you hear them say, "And we're out." Watch enough daytime television and you'll see that many a long glance is held at the end of the scene. It's called a tag, and usually they'll tag off a lead actor. Still, stay in the scene.

In the most recent episode of a soap opera I shot, where I played a morgue attendant, I picked up some clues from the script. It was a dark and stormy night (of course), with thunder and lighting. Translated: Be ready for random flashing strobe lights on the set. The actor with whom I had a scene thought his daughter had been killed in an accident, and I was to show him the body. Translated: high stakes for him. Technically I was a day player, but really, my dialogue was sparse. I only said things like, "We're not releasing information to the press," and, "I'll see what I can do."

Here's how it went when we finally got around to shooting. The actor, who's a really talented guy with a huge theater background, was working himself up emotionally—stepping aside and getting to the heart of his grief. This hadn't happened in rehearsal. I was cued into the door and started to walk by him when he stopped me and asked about his daughter. We had a brief exchange where I mistook him for a reporter; then, when I found out he was asking about his daughter, I told him I would look into it. *And we're out.*

I wait. We need to do a pickup. The stage manager gives me a line, telling me that they're picking up from a certain point. Because they're cutting as they go, the scene will be cut from the last moment you acted that preceded this. There's lots of stopping and starting. Naturally, with the amount of text getting learned, shot, and blocked in a certain day, there are going to be mistakes. Plus, the director is calling camera angles for the first time that day. And she might want to do a better job of it. Still, your job as the hired hand is to not cause any more problems. Because aside from screwups, there's usually only one take before they move on. No "I can do it better."

This time, I enter and try to walk past him. In the script, he says something like, "Excuse me," then repeats himself before saying, "Hey, don't ignore me." In rehearsal, he and I had a brief discussion about me continuing past and him needing to stop me. I agreed that this was what the scene should be. So I did just that. Continued on.

I swear to God, he nearly tackled me. It wasn't at all what I was expecting. Nor was it the way the scene had played in rehearsal, or in my mind, for that matter. I figured he might put an arm on my shoulder, which would be enough to make me stop, turn, and talk to him. He grabbed me full force and pulled me back to him.

In that moment the scene changed. Everything I had prepared went out the window. It had to; otherwise, I'm left being the guy trying to act an imaginary scene. Now, I needed to calm this guy down, ease him into a position where I had the authority and control over the situation, and I didn't have lines to do it with other than "Just give me a few minutes."

What a fun challenge, right? But nerve-racking as all hell when I came out of it. The actor apologized for grabbing me so hard after we taped, but that's his job, and mine is to be ready to react. We are, after all the craziness, actors. And that's our job.

On to the next scene, and then that's it, you're done. Maybe, for a day play-er with a couple of scenes, you've had an hour of time in front of cameras that are rolling. You'll be released, you'll fill out your W-4, and you're back out in the world, looking for your next job.

When I got home from shooting that day, I sent an e-mail to a friend describing my experience on the set. *Soaps are like an improv,* I wrote, *only you don't know you're in it until you're actually shooting. Your cue line might resemble your cue line, or it might not. It may just be, "I think that's sort of my cue line, so I guess I'll say my line . . . now."*

Expect to have a good time. The soaps are actually a lot like the theater. They are linked by the actors and directors who work in both. Terms like *upstage* and *downstage* are used, and you rehearse in a rehearsal room, not on set. So it's kind of like theater, only instead of five weeks of rehearsal, you have five minutes.

Working in the Theater

In high school, I thought, *I can't wait to get to college.* Bigger sets, better actors, more time to focus on rehearsing a play. I'll be working with true professionals.

In college, I thought, *I can't wait to get out into the real world, where I'll be able to put all my time and energy into my craft, rehearsing plays with dedicated, creative people, devoting all of our time to our art.*

In my early New York days, I thought, *I cannot wait to graduate from the cold, black-box theaters I'm performing in to an Equity contract. I'll get paid, I'll devote all my time to creating my role, and I'll be living a comfortable life.*

Now, I think, *I wish it was like high school again.*

It doesn't get easier, it gets harder. It doesn't get simpler, it gets more complicated. Egos and opinions and artistic temperament do not go away with age, they strengthen. And guess what else? Your high school probably has more money than any theater company in New York.

Actors' Equity has a wide range of contracts governing the array of theatrical presentation both in New York and in the regions. Working in NYC is different in many ways from working out of town, mainly logistically and fiscally. But when it comes down to the nitty-gritty, the *What do people do all day?*—as Richard Scarry put it—well, not much changes from your freshman year in high school to your Broadway premiere.

Understudying

Someone's got to be there if an actor gets sick, or if he books a higher-paying job that conflicts with the show schedule. *Understudies,* also know as *standbys,* generally cover for more than one actor in a show. Often producers will hire one man to cover all the men and one woman to cover all the women. It's a ton of (usually) thankless work for an actor, in terms of exposure, but it can be a great way to gain credits and experience in New York. However, there's no guarantee of performing or of taking over for another actor if he leaves a show. And to make matters worse, some actors get typed as understudies, and are never considered for lead roles at theaters where they have worked as a standby.

Regional Theater

Generally, regional contracts run about nine weeks. Four to five of those weeks are spent in rehearsal, the rest in performance. Weeks, in this case, are Equity workweeks, which means six days a week with Mondays off. Going from not working to working in the theater means making a significant shift in your life. You've been auditioning during regular business hours for months, and then suddenly you change schedules so that your weekends are full and the only day to get anything done is a Monday. The rest of the world is happily unaware of this, but when it comes to spending time with family, wives, husbands, children, and friends, life takes a dramatic shift once rehearsal begins.

It's exciting. They're going to buy you a plane ticket, house you, even ship a set amount of your stuff for you. Pack as you wish, but remember things like sheets and towels if you're particular about where you sleep. There's no guarantee on thread count in the Equity contract.

Individual housing is required—you're not going to be bunking with anyone, except later in the run when you've begun that torrid affair with your costar—the one where it all seems so perfect until you set foot back in New York and realize that you've been living a completely alternative life in Dallas for the past two months. You will be provided a frying pan, silverware—the basic cooking needs. There will probably be a TV but no VCR, and you can pay for cable if you wish. There will be no transportation; chances are you'll be walking to work at the theater most days.

There's more money in regional theater budgets than there is in New York, thanks mostly to the subscriber base that keeps these theaters going. This means you'll be saving a chunk of change while you're out of town, if you're smart. Though you know nobody in this new town you're calling home for the next two months, you'll soon be making friends, and if there's one thing actors like to do when out of town, it's run up bar tabs. Working in regional theater can be a surreal existence, where you declare to yourself that the life you're living is a slightly pretend life. You're not paying rent. You're working every day, and you'll be performing for a paying crowd.

There's something wonderful about stepping out of your life for a while as an actor. I mean, isn't that what we get paid for? "I've has a lot of good experiences working out of town," Michael tells me. "I think in some ways it has been a second training for me. . . . There's less pressure. I'm sort of able to focus more directly on what I'm doing because there aren't the distractions of my friends and my life here."

And the converse?

"There are times when I felt like I was going to go insane, being out of town."

The Rehearsal Process

Settling in is really the only difference between working in town and working out of town. After that, it's the same thing everywhere, meaning, it depends on what your director wants.

What Does a Producer Do, Anyway?

Because my mother has asked me this so many times, I'm including a quick reference guide defining the tasks of those who don't perform on stage in the theater.

Producers—can take on a variety of roles, from the creative to the financial. A producer generally has put up the money for a show, and therefore likes to have some say in most aspects of the process. Producers hire directors, and are involved in casting decisions. Some producers lean toward more involvement, some less. In addition, they delegate responsibility for many other facets of the show, including marketing and publicity. They are the CEO of the play, as it were.

Directors—usually have overall creative control, which exhibits itself in working with actors and designers. If a new play is being rehearsed, they will collaborate with the writer.

Lighting/Scenic/Sound Designers—work with the director to design each aspect of the production. Once a show opens, they're gone.

Stage Managers—are the actors' adversary on the production team. They eventually become responsible for running the show, once the director has left the production. They run the rehearsal room, call breaks, take blocking notes, and do many other thankless tasks.

The first day of rehearsal begins with a *meet and greet*. A roomful of nervous actors, directors, designers, and board members all come together and realize, in communal terror, that in five weeks, there will be a play. After going around the room with introductions, the design presentations begin. Everyone will ooh and ahh at the model of the set. Then the costume designer will show her renderings (more oohing and ahhing). Lights and sound will talk about their visions briefly, and then the director will launch into a speech about how happy she is to be there, working with this group of people.

Then the first read-through happens. Everyone will probably try a little too hard to make the play work and sound funny. There will be a break. The board members, who have sat in on the table read in order to feel a part of something creative, will scatter and part ways, not to be seen again until the opening-night party. Designers will go forth until tech. You'll go off for your ten-minute break. When you return, the table will be a lot more intimate.

I've found that one of the major differences between "professional" theater and the work I did in college and in downtown New York is the amount of time spent at the table. Part of this has to do with the professionalism of everyone involved, and the level of intelligence. Time spent at the table varies from director to director, but there will be anywhere from three days to two weeks spent around the table, reading and discussing the play. Some directors work at the table so long, you find yourself off book before you ever get on your feet.

Blocking rehearsals begin sometime at the end of week one or the beginning of week two. The task of staging the play occurs in a rehearsal room. The floor is taped out to resemble the set. Alternate sofas, chairs, and tables mark the actual set pieces that will appear later. Each director works differently, of course. Some like to block a show start to finish, then go back scene by scene. Others work one act at a time, progressing forward at a slower pace. As an actor, you never know what you will run into. There's no one way of working. Hopefully, after a sum total of maybe twenty minutes in a room together at the audition, the director has chosen you not only for your talent and ability to fill a role, but for the way you work, a way that complements her own.

Scene work and run-throughs will comprise the next two weeks. The five-week rehearsal is a generous one. Most theaters do four weeks including tech, because everyone is getting paid for their rehearsal time at the same rate as they are during performance. As far as getting off book goes, that's an individual question, but most directors like to have you off book by the time you make your second pass at a scene, once blocking has been completed. A run-through for the design team usually happens sometime in week three, so the sound and lighting designers can engineer cues.

Then it's time for tech. It's that magical time when actors are forgotten and the technical elements of the show are put into place. The show moves to the theater. Working from one cue to the next, tech proceeds at a sluggish tempo, and that's on a good day. Depending on the theater, and on the contract, tech can run anywhere from two days to two weeks. On Broadway, they may only tech one scene in a day. The more money, the heavier the tech. The heavier the tech, the more time it takes.

More often than most theaters would like to admit, the show goes into tech underrehearsed. This is why previews exist. Preview performances run anywhere from a week to over a month, again depending on the venue and the amount invested. Previews are when the kinks are worked out. In a new play, there may be rewrites. In a revival, there may be cuts. Cues change. Scene changes change. Occasionally, actors change, as producers or directors take odds with the performance.

During previews, the cast is rehearsing during the day and performing at night. It is not until a show opens that no further rehearsals are permitted. Plays need audiences to help them figure out the tricky spots and in order to find a rhythm. In a comedy, one has to find the laughs. Audiences tell the play, and the players, how to pace a show—when it's too slow, when to take that extra beat.

The different tones of silence, or coughing, can inform the play a great deal.

It used to be the case that the press came on opening night. Now, however, with the number of shows that get reviewed in New York, and with the liberty of previews, press often attends a preview somewhere in the week leading up to opening night. Press, at least in New York, will make or break a show. The celebrity factor helps producers counter this problem, but a good review in the *New York Times* translates into ticket sales. Thus, though actors are loathe to discuss press, and most want little knowledge of when press is in attendance, something changes in the air when the critics arrive.

Opening night is not a first performance, but rather a first official performance. It's a celebration. The house is packed with friends and people from the industry, and there's a big party afterwards with free cheese cubes (nonprofit) or tenderloin and martinis (Broadway). Everyone gets dressed up and feels special. Rehearsals have officially ended. The director's involvement with the show has come to an end. There are no more notes. There is just performance.

It's now in the cast's hands. The stage manager calls the cues for the show and lets you know if you're doing anything drastically askew from the director's vision. Her job is to maintain the running shape of the show. This means that if the kiss takes too long, or the show is running ten minutes over, you will hear about it. Other than that, it's business as usual. You arrive by your Equity mandated half-hour call (earlier if there is a fight call), you perform, and you go home. Seven to eight shows a week, maybe five over the course of a weekend. Weekends are killer. As you become the thing everyone does with his free Saturday night, your Saturday night, and Sunday morning, and Sunday night become progressively more exhausting.

And then you settle into the run. Your days become free. If you're in NYC, this means you begin auditioning again, looking for the next job. If you're out of town, you take up the guitar, or explore, or watch DVDs, or think up an idea for a book about the acting business and write it (guess who?). You will have a ton of time on your hands for anywhere from three to ten weeks. Most runs don't go much longer than that. Contractually, for nonprofit contracts, they can't extend without upping your paycheck in New York. So unless a commercial producer gets involved and transfers the show to a commercial venue, you will run until you close. Have a drink with your cast, promise to keep in touch, and then go your separate ways.

And then where are you? After work, it's usually back to the land of unemployment, a place where the only artist subsidy that can be found is with the N.Y. State Department of Labor at $405 a week, if you qualify. It's why you could be under the hot stage lights one week and back to catering the next.

11

**TURKEY DOGS
AND THE ECONOMIC
REALITIES OF ACTING**

"I've made sacrifices, lived sacrifices until this moment—I'm living in a place CNN would casually dismiss as third world. The people who are my age who don't do what I do have homes and cars and—I scrounge for subway fare. So I have my nine-years-in-the-making overnight success and you know? I'm thinking, Oh, this is where they pull back the velvet cord and I get to meet whomever I want to meet and do whatever I want to do, and I'm still looking for temp work to hustle together rent. Because no one ever tells you about that little breather period between critical success and financial success."

—Evan Wyler, *As Bees in Honey Drown* by Douglass Carter Beane

"Well, I'm not doing catering at the Holocaust Museum anymore. Ever again." Patch pauses and looks up at me.

"You should put that in your book, too. I say that to people and they think I'm joking."

He's not. Talented people are working menial jobs because it fits their time frame, allows them to go on auditions, and gives them the ability to pursue the thing they love to do. It is wearying, both physically and emotionally, because you so rarely work in the occupation that makes you happy, and so frequently get treated like, well, a waiter.

Not that this should be any surprise to anyone. On the U.S. Bureau of Labor Statistics' Web site, where they take great pains to analyze and evaluate all fields of our economy, the acting profession is bullet-pointed with these warnings:

• *Actors endure long periods of unemployment, intense competition for roles, and frequent rejection in auditions.*
• *Because earnings for actors are erratic, many supplement their incomes by holding jobs in other fields.*

For comparison's sake, here's what they have to say about dentists.

• *Job prospects should be good.*

It's not like we haven't been warned it's a tough profession, especially at family reunions, when it resurfaces in your interrogation by your Great-Aunt Jean. Many actors, however, have the professional training equivalent of lawyers. They have studied just as long, and just as hard—three years postgraduate for an MFA—and therefore it is understandable that there might be some sense of entitlement attached to one's career, especially coming out of school $50,000 to $100,000 in debt.

Note, also, that an entire sub-industry has cropped up in the fringes of the acting business, feeding off the dreams and hopes of actors. There are headshots to be reproduced, classes to take, seminars on the business, casting workshops, and forums where actors pay to meet agents and casting directors. Some of these are necessary evils, some are just evil. Nonetheless, acting is becoming an industry where you have to pay money to get noticed.

It's a difficult balance to strike economically. You feel successful with a large paycheck for a Guest Lead on an episodic, but it won't support you for a year. That's why, no matter how successful they are, most working actors are still picking up scrap jobs in between.

So acting becomes more than a job—it becomes the individual as a corporation: taking strategic risks, working the market to your advantage. Maintaining an acting career requires a keen sense of business savvy in addition to talent. So here's the economics class you skipped in college, a financial primer for the artistically inclined. Read on, and you might just qualify for a matchbook MBA.

Taking a Loss

You are about to become very familiar with a wonderful part of the U.S. tax code called the Schedule C.

The Schedule C declares profit or loss for people running their own business. I first learned of it on a visit to an accountant. No one had bothered to mention it to me before. This is unfortunate, because the fact of the matter is that as an actor, you are running your own business. You're much like an independent salesman, but you are selling yourself as a product. In doing so, there are costs, some which can be claimed as a business expense on your taxes, thus offsetting your income and allowing you to pay less to the government. There's only one problem.

You have to make money too.

As you enter this profession, you will immediately be hit with a loss. You must incur these costs before you make a penny. You are investing in your own future.

As I mentioned in chapter 6, you must have headshots. The business operates on 8" x 10" photos of you with a resume stapled to the back. For each and every audition, a headshot is submitted. The digital world is slowly beginning to change this, and there is an increase in digital submissions, but only to a middling degree. While the rest of the world is e-mailing photos to each other, actors and agents are still stapling resumes onto the backs of photos, sticking them in envelopes, and messengering them to casting offices around the city. By pony.

Just kidding about the pony. The rest of the system, however, moves along with the bureaucratic innovation of the U.S. Post Office. Photos are sent back and forth. And so, to get auditions, you must have many of these photos. Get out your calculators.

A session with a reputable NYC headshot photographer will run you from $600 to $900. Most are in the $800 range. Some offer discounts of the "bring a friend" or "peruse the Web site instead of coming to the studio" variety. The package usually includes several rolls of film and one to two original prints. Digital photography and digital color photography are coming into vogue, but have yet to fully take off. Still, even with digital, photographers' rates are only negligibly lower.

Once you've selected the print that will represent you to casting directors everywhere, you have to get reproductions. These run anywhere from $1 to $1.50 a print, depending on the method of reproduction, the number of pictures ordered, and the stock used for printing. Let's say you get 500. The major house in the city, called Reproductions, charges $342.50 for this order on photo paper.

You're over $1,000 already. Those 500 prints will last you a year, maybe, depending on who is submitting you and how often you're going out. Should you choose to order postcard photos for promotion, you're adding another $200 to $300 on top of this. Then there's postage for mailings, which you'll have to do at first, even if it may be a fruitless endeavor, because you have all those goddamn pictures and nothing to do with them, so you might as well occupy your time—like playing the lotto. At $.63 an envelope, for 45 agents, that's $24 per mailing operation. Let's say you do postcard follow-ups for six months or so, monthly progress updates, at $.24 a card, for 40 agents a month. That's $57.

A rough estimate of your expenses, for promotional materials alone, for your first six months as an actor, is:

Headshot Originals:	$850
Reproductions:	$350
Postcards:	$200
Mailings:	$80
Total:	$1,480

You're $1,500 in the hole. And though some of these expenses disappear, the cost of reproductions remains for as long as you are an actor vying for jobs in this business. It doesn't matter how many times a certain casting director has seen your face. Each and every time you are submitted for an audition, it's costing you a dollar. Those are the legitimately sanctioned ones.

Of course, there is the other route into the profession. Graduate school. And just like everywhere else in this society, the value of art leaves actors with few scholarship opportunities. Training is one of the easier entrances into this world. Get into one of the top graduate programs, and almost every agent and casting director in New York will see your work. A three-year graduate school— let's take NYU as an example—costs $31,270 a year—before living costs. At three years, you're over $100,000 in debt. Loans for higher education make it possible to defer much of this cost. But look carefully at this expenditure before you head off to school. It's debt that will stay with you for life.

You're in New York because you have to be. It's New York or L.A. for actors, with the soft exception of Chicago, but they all eventually end up here anyway. The cost of living in New York City is astronomical. Expect to pay, at minimum, $700 a month on rent. That means roommates and a bit of a commute, which means a MetroCard, now at $76 a month. Plus, you have to eat, too. Often you're stuck between auditions without a chance to go home for lunch, or there's the inevitable hour to kill at a Starbucks on a rainy afternoon. Maybe you want to go out a little, especially to network with other actors at bars.

Factoring all these costs together, your bare minimum turkey-dog diet annual cost of living is about $18,500. Okay, you can make that as an actor, right? Let's see.

Income: What You'll Make Working in Theater

If you had told me ten years ago that there would be a full-color photo of me alongside a nice review in the *New York Times,* I would have been elated. That, I would have told you, would surely signal my arrival in the New York theater. It would herald the end of working other jobs. Casting directors would be calling my agent, trying to find out who I was. Job offers would begin to roll in. I would have found success, financial health, and, in a word: security.

If you had told me I would be making $340 a week for this show, I would undoubtedly have called you a liar.

If you had told me I would be unemployed as soon as the show closed, I would have doubted your grasp of the way this business operates.

If you had told me that my fellow cast member, who played the title role "with an intriguing opacity . . . in a promising New York stage debut," according to the *New York Times,* would be back waiting tables at the restaurant where she worked *during rehearsals* because we were barely making minimum wage, I would have had you certified as insane.

Are things better for me and for her, having completed an Off-Broadway run? Sure. Do we have slightly more recognition? Yes. Are we working?

No. We're collecting unemployment and waiting tables and maybe living off some residuals from a commercial shot last year. Auditioning. Waiting by the phone. Watching *Dr. Phil.*

Let us return to the dream. Broadway. The pinnacle of theatrical success. The place where stars are made, careers launched. Every stage actor, and an increasing number of film and television stars, dreams of working on Broadway. So what are the job opportunities?

Number of Contracts AEA Issued in 2004

Here are Equity's numbers for contracts for the calendar year. However, these numbers do not directly translate to number of actors working. Some of these are the same actor working again and again.

> *Production (includes Broadway and some Tours):* 3,241
>
> *Off-Broadway:* 935
>
> *New York Letter of Agreement:* 466
>
> *New York Mini Contract:* 397
>
> *LORT (League of Resident Theatres, mostly regional):* 8,216

This week's *Time Out New York,* the great democratic platform of theater listings, provides information on thirty-six Broadway shows. It's Tony season, so things are at their peak right now. Of these, twenty-three shows are musicals, so if you sing, your odds of employment just increased. Two of the plays are one-man shows, so unless your name is Mason or Crystal, as in Jackie and Billy, you're not getting in there. This leaves, for the actor who can't sing, or who opts not to do musical theater—i.e., most of us—eleven plays.

Let's take those eleven plays and give them each a cast of ten. A generous number, since most probably average five. That's 110 roles available on Broadway. Now, calculate in the celebrity factor. Right now, Jessica Lange, Rebecca Gayheart, Alan Alda, James Earl Jones, Christian Slater, John C. Reilly, Liev Schreiber, Billy Crudup, Jeff Goldblum, Denzel Washington, and Kathleen Turner are all on Broadway. Not all of these actors hail from the screen alone. In fairness, many have performed on Broadway before and trained in the theater. But here's the point. Those jobs were never going to be jobs you could get. Those jobs go to stars. Period.

So let's lose twenty of those jobs to star offers right off the bat. Thus, without considering factors such as sex, type, age, and all the things that casting entails, we'll just assume that each of the 15,000-plus members of Actors' Equity in New York are right for all of the roles. 15,000 actors into 90 roles equals: .006.

That's just over *half a percent chance* of getting a Broadway show.

I'm no statistician. My figures are rough. But there's no way to make *one half of one percent* look good.

And if you do book the role? Broadway minimum at the time of this writing was $1,381 a week, which is $1,242.90 after 10 percent agent commission, which is a yearly salary of $64,630. That's a yearly salary. The show must run for a year.

Of those straight plays I used for my calculations, guess how many have run for a year?

None. The closest any of them came to it is having transferred from Off-Broadway to Broadway. Close, but not quite the same monetarily.

Off-Broadway, I hear you whispering. More jobs? Better opportunity for the young upstart actor? Let's play the game again.

Sixty-one shows. Of those sixty-one, only about half are paying contracts. This includes several one-person shows and long-running gigs like *Blue Man Group* and *Stomp,* which do, every so often, recast their shows. So thirty shows with eight actors each is 210 roles. That's 15,000-plus union members and: .014.

A 1.5 percent chance of employment in a paying Off-Broadway show. And mind you, the stars are taking those jobs now, too (this year saw Jason Biggs, Amanda Peet, Ben Stiller, Molly Ringwald). Say you get a job under an Off-Broadway contract—a commercial venue, not one of these letter of agreement or nonprofit deals, which pay as low as $200 a week. You're working Off-Broadway at something resembling the scale below.

Off-Broadway Minimum Weekly Salary Schedule

SEATS	100–199	200–250	251–299	300–350	351–499
SALARY	$493	$574	$665	$765	$857

By the way, no one ever gets paid above minimum.

These are pretty decent weekly numbers. But first, take out 10 percent for the agent, every week. (I'm cheating here slightly for the 100–199 seat category because agents cannot get commission on weekly salaries below $500. Managers, however, can.)

SEATS	100–199	200–250	251–299	300–350	351–499
SALARY	$443.70	$516.60	$598.50	$688.50	$771.50

Oops. Dropped a tad. But still, if you work one of these shows for a full year, all fifty-two weeks, here's your yearly salary.

SEATS	100–199	200–250	251–299	300–350	351–499
SALARY	$23,072	$26,863	$31,122	$35,802	$40,118

Wait a minute. Off-Broadway is a major venue in New York City, the heartland of American theater. Hackman, Duvall, and Pacino have walked its storied path. Hundreds of actors are out there killing themselves, trying to make it, and this is what *making it* means? No. Acting must provide more than my cousin makes in his temp job at that accounting firm.

It doesn't. Then, add to the mix the number of shows running for a full year Off-Broadway—six this year (that's total Off-Broadway, not just commercial). Most close in three months. Maximum. Here is a prestigious acting job in New York that, at the top end, makes what many New Yorkers consider a starting salary. There is not going to be any promotion or raise, and there is no guarantee of how long the show will run.

This is the salary for an actor doing seven or eight shows a week. Though the traditional forty-hour workweek doesn't apply in this business, when you calculate the time an actor logs, from performance through rehearsal, things even out. A show runs two hours—that's sixteen hours of performance a week, which is more than a professional basketball player, for comparison's sake. Add in time for warming up and getting in and out of costume—an hour before every show when all is said and done—and we're up to twenty-four hours a week. That's just performance. There were about four weeks of rehearsal, which are eight-hour days, plus at least a week of tech, which is comprised of ten-hour days, and things start to even out.

Median annual earnings for an AEA member in 2004 were $6,638. The average beginning salary, across all professions, for a person with a Master's degree is $62,820.

When they say there's no money in the theater, they ain't lying. Which brings us to the wonderful world of the Showcase code, the agreement that Equity has arranged so that union actors can actually work for no money. It affords actors the chance to be seen. However, as Patch tells it, "You have producers who are basically taking advantage of the fact that actors just want to work and be seen." It's an opportunity that comes with a price tag as well. For a recent showcase, which was written by an up-and-coming writer who had work previously produced by Second Stage, as well as regionally, Patch received a stipend of $150.

That's $150 for eight weeks of work. Get out your calculators once again, friends. Eight weeks, six days a week, three hours a day, at least. That's . . .

$1.04 an hour.

No one is saying that actors are doing these shows for the money. They're not. But the residual sacrifice that one must make in order to do these shows—and one *must* do these shows—is enormous. Did I mention Patch has a Broadway credit on his resume? Yet he's still faced with this conundrum.

Patch recalled his agent's response. (Yes, actors who work for free have agents.) "'The big question is, can you afford to do another showcase?' And, well, I can't afford it, money-wise. I'm in terrible debt because of it. . . . But a lot of people got to see it, and we got a *New York Times* rave review. Can I afford *not* to do that?"

From top to bottom, in New York City, making a living in any part of the year as an actor in the theater is a near impossibility. Making a living with any consistency . . . well, that's just a hoax. There is, however, the opportunity to go out of town. Regional theaters pay much better than do theaters in New York City. Of course, in order to go out of town, one must be in town, paying all of those living expenses. And to afford to go out of town, one must sublet his apartment. And if all these things happen, you can leave and make, at the top end, about $900 a week in the regions. Your housing is paid, your expenses are low, and you can save. But you can't audition while you're away, which means that you are, once again, returning to the land of unemployment upon your arrival in New York, for at least a month.

The truth of it is, a man cannot survive on theater alone.

Income: What You'll Make Working in Television and Film

Be honest: A little part of you wants to strike it rich.

I'm no exception. Though I act because I love acting, I'd be lying if I didn't admit to that kernel deep down that craves more than making a living at it, actually striking it rich. And it does happen. People do book commercials and pilots and film and get phenomenal paydays for one day of work. One actress quoted $160,000 for two national commercials when I asked. The money can come suddenly, in great heaps, and you'll think you're rich.

You're not. It doesn't keep coming like that, so save and spend wisely, because there is always a rainy day around the corner in the acting industry.

Getting the job in a commercial, or a part on a television show, is generally thought to be the way in which theater actors support themselves. But it ain't that easy. The competition is just as fierce, and it's not like there is a ton of interplay between the different worlds. The agents and casting directors are different.

Even if they appreciate the theater, it can still be a complication. Say you're doing a show in New York, as I recently was, and you get called in to audition for a Guest Lead on *Law & Order*, as I recently did. They don't care that you have a performance every night at 7:30. If they hire you, they own you. They have bought that time. Say a soap opera offers you a week's worth of work, which could turn out to be several thousand dollars in supporting income. On one of those days, they can't guarantee that you'll be released in time for your curtain. Most likely you'll be fine, but if push comes to shove, they own you.

You're faced with a decision. Most of the nonprofit agreements in New York give the actor a brief out clause for *more remunerative employment,* meaning that one of the caveats to the deal is that they have to let you take the higher-paying job and not fire you. Fine, you can finagle it legally and contractually. But what about the relationship you've built with these people? What about your castmates, who are counting on you? What about your own sense of duty to the production? Plus, when it comes to making the decision, you'll be on your own. Agents and managers and casting directors don't like to deal with such quandaries.

I brought up my recent situation of having to turn down work for a show while talking to Rob.

"What are you getting on that play?" he asks.

"Three hundred forty a week."

"So you would have made that in a day . . . and there would have been days when you made two or three times that." But he agrees with my choice. "Listen, I think that there's legitimacy to *That's too close to call, and I've already got a commitment.*"

Unfortunately, legitimacy doesn't buy MetroCards. Had I risked it, I would have made as much in a week as I had for the entire run of the show.

When you work, you're going to be faced with these problems. Complications aside, however, the basic picture is quite simple. There are minimums that the unions dictate based on the categories I described in chapter 2 (Under 5, Day Player, Guest Lead, etc.) We're not exactly talking about the striking-it-rich category. Absolutely, this is a wonderful amount of money to make for a day's work, perhaps a ridiculous amount for an eight-hour call, even more insane considering the actual time that you're working on set.

SAG TV Pay Rates ⎯⎯⎯⎯⎯⎯⎯⎯⎯⎯⎯⎯⎯⎯⎯⎯⎯⎯⎯⎯

    Day Player - - - - - - - -$678

    Week - - - - - - - - - - - -$2,352

    3-Day - - - - - - - - - - -$1,714

    Major Role (hour-long) $5,831 (minimum per episode)

But that one job on an episodic show means you are now finished with that show for a year. It's an opportunity gained and lost all at once. Plus, you'll be surprised to learn that, thanks to the differentiation between Series Regulars and recurring roles, many of those actors on television are not being paid as much as it may seem. One actor I spoke with just booked a recurring role on a new show on FX, which, as a general rule, pays far less than the networks, and so even Series Regulars on the show are making less per episode than they would on ABC. She was a recurring character in this show, covered by AFTRA, but the producers opted to shoot all six episodes' worth of her scenes in one day. She was paid an AFTRA scale rate, not a Series Regular rate. This day, which went well into overtime, paid her well. Plus, the union mandates that a performer receive her negotiated rate per episode, even if all the shooting is done in one day. But this actor, whose character may grow a better storyline, who may become loved by the show's audience, who may seem like another member of the regular cast—she's in five of the first six episodes—is not making money the way you think she is.

The good news, then, is that the unions have gotten minimum rates for actors that reflect the lack of employment opportunities and exposure, so that when one does book a job, it might stretch as far as a rent payment. Usually, it's no more than this. And what the union has achieved in minimums, it has completely disregarded as far as maximums are concerned. While in most industries, a minimum might be a base where negotiations begin, in acting the general feeling is: *You're lucky to have this job, I could easily give it to someone else, and therefore, you will be making scale.* Our scale is nice. Our scale is anywhere from $20 to $60 an hour. But it is important to remember that this is both your minimum and maximum rate, at least until the roles start accumulating, or you book a Series Lead.

For work on any network television job, you can expect to ultimately receive about three times your original day rate. This is thanks to our new favorite friend, the residual. For primetime reruns on network television, an actor will receive a check equal to his or her original day rate. This does not include any overtime you might have made the day that you worked. It can be a nice chunk of change; the only problem is that one never knows when it might arrive. Therefore, you cannot count on it as definite income. Shows are rerun all the time, sure, but it's not like network executives are sitting around thinking about your fiscal health. They're thinking about programming and advertising. So, though there is an incredibly high chance that your day player role will be run again during primetime, no one is going to advance you that money.

Payment

It takes forever to get paid.

The unions have regulated talent payment so that a check must be sent within two weeks of the completion of work—a reasonable amount of time. That check is sent to your agent, who then deposits it, usually waits for it to clear, and then cuts you a check. If you have a manager, there's a third stage to the process, where the agent sends the check to the manager, then the manager deposits it and cuts you a check. All told, don't expect to see the money from your job for about a month.

If a show is put into syndication, residual payment goes down significantly, eventually to as low as 5 percent of your day rate. Discussions of residual checks in the amount of $7.14 are a common occurrence in audition rooms throughout this city. That's about what you get if you make day player scale and the show is sold to TNT for reruns. Of course, if you're a Series Regular, your percentage of that rerun money turns a bigger profit, because your per-episode rate is the determining factor. And so, in the way of all labor history, the rich get richer while the day laborer struggles.

Yet, mom and dad still want to know why one thing hasn't led to another and landed you a role on television. I've taken a careful look at market opportunities with the help of this week's *TV Guide,* and have come up with what I'll call the "Impressing Mom and Dad Television Survey."

Forget New York versus Los Angeles for a minute and pretend you have opportunities in both cities. You don't, but why not play along for fun? It's a week in May and I'm narrowing our field to the main producers of television covered by SAG. Though there are plenty of new shows on cable, we're gonna pretend Mom and Dad don't have HBO at home. I am including all the major networks (ABC, CBS, NBC) plus FOX, UPN, and the WB, in the survey.

Reality television still rules the roost, and networks are airing their season finales this week. It's not the height of the season by any means—that time when all the new shows come out in the fall before natural selection winnows the quality shows from the stinkers, keeping some of each on the air. However, this seems to be a reasonably representative survey. It's a week in TV land, and here's what's on.

Sunday there are six hour-long dramas on TV. FOX runs all cartoons, which do offer voiceover work, but which I won't include for the purposes of this survey. Mom and Dad want to see you, not hear you. The rest are newsmagazines and reality programming. And there ain't no work for actors in reality programming.

Monday is a good night. There are ten shows on the networks, a mix of half-hour and hour dramas. Plus there's a miniseries. Doesn't count—not produced week in and week out.

Tuesday there are eight shows, and CBS has the country music awards.

Wednesday has the heaviest turnout. Twelve shows for actors to do acting.

Thursday there are six and ABC is showing a movie.

Friday and *Saturday* there are three shows total, plus a bunch of network *Law & Order* reruns, some baseball, and the Daytime Emmy Awards.

All told, this week in May, there are forty-five shows. Let's say that each has five Series Regulars: the actors who show up at work every week and get paid per episode. Now, in the Screen Actors Guild, there are roughly 118,000 members. Your chance of being a Series Regular, then?

It's .001906779661. Rounding up, that's half of half a percent chance.

Say there are five Guest Leads per episode, per show—people who make a good amount for being on the show, multiplied by twenty-two episodes a year.

That's .04194915. Or 5 percent.

Maybe twenty day players per show. That's a 15 percent chance of employment for the year. Of course, there are myriad factors such as who your agent is, the number of non-union actors you're up against, factors of age, sex, and race. So really, these are generous numbers.

I am reminded of a conversation I had with an agent who was interested in me. I had just finished performing two monologues for him in his office. You know what he told me?

"You're top 10 percent, but not top 2 percent."

What did he really mean? *You're a day player, not a Series Regular,* he might have been saying. Or, more matter-of-factly, *You won't book work, because only the top 2 percent book real work.* And, for what it's worth, he was wrong. I do book work.

There are actors and models who are not yet union members who will take some of these roles. There are shows that run and shows that die. There are celebrities who take all the Series Regular parts. I'd love to get a statistician to do a real analysis of all of this, but I'd venture to guess that the numbers, once we weeded through it all, would be about the same.

Income: What You'll Make Working in Commercials

Commercial money, namely residuals, is an entirely different enterprise. The SAG commercial contract bases residual payments on commercial usage, and thus the actor is getting paid based on her exposure attached to a certain product. When you do a commercial, you are paid a day rate. This day rate then becomes your first holding fee.

When you do a commercial, you are signing a contract that says that you will not advertise for competing products. If it's Burger King, this means you cannot do McDonald's or Wendy's; if it's AT&T, no Verizon. You get the idea. Agents can get creative when it comes to the rates you get paid for holding fees depending on what kind of exclusiveness the client is asking for. For the most part, however, your scale day rate becomes your holding fee.

For the next two years, then, you will receive this holding fee for each thirteen-week cycle where the commercial runs. As long as they pay you this fee, you cannot do a commercial for a competing product. The advertiser can stop paying you this fee at any time, but most hold you for two years.

Again, you're going to be on the losing end of this proposition as far as economic principles go. Any sensible businessman, knowing that he was going to be attached to a product for two years, would ask for that money up front—a buyout, as it were. For example, $500 every thirteen weeks for two years is $4,000. Plus, in most cases, a few versions of a commercial are cut, and you'll be paid a holding fee for each of these spots. You could be looking at $10,000 over two years. But because it is coming in installments, you won't be able to make a down payment on that apartment, or pay off a chunk of your student loans, or even collect interest. When it arrives in small increments, the money has a funny way of disappearing.

The good news is that this is your bottom line. Because of usage, you'll be making a lot more than just holding fees if you do a commercial. The intricacies of commercial residuals are tricky, and advertising agencies have entire business affairs departments devoted to figuring out the math, but the basic premise rides on the exposure scale. Regions and markets are given weight in terms of units, e.g., New York carries more units than Boise. A commercial may run in all major markets, meaning you'll be paid for these cities. Or it may run as a wild spot, which refers to a regional advertising buy. The jackpot is a national commercial. It can support you for years, if you save and spend wisely.

As an actor, you've waited and waited and then finally you open your mailbox a month after having done a commercial and there are four thick envelopes from your commercial agent. Inside each is a stack of checks. Literally, a stack. You get out your calculator and add it all up. This morning you went to the gym and bought an egg-and-cheese sandwich with change from your desk. Now, pressing the EQUALS sign on the calculator, you realize you just made seven thousand dollars. You decide to make a reservation at Per Se.

It's tempting. You want to celebrate. You want to go buy new clothes and new sheets and new towels and take your girlfriend out to a fancy dinner and buy all the drinks for your friends because you just did something that so few actors do. You just made money, something approximating a living, even. I encourage you to celebrate. You should. But keep it to a healthy level. Because even if you make seven grand or three times that amount from that commercial this year, it might be *all* you make this year. It might be all you make for the next two years. The sum of $21,000 a year is not a lot of money in New York City. People scrounge by on that amount. The fact that you got it all at once doesn't mean it's more money than it is. It just means you're going to spend it faster.

As actors, we need a big checkup in the financial health department. Because of the way we make money, and the way in which we move from job to job, on unemployment and off it again, things get fiscally complicated. None of these production companies pays you directly from their payroll. Instead, they hire a talent payment service, with a name like Talent Partners or Entertainment Partners. For a fee, these firms handle talent payment, thus covering unemployment insurance liability as well. When it comes time to do your taxes, and you have W-2s from nine different talent payment services in five different states, you'll begin to understand how messed up it is. Then, because you make lump sums of money, most of your original earnings are taxed at an incredibly high rate. Make $800 in one day and the government assumes you make that every day, all year long. That puts you in the highest tax bracket, even though you will probably fall closer to the poverty line, according to the government's own statistics.

W-4s

When filling out a W-4 for an acting job, remember that you will be taxed as if you made that much money every day, or week, of the year. A paycheck of $600 a day is fine if you're getting it every day, but since you won't be, you might want to make an adjustment on your W-4 form so that you get to hold your money, not the government. The way to do this is to claim a higher number of dependents. Instead of the usual one dependent, claim six. You don't have to prove it, and it will mean that you are taxed on your earnings in a more judicious manner. However, should you owe money at the end of the year, you'd better be able to pay. Otherwise, the IRS will write to your employers, demanding they withhold a certain amount from your earnings. Of course, it's always best to consult an accountant.

Dale Daley*, mental health coordinator for The Actors' Fund, an organization that provides all manner of assistance to actors in need, worries that actors aren't taught financial health. "When kids are being trained in the theater," he says, "nobody's really saying to them, 'Develop a secondary career that you can use until you do become a star, because we know you are, but you need to do something in the meantime so that you can hang out until you catch on.' Or saying to people, 'We're going to do a finance class. This is going to teach you just how to do a budget, so you can figure out how much money you need.' Because the big thing we're seeing now, which is unfortunate, is people who get in such credit card debt, which is hard for anyone but is really hard for people in the theater. Credit card companies love actors because they get to a place where they're paying the minimum—they'll pay until the day they die."

There's a simple phrase Dale used while speaking with me that actors should plant in their minds and repeat like a yoga mantra: "You have a varying income."

For an artist, dealings with money can create real psychological baggage, and Dale didn't mince words when he spoke to me about the way in which eco-

---

*Dale spoke with me as a professional social worker, not as a spokesperson for The Actors' Fund. His comments reflect his own personal experience working with actors in the industry.

nomic factors emotionally affect the actor, calling the actor's life, at its most extreme, a "constant state of poverty and anxiety." It's not just actors whining about it being hard. "It's a clinical issue," he said. "It's a psychological issue, because if people can't take care of themselves, over time we really find that it takes a toll on people's psyche . . . how they look at themselves as people, professionals."

Unemployment Benefits

"Frankly," Mandy says, "it's the only way for working actors to get from one job to the next."

There will always be joblessness. Call it a vacation if you like. Or a little break in between jobs. Or call it what it is: unemployment.

As an actor you will, at some point, be unemployed. Hopefully, you will be eligible to collect unemployment. Let's get one thing clear: Unemployment is okay. It is not welfare. It is not money coming out of personal income tax. It is a tax levied on businesses. Your employer is paying this money as a security in order to have the right to employ you. You are not robbing from the poor working man. You are taking money that has been set aside for you because your business—the acting business—lays off a ton of people.

I once wanted to claim unemployment early in my acting days. I had heard about it from other actors, and it seemed fair to me. When I brought it up with my girlfriend, she was adamantly against it. It was, to her, the equivalent of being lazy and jobless. She, and all of her friends who worked in advertising, would hear nothing of it.

Then, guess what happened? The dot-com bubble burst and many of these people got laid off. Every single one of them filed for unemployment.

Technically, every time you begin and end a job, you are getting hired and getting let go. (If you are fired with cause, you are not eligible for unemployment benefits.) It just happens a lot more often to you than it does to anyone who works in advertising. Most other civilized nations in the world support the arts and recognize them as an important part of the national fabric. Therefore, they offer things like artist subsidies. Our country has determined the arts to be a less valuable, even nonexistent, part of our national consciousness. The National Endowment for the Arts budget has been sucked bone dry.

"Thank God for unemployment, because we live in a country where there are no grants for artists," Mandy says. "We're completely unsupported by the government. What would we do if there was no unemployment? There could be no artists if there weren't unemployment." But it's not a source of pride. "I mean, I would love to not be on it, and I try to use it as little as I can."

Health Insurance

New York State recently passed a bill that provides a 50 percent subsidy to actors who have COBRAed their health insurance. This means that should you choose to pay to continue health coverage once your benefits expire, the state will pay for half. It actually makes continuous coverage affordable. Consult The Actors' Fund, or one of the unions, for more information.

Fiona did five shows last year, more than most actors would dream of. But when I ask her if she makes a living as an actor, she says no. "I don't. You would think I would. I do temp work and my mom bought me a winter coat this year." I stop to calculate her year in terms of workweeks and figure that five shows is about forty weeks of work. Add two weeks off in between shows, and it would be nearly impossible to find room for a sixth. But during those times, she's unemployed. Not making a dime.

"I'm in the lowest tax bracket," she continues. "I was excited last year when I earned $20,000. But there's still temping in there. And I collect unemployment. Unemployment is your grant from the government."

Got it? We need it. So take it.

In order to collect unemployment, you must meet the following conditions: You must have worked for an employer who pays W-2 earnings—that is, earnings that are taxed. You must have earnings in at least two calendar quarters during your base period, which is four or five continuous calendar quarters, depending. You must have earned one and a half times your highest quarterly wages within your base period. You must have lost your job for *lack of work*, not have left of your own volition. If you meet these conditions, you can apply.

Your benefit will then be 1/26 of your high quarter earnings, maxing out at $405 in New York State. Your earnings will be calculated within a defined base period. The base period is the first four of the last five completed calendar quarters of work prior to the quarter in which your claim begins. For example, if you filed in February 2005 (part of Q1), your base period would be October 2003 through August 2004. An alternate base period of the previous four quarters

(January 2004 through December 2004 in this instance) can also be applied.

Now, they're not going to tell you all this when you apply, so be careful about when you decide to do so. You may want to wait until a certain calendar quarter has passed before applying for benefits so that the money from the commercial you shot gets calculated. The money will be put in the calendar quarter for which you were paid when it comes to filing your original claim, meaning residuals apply for when you get them, not the day you worked. Once you have begun collecting benefits, your residuals technically count as wages paid from the day you worked, because work is defined by the N.Y. State Department of Labor as "any day when you perform services, even an hour or less." Though this is a shady area, most actors continue to claim benefits while getting residual checks.

The other caveat is that you must be actively seeking employment while you're unemployed. But what actor isn't? And though this means you should technically be looking for work in any industry, not just acting, I see no reason why, as a trained professional with an MFA and a mountain of debt to prove it, you need to take a job waiting tables any more than your friends from advertising should when they get laid off. But that's a judgment call.

Unemployment doesn't last forever. In New York you get twenty-six weeks in any year-long period. Rules change, so consult the Department of Labor before you apply. Use it sparingly, when the need arises, but be aware that it can bridge some difficult financial gaps.

A Financial Year in the Life

So how does all of this translate for the working actor? A show here, a day player job there? I'll take you through a year of my life, my 2004, a year where I—and I say this with pride—made a living as an actor.

I began the year woefully unemployed. The show I had just finished Off-Broadway in November had not led to any more employment. I was temping at a bank in a job my friend hooked me up with, answering phones for traders in the Latin markets, literally listening as millions of dollars changed hands in the blink of an eye. Two weeks in, I get a job at the Actors Theatre of Louisville doing two plays in the Humana Festival. Even though I'm doing two shows, I still get paid the same LORT rate, which is approximately $600 a week, minus $120 for agent and manager commissions.

I booked the job January 19. I start work on February 6. Thankfully, I was house-sitting for a friend at the time and had already sublet my apartment. Otherwise, I would have had two weeks in which to do so. The rest of January, I had eight commercial and four legit auditions.

I work in Louisville from February 6 to April 4. In total, I make $3,350 after taxes and commissions. Then I return to New York. Throughout April I audition—four commercial auditions and eight legit. I also begin catering. In the middle of May, *Guiding Light* calls to offer me two days of work. I make $875 for each day, less commissions, of course. In May I audition for twelve commercials and three legit jobs.

Then, nothing until the end of June, when one of the shows I did in Louisville is remounted in New York as part of a new play festival. We begin rehearsals and the gods smile upon me. I book a commercial, requiring me to miss two days of rehearsal—the director was gracious enough to let me do so, although anyone who doesn't understand the financial necessities of taking such work should be given a serious talking to. I shoot the commercial, and some print ads to go with it. Because the shoot is in Chicago, I am paid for travel time. Basically I'm on the clock from the moment I leave JFK. Over two days I earn $1,600 after taxes and commissions. In June, I had five commercial auditions and one legit.

July is dead. Eight auditions total. I have a vacation planned for August and assume that it'll be dead then, too. My agent supports my need for this vacation. Of course, what happens as soon as I buy my ticket? I'm offered two jobs: a workshop in upstate New York and a short summer stock play as part of a festival on the Bard College campus. After some deliberation, I turn them both down. I like being a real person who gets to plan vacations and actually take them. Right before I leave the city, I book a radio voiceover.

I return at the end of August. The client for the commercial I shot in July wants me to do a radio ad that is essentially the same as the TV spot. I do. Then, in early September, I do a workshop in New York City for Actors Theatre of Louisville ($300). See how it comes in weird bursts? I have ten auditions in August and eight in September, an even split between commercial and legit.

October, eight commercial auditions and two legit auditions lead to . . . nothing. Beginning of November, I book another radio voiceover for America Online. It's the same voiceover that Julia Roberts does in the television ad. I think it'll pay well, but I've since learned that they did it under a little clause called *dealer usage.* This has something to do with buying and selling ad space.

I don't really care. Dealer usage to me means, *I get fucked.* I'll bet Julia Roberts didn't get dealer usage. I'll bet Julia Roberts got bank.

In November my commercial stock rises: twelve auditions. I have six legit as well. I do several readings during this time. They don't pay. But I am working on plays, meeting new people, and keeping active. All good things. December, ten commercial auditions, three legit, and no work. The industry slows to a halt as everyone gets ready for winter vacations. Only problem is, they all have jobs to come back to. I'm an actor. I don't.

I read a script and audition for a new play before I leave town for the holidays. I hear nothing. When I return in January I get a callback. Okay, fine, we're into another year, but I got the show. So there.

I made a living. I had seventy-one commercial auditions and booked four jobs. That's a 6 percent work rate. Of the sixty-eight legit auditions, I got three (although one was a direct offer, but who cares). That's a 4 percent work rate. My total employment rate was 5 percent.

And that, ladies and gentlemen, is a good year.

As you can see, the more auditions, the better your shot at working. Even though the numbers are low, 5 percent is still making a living. So within these pitifully low numbers is some good news. You can bat a ridiculously low average and still make it in the acting game.

That really should be a hopeful message. It should keep you moving during those hard times. Though each of those little jobs is not enough in and of itself, if you can string three or four of them together, you might get by. You might be a working actor. And, essentially, that should be the goal. That should be what you tell people and that should be the expectation. Stardom, Series Leads? Yes, that would be nice.

Let's start by making enough to pay the rent.

DON'T CALL US:
Dealing with Rejection

"Anyone getting into this business, you have to be like a duck.
It has to be like water that rolls off your back."

—Mandy

You will face more rejection than you ever thought possible. Even the most successful actor is told no more times than yes. That's the lucky actor, because at least he's told something. Most are told nothing at all. The audition occurs, you take the elevator down to the lobby, step back out onto Eighth Avenue, and go on with your life. That four-minute audition, which you spent hours preparing for, floats off into the great abyss of performances lost and jobs gone to another. This happens, at least in my case, 95 percent of the time.

You'll never get used to it, but you can try. Certainly, you need to come to some understanding with yourself. This entails unraveling the confusion between your self-worth and your acting worth, because the two are entirely unrelated, though they feel, at times, inseparable. Where else would one derive his worth? From the catering job at the Holocaust museum? How does one take pride in what he does if he never gets to do it?

As our casting director friend, Kimberly, described with her box theory, you must remember that, although your professional life has become one of constantly subjecting yourself to the judgment of others, this judgment is not personal.

But it never stops being painful.

You are, after all, spending your life going on job interviews. Every day, all day, your job is interviewing for a job. The relief of getting a job is enormous, but within anywhere from a week to three months, you are certain to be back on the job hunt again. As you become a known actor in town, you will have an easier time getting the auditions that lead to the potential jobs. It will never get easier, and you must change the perception that it will at the start of your career. One job does not necessarily lead to the next.

In the past year, I have sat in audition rooms with actors whose careers I would kill to have. Actors like Robert LuPone, or Illeana Douglas, or Debi Mazar, or character actors from HBO shows like *The Wire* and *The Sopranos*. Together, we have waited to read for commercials and independent movies and television shows. And you know what? They came in just like I did, signed in on the sign-in sheet just like I did, sat for forty-five minutes just like I did, read over their sides just like I did, read for the director or casting director just like I did, and did not get the part, just like I did. These are actors with resumes that stretch on—great credit after great credit—and they still do it the way I do it, the way you'll do it.

One actor, who spent most of her career in Los Angeles before moving to New York, told me about a final callback for a pilot. She was sitting in the waiting room and Carol Kane walked in. Carol Kane, if you don't know, is one of the great female comedic actors of the twentieth century. It's not as if the producers don't know her work. It's not as if they're wondering how she'll play the role. She's Carol Kane; does *Taxi* ring a bell? You couldn't ask for a more specific type. You know what you're gonna get, and it'll be brilliant.

Carol Kane still had to audition.

"I do remember when I was younger, going into auditions where there would be much older women and men," Mandy says, "and I remember being surprised. I was like, 'Oh, they audition too?'"

So get used to auditioning for the rest of your acting life, and get used to rejection. It comes in all shapes and sizes, each providing varying degrees of emotional pain. There are four basic types:

Wrong the minute you walk in the room. You're either not right the moment they see you, or it's late in the day and they've already found their top choice, and really there's very little you can do to beat him out. The auditioners will have heavy eyelids and are already anticipating their dinner reservation downtown.

No response. This is what will happen most of the time. You will go to the audition, do a bang-up job, perhaps even be called back. The director might give you some notes, there will be some fawning over your talent and your interpretation of the role, some compliments on your choices. You will go home, keep your sides tucked away in the corner (just in case), and hear nothing. Ever. You will never know why they didn't like you unless your agent finds out, in which case the response will usually be something like "They went with the blonde with the ponytail," or "They wanted older." You will try to use this to make yourself feel better, because you are not older, nor do you have a ponytail, nor could you ever be or have either of these things. But somewhere in the back of your mind you will think, *I could have nailed it, and then they would have hired me.*

Utter heartbreak. This one usually involves three to five callbacks. You get closer and closer and closer to getting the part. With each callback, the director gets a better sense of you as you try not to screw up the previous good impressions you made. You are eventually placed on hold, or perhaps told it's between you and one other person, or even, if it doesn't go to a star, it'll go to you. You've given copious amounts of time and energy to your many auditions, and are now invested emotionally in the role and the project. And then, one day, you are released, or the news is broken to you that someone else got the part. That someone usually is not the person you had thought it would be, and you've had so much sunshine blown up your ass that you, in an entirely reasonable assumption, thought that if the role didn't go to you, it was going to someone bigger and better. You hate everyone who led you along: the director, the producers, the casting director. You wish that your agent could have done something more aggressive, or that you had skipped all those callbacks and said, with some tone of empowerment, "You've seen my stuff; now hire me or end this thing." You rethink every moment of every audition, wonder where you could have made the different choice that would have changed it all. You sit in a funk of utter depression for a week.

Getting fired. You get the job. You may even begin rehearsing it, and then at some point in the process, the director, the producer, or maybe the leading lady who happens to be famous and have more clout than anyone, decides she doesn't like what you are doing. It doesn't matter that you're under contract—most likely they'll pay you out—you're getting the axe. This has been known to happen as little as a few days before a show opens. In television, recasting often occurs once the entire pilot has been shot, depending on reactions in audience testing. Perhaps you turned down other work to take the job from which you got fired. Oh, well, too bad, that job is gone now, too. You are back in the unemployment line.

Actors entering this profession do not realize how constant the rejection is. There is a common belief that, after a little while, the rejection lets up; that you're in a world of being offered jobs and declining them, or only auditioning when they really, really want you. This is not true. Rejection, in all its forms, beats a continuous pulse through actors' lives.

Every actor has more tales of rejection than they do successes. Most tales bleed into the norm, but some stand out by the sheer cruelty of the situation. Don't let rejection get the better of you. "Part of the thing," Fiona says to me, "is not to get fascinated by your failure. . . . Otherwise you make it insurmountable."

Or you can imagine yourself alongside others facing the same levels of competition. "It's like being an athlete," she continues. "Is there any actor who watches the Olympics and doesn't cry? It's so similar, because you see people who have worked—they're the fucking fastest people in the whole world. There is nobody faster. I mean, it's *ludicrous* that these eight people are now going to race each other and one's going to be the fastest."

But that's the job you signed up for, and it's every day, not every four years. The race is the audition. Winning is getting the job. And only one person on that particular day is going to be the fastest. The other seven, with their fraction-of-a-second lapses, will have to wait.

Actors have bad days too. Just like teachers who might not connect with their class one day, or lawyers who might not make the best cross-examination, we can stumble over some lines or just not be as connected to the material as we were the night before. This happens. It happens when you are feeling the pressure of unemployment, when you're sitting in a waiting room for half an hour with ten other actors and then have to be *on* at a moment's notice. Some days you just don't have it.

It's the psychology of rejection, and the risk of becoming mired in it. You can't get over the hump.

An actor's challenge is in living between jobs and auditions in isolation. "I did a vocal warm-up today" isn't the same as running ten miles to prep for the race. For one, you know you can be in the race if you run fast enough. In acting, sitting at home learning lines may be a part of the craft, but you can be the best line learner in the world and not get the part. As the athlete, the run is both the practice and the performance. But acting is a profession of interaction, not of solitude. "It's difficult when you're not working on your craft," Fiona observes. "You need other people and you need an audience. You feel like you're spinning wheels. You can read stuff out loud. You can challenge yourself. You can find a monologue and . . . try do it, but the fact that you can do that monologue in your room by yourself is absolutely no indication whatsoever about whether you can do that monologue in front of other people or at the moment when it's supposed to occur in the play."

So in addition to the rejection, what you're really facing as an actor is something far more dire. You're facing loneliness and isolation in between jobs. Acting is indeed the most social and the loneliest of professions, both at the same time.

Its highs and its lows and this mania can lead to some really trying times.

The Human Toll

To get a better sense of the trying ways of the actor's lifestyle, I consulted Dale Daley. He and I spoke for nearly an hour one afternoon about the difficulties actors face. He spoke of the complexities of the career choice—of the juggling act it takes to balance art and life and money.

Dale started his career as an actor before becoming a social worker. "People have such unrealistic images of what this industry is about," he began. "We see the people who are fabulously wealthy." With the romanticized nature of celebrity, and the recent overload of celebrity culture and magazines, it seems that "if you succeed, you're all over the place making lots of money"—when in fact, most of the actors Dale knows, actors who are working, are living close to the poverty line.

When I ask about the highs and lows of this profession, the constant jolt from unexpected auditions and callbacks and rejections, Dale says, "It's almost like a drug addiction. That's a wonderful high, and it's fine to have it, but that's not what sustains you over the years."

"It's a business, and there's nothing shameful or embarrassing about taking care of yourself as an actor."

The constant rejection and financial hardship can easily lead to bitterness. Dale sees this all the time. "People who say, 'I feel like I've worked all my life for something, and I feel like I have nothing to show for it. And I look forward and don't see that's going to change very much.' And a profound kind of existential depression sets in. . . . They are no longer operating with any kind of feeling that their job is satisfying for them, or that there's an art form, or that they are artists.

"They feel they have no choices anymore."

I warn you right now, this feeling will inevitably hit you at some point in your acting career. And as soon as it does, do something, anything, to prove that you have the power to make a choice. "We try to help people realize that they need to kind of start taking some responsibility because it will really make their lives better. And their careers better."

Perhaps most importantly, he adds, "They'll be better actors."

The glorification of poverty, what Dale calls "*La Bohème* syndrome," is bullshit. A starving artist is an unhappy artist, and an unhappy artist becomes bitter and angry and, from a practical perspective, unhireable. You must take care of yourself first. That doesn't mean you won't be working overtime. To make a living and pursue acting, you'll most likely be pulling sixty-hour workweeks for a long time. There's certainly a tendency for the rest of the world to place judgment on actors who are doing jobs other than acting, as if the only successful actor is one who only acts and does nothing else to make a living. That's the cover of *Us Weekly,* okay? That's not reality.

"People start saying, 'If I start doing something else, the gods of theater are going to curse me because I don't have faith.' So they will live for years, again, in a kind of deprived state, saying, 'I have to do this.' We try to address that personally," Dale continues, "plus we find that people usually come from environments where that's what they've grown up hearing. And many times, they're trying to prove it to themselves, because they're still trying to prove it to their families. 'Look, I am a real person, I do have a real job.' We find, for instance, that when [actors] work with mental health individuals, they'll go to a therapist and they'll tell them about what their lives are like, and the therapist, if she doesn't understand where actors come from, she'll say, 'The first thing we have to do is look into getting you a real job.' And, of course, an actor will feel totally unheard, because here's this person that they've come to talk to about that, who basically invalidates them by saying, 'You're not really working.' When, of course, actors work as hard as"—Dale remembers his own days as an actor, before carefully stating—"It's a hard-knock life."

The rejection one feels as an actor occurs on many levels. There is, of course, the day-to-day auditioning and not getting parts. One might think this gets easier over time, but there can be a final straw that breaks the camel's back. Dale tells me the story of an actor who came to see him. The perfect role had finally arrived. "It was an overweight, balding man who dances." And the actor thought, "That's me. I would be perfect for this. I've paid my dues. I've been in a lot of shows." And he auditioned several times for the role before the director and producers decided that the role wasn't going to sell on Broadway. And so instead of casting a talented man who's paid his dues and finally found the part that was written for him, the director and producers ordered a rewrite. "He came in really feeling as dejected as he ever has in his life. He's in his early fifties, and he basically said, 'I'm thinking I may get out of the industry now.' Because, he said, 'That was the role that was made for me, and I'm not going to get it.' And he's pretty sanguine. He's been able to face rejection in the past. But he felt that this was finally his role to shine, and he lost it."

That wasn't his fault. There was nothing he could do to change it. But one can only take so many knocks before a wound stops healing.

"People talk about the narcissism of actors," Dale muses toward the end of our conversation. "On one hand, yes, there's a certain narcissism that's necessary to be able to get on stage over and over again and have people say, 'No, not you.' That's a very helpful narcissism. On the other hand, what's sometimes missing is people's sense of identity to say, 'You know what, it's not just about the show and it's not just about the production, it's about what I need.'"

Indeed, living a life close to the poverty line in order to pursue your art is not self-centered at all. It's selfless, and that selflessness can become highly problematic.

This is not easy stuff, but it's eminently present. It's better to witness the reality here in these pages than to become shocked by it after a year in New York City. The problem is, to be an actor is to be inherently vulnerable. You are working in an arena of truth and emotion, you are called upon to be a thoroughly feeling being. And then, time and time again, you are told you are not right for a role. So one must find a way to keep his guard up, while keeping his instrument intact.

You must know that you're not alone. You must have a life. You must develop coping mechanisms and a support structure that enables you to get through tough times. You must realize that there is nothing to be ashamed of when you don't work. That this industry does not have enough jobs for all of the talented people who occupy it.

Coping

"I think unconsciously it's about being a part of a group," Kat says. Being part of a collective, working together toward a common goal: This is what the theater is about. "This business is so full of self-doubt that you need someone in this world to believe in your choices unconditionally. Because you're not gonna believe in your choices all the time."

Most actors are at their best while they're working. So to remain at your best while you're not working requires keeping a supportive community nearby. "It's difficult when you're not working to work on your craft," Fiona says. "You need other people and you need an audience. You feel like you're spinning wheels."

After a bad audition, or after a good one where you swore you were going to get the part, but didn't, be very careful about judging your work. Agents and casting directors might think that there's a rhyme or reason to booking work, but most of the time it's luck. "I've had so many different experiences, I don't know what the hell to do," Fiona says. "I have gone into auditions that I have not prepared for and I've gotten the part. I've gone into auditions that I prepared for and I've gotten pretty far, but I haven't gotten the part."

For the day-to-day rejection, Marin offered the best advice I've heard. "I go to the movies," she said. "The only thing I have learned about going to shitty auditions is that you can't stop thinking about them, and really, you just need it to be another day. Because it gets better the more hours go by, so you really just need to make time go by." Time heals.

But, barring all this, there's one more thing that might help: *schadenfreude.*

One Line Does Count

No, really, it couldn't be much worse.

This is the worst audition story I've ever heard. An actor, whom we'll call Trent, went in for a one-line role on *Law & Order.* He walks into the audition sans script, because hey, it's only one line, and he's been running it over and over in the parking lot. Something about pointing at shoeprints as evidence and saying that he'll collect them.

He's called in from the waiting room, strolls into the audition room, and greets the producers and directors with a smile. He makes a joke about the one-line audition before getting started. There's a chair, but he wants to kneel on the floor, so he asks if he can. They say sure. He does.

Somewhere in that moment, he panics. His brain freezes up, and that one line about the shoeprints goes floating off to Neverland. But this isn't going to stop Trent. He says what he thinks is the first word, then stops.

"Can I start over?"

Sure, they say, the room temperature rising. He cracks another joke. "One line, right? Ha."

He looks to the carpet. Second try. Still no line. And, of course, there's no script anywhere near him.

He looks to them again. "Sorry. Just one sec."

Try number three, everyone is now totally bemused. Producers are wondering how this guy ever made it into the room. And so Trent, knowing he cannot just walk away, decides to improvise his one line about the shoeprints.

"Looks like, um, the size nine from the . . . uh—"

Thank you, say the producers. He leaves the room. He went up on one line three times in a row.

As soon as he hits the parking lot, the line comes to him.

Trent is now happily working, by the way. Even good actors have bad days. In fact, it's probably the better actors, the ones who create their own shows, run them successfully in New York before taking them to the Edinburgh Fringe Festival and the Mark Taper Forum in Los Angeles, who have the most difficult time with the mundane one-line audition.

You Can Get Arrested in This Town

"One of the first things that I went out for in L.A. was a movie directed and written by Bobby Moresco and Chazz Palminteri," Jon begins in a foreboding tone and with a smirk on his face. "It was a great role for me. Val Kilmer was attached to it, Dennis Hopper was attached to it, Christopher Walken was attached to it, a lot of really good actors that I love and respect. It was a really good movie with balls; it was something I was really attracted to. I went to the first audition for the casting director. She had me in there for an hour and forty-five minutes, trying it a million different ways. She thought she had found her guy. She went back and I met with Bobby Moresco, one of the directors, and it went great. Bobby Moresco and Chazz Palminteri invited me out to their house to have lunch and discuss the role. At this point, it was really looking good for me; I was very excited."

So Jon hops in his car and heads out to Burbank. He arrives early, as he usually does, parks, and then paces around the neighborhood. He runs his lines.

Occasionally he reaches into the car to pull out his sides to check the lines. "I had my skullcap and my sunglasses on, and I started walking through the posh residential neighborhood, going over my lines, calling my mom and telling her that this was going to be the biggest day of my life."

Finally, having killed enough time, Jon begins walking up the front steps of Chaz Palminteri's house. "All of sudden I heard a siren. A police car pulled up on the side of the road. A policeman gets out of the car, draws his gun on me, and tells me to take a seat on the curb."

Now, Jon has a little bit of an authority problem, his view of cops is not idyllic, and he's amped himself up for this audition at the director's house. So when the cop pulls his gun and tells him sit on the curb, "I tell him, why doesn't he take a seat on the curb. He didn't like that, obviously, so he said, 'Sit on the curb right now, or we're going to have a problem here.' I asked him what I'd done. He didn't tell me. I said, 'I'm not sitting down on the curb till you tell me.' He pushes me, gun drawn. Another squad car comes up, policeman gets out of the car, throws me up against the side of Chazz Palminteri's house."

"Remember," Jon says, "this is the biggest day of my life." Realizing that he's now pretty screwed, he says to the cop, "'Please tell me what I've done, and I will totally cooperate.' He doesn't tell me, calls me a tough guy, gets a billy club, pushes it up against the back of my neck. I get thrown in handcuffs and put into the back of the police car."

By this point, he's screaming, "'I'm an actor, I'm going to an audition, I'm going to meet Chazz Palminteri.'" He's locked in the back of a squad car, freaking out. Late for his audition, about to be carted away by the LAPD on the biggest day of his life. Completely freaking out.

As if this were a Marx Brothers routine, the casting director pulls up as Jon is banging his head against the window of the backseat, where he sits handcuffed. Seeing Jon, the casting director explains to the police that Jon is indeed an actor who does have a personal appointment at Chazz Palminteri's house. The officer lets Jon go, and explains the situation.

"Supposedly somebody had called the police, said that there was a very sketchy-looking character walking around the neighborhood talking to himself, going inside of cars and pulling things out—which was my car, and I was going over my sides in my script, touching my various good luck objects that I like to fondle before I go into my appointment."

Completely shaken, Jon then finishes his walk up Chazz Palminteri's front steps. He sits down, tells them the story. "The meeting went great; they basically told me I was their man. I was on cloud nine until a week later."

That's when they called him and told him the role went to Freddie Prinze Jr. and they're very sorry.

13

THE REWARDS:
Charting Your Success

"Eighty percent of success is showing up."

—Woody Allen

Still reading? Good.

That gives me hope. That should give you hope. Acting is 95 percent rejection; the other 5 percent is the reason we do it. Dealing with percentages that small requires a shift in the way you think about work, the way you reward yourself. You must find a new way to calibrate success. You must set your own goals, create your own framework, and you must have the patience of a Buddhist monk.

If, as I said when I began this book, you are willing to endure, to take the temp jobs, to take the knocks that will invariably come, you could be in the fortunate position of finding yourself with an acting career. And I can tell you, though it never gets any easier or less daunting as a profession, working in this business is the most wonderful feeling there is.

We'd all change the business if we could. "We want there to be less people," Kat said. "We want people to be eliminated from the starting gate if they're not any good. Someone who goes to one of the top business schools, if they don't get a job at one of the top ten firms, they go back to Kansas. We have so much hope and it's constantly dashed and we keep coming back for more." But we do come back. And that must always be a point of pride.

The system is against you. It is not set up to be actor-friendly. It runs around casting and production and budget and time constraints. In my interviews, one constant gripe that actors had was that celebrities were taking all of the good theater jobs. "I would not have stars from television and film be in shows in New York," Fiona said when I asked her what she would change about the business. "I mean, obviously the reason why they're in those shows is that theaters need a way to draw nontheater audiences to the theater so they can make money, so I can't get my panties all in a bunch at the theaters, because they're just trying to create an environment where they can keep doing theater."

"However," she continued, "I've made a choice to be in New York and to be in the theater, and I have a real commitment to New York and the theater, and I want that commitment to be valuable. I know wonderful theater actors who are looked over for a part so that Ashley Judd can be in *Cat on a Hot Tin Roof.* And the thing that's so funny about it? It's not like they get great reviews.

"I want theater producers to give up on this. I want them to sit in a room together and think, 'How can we make our own stars?' I want to see an article about Cherry Jones in *Vanity Fair."*

But until the theater makes that change, celebrities will be a constant part of your life. Thus, it becomes imperative not to allow our societal celebrity fascination to color your view of success. Look for joy in small corners of the day, in the subtle nooks of daily life. The subway ride to work becomes more pleasurable when work is a rehearsal in the Manhattan Theatre Club building. Showing up on a film set makes all those moments of waiting in an audition room less painful. Sharing an after-work drink, paid for with your paycheck from an acting job, makes the beer that much colder.

Overnight Success

Careers are built, not bestowed. Everyone does his time in small roles, in extra work, in Off-Off-Broadway theater, and in Co-starring roles on television. In a movie called *No Man's Land,* Brad Pitt played a waiter. In *Less than Zero,* he was a partygoer. Michael Chiklis, star of *The Shield,* was doing his guest work in 1989 on *Miami Vice;* in 1990 he was on *L.A. Law.* Jennifer Garner, in her pre-*Alias* days, paid her *Law & Order* dues in New York, then did a guest stint on *Spin City.* I'll bet they all had day jobs, or night jobs, in between television appearances. They weren't pulled out of a magic casting hat. They did their time, and a lot of it.

Yes, getting these jobs is hard. And yes, you must get them in order to continue on in this business. But reframe the equation. Give yourself a little more time than you might have thought. Realize that Jennifer Garner's *Law & Order* did not earn her the job as a Series Regular on *Alias,* that Brad Pitt's waiter wasn't so conspicuous as to get him cast in *Thelma & Louise.* They all auditioned, and didn't get parts, many more times than they were cast.

Soon the herd will thin. Many of the actors who crowded the business when you first entered it will be gone within five years. Those who remain will have a better shot at landing the jobs. Endurance is as much a factor as luck, talent, and type. Sometimes it just takes a while for people to notice you.

Rid yourself, and those around you, of the idea of overnight success. It is a grandiose scheme peddled by those with no insight into this industry, and it is nonsense. Every agent loves to tell the story of the girl who walked into the office, signed, went out on her first audition, and booked a pilot. By this point in my career, I feel like I should have met at least one of these actors. I haven't. Don't live in the dream world created by those you endow with power—those whom you've decided know how this business works. No one knows how this business works. If someone could figure it out and explain a tried and true method of making it, you would have heard about it by now. So nod intently when the agent tells the story of the overnight success, and of you being the next version of that, or of you being nowhere near the next version of that, then walk out of the office and live a normal life. If you sit around waiting to be an overnight success, it's going to be a long, lonely night.

Rid yourself, too, of the idea that success is lasting. It isn't. It's fleeting; it comes and goes without rhyme or reason. You might have a string of jobs, then go without for six months. This has nothing to do with your talent. It is the whim of the beast called showbiz.

In the back of your mind, a certain hope will always exist: that a particular play, or Co-starring role, or commercial will be the one that gets the attention of that magical, mystical figure who has the project that will launch you into a career. That dream will never fade, and it's part of the kernel of hope that keeps the actor alive. But it must be kept in check. For the most part, each job lives and dies in its own universe.

For a while, anyway. Because though everything I've written so far explains how one job doesn't build to the next, it is a time-tested truth that work begets work. I have no way of explaining this in a literal way. But the fact remains that actors often go on hot streaks—booking three jobs in a row, one right after the next. The only way to truly explain this? Work makes actors happy and relaxed, and they exude a certain glow. A happy, relaxed, glowing actor is the kind of person you want in your play, your movie, and, perhaps most importantly, your living room.

One day, the project will arrive. One day you decide to do a showcase that you knew in your heart was the role of a lifetime. And it gets a good review, and an extension with an Off-Broadway contract, and the attention of writers and directors throughout the city. And the next thing you know, you're performing in two shows at Williamstown and in your final callback for a Broadway show. That's what happened to Laura. "It was the best role that I've ever been offered in my life," she says of the showcase. "And it was an incredible play. The director, the production, the design, all the actors. . . . It was like the mother of all showcases. Everything was right. . . . What has happened from it is, I think, just a sort of sense of people knowing who I am and the word spreading about a play that I just did."

Or Mandy's case, where the biggest show she's done, *Noises Off* on Broadway, was by no means the one most beneficial to her career. "You just never know. We've all been in productions that everyone thought were gonna be huge and change your career and don't." Two other shows, both of which paid far less money and offered less prestige at the time she was hired, turned out to be far more valuable life and career experiences. The two often go hand in hand. "*Stupid Kids* and *Blackbird* were the biggest shows in the fact that they generated their own significance, and people's response to them was like nothing I've really ever experienced."

Or Fiona, who is about to do her third play with the same director, a director who offers her roles without seeing anyone else, because they have developed an artistic relationship. Laura's overnight success, the play where everyone suddenly noticed her, took eight years to happen. Mandy's took three. Fiona has been at it just as long. "Overnight" isn't overnight. "Overnight" is years.

Slowly, we build one job on top of the next. We work more often then we don't. We begin to feel like actors, not auditioners. Success is arrived at only through perseverance and trusting your gut. Like Woody says, 80 percent is showing up—every single day.

The actors I interviewed for this book are all successful working actors. They have worked on Broadway, Off-Broadway, and regionally at such venues as Actors Theatre of Louisville, La Jolla Playhouse, Yale Rep, Pittsburgh City, Berkeley Rep, Shakespeare Santa Cruz, Dallas Theater Center, Alabama Shakespeare Festival, Guthrie Theater, George Street Playhouse, Old Globe, Cincinnati Playhouse, Denver Center, Alley Theatre, Woolly Mammoth,

Hartford Stage, New York Stage and Film, Eugene O'Neill Festival, Summer Play Festival, Humana Festival, Williamstown Theatre Festival, Roundabout Theatre Company, Brooks Atkinson Theater, Atlantic Theater Company, Cherry Lane, Rattlestick Playwrights Theater, Primary Stages, Playwrights Horizons, and Public Theater.

They have appeared on the television shows *Law & Order, Law & Order: Criminal Intent, Law & Order: SVU, Jonny Zero, CSI: Miami, Boston Legal, Without a Trace, Guiding Light,* and *All My Children.* In commercials for America Online, Flonase, Hebrew National, Breyers yogurt, Miller Lite, Bud Light, Campbell's Chunky Soup, Burger King, McDonald's, and MTV.

In the films *Winter Passing, Tony 'n' Tina's Wedding, School of Rock, Two Weeks Notice, The Out-of-Towners* and Oliver Stone's currently untitled 9/11 project.

They have agents, but they didn't always. They come from different backgrounds—some with school, some without. I chose them because they represent the fabric of this business—the people you should aspire to become, the people you must learn to admire—because they all work. But not one of them has a guarantee that he or she will work tomorrow, or next month, or next year. Still, they are the success stories. Despite the temping and the catering and the turkey dogs, they are working actors.

You've never heard of any of them. Recognition helps a career, but it does not make one. A career is something one looks back on a resume to find. As an actor, you will be hard-pressed to find a career. Job after job, and then maybe one more job, makes for a good year. Good year followed by good year makes a career.

Advice

"At one time in this business," Stephanie Klapper said, "people went into it solely for the love of it and the creativity of it. And I think it's gotten increasingly more difficult, but it is about all those things. It is about the calling, the passion."

That's worth remembering. You chose this profession. No one is holding a gun to your head and making you be an actor. You've entered into a rough, unpredictable, emotionally and physically demanding profession. You do it because you love it.

When I asked Dan, the agent from chapter 7, for his advice, he offered this: "Surround yourself with powerful people. And I don't mean like directors, producers . . . I don't mean powerful in that sense. I mean powerful in the positive sense. . . . Be a nice person. It matters. Everyone wants to work with a nice person." And most importantly, he added, "Never listen to anyone telling you, 'You can't do it.'"

Your support network is imperative. "I think of it as my team," Fiona says. "My yoga teacher, my therapist, my parents." Almost all the actors interviewed for this book mentioned how supportive their parents were. "They're parents and they worry. I think they would be happier if I had chosen an easier life," Mandy said. "But they always express how much they enjoy watching me as an actor. They're so proud of what I've accomplished."

Parental support, both emotionally and financially, can get a young actor through the inevitable tough times that lie ahead. It is difficult for anyone, parents included, to understand just how thorny this industry is, and the way in which one navigates through a lawless, petty, and at times, glamorous world. Not only does it become your job to face this world, it becomes your job to try to paint it in a way in which your parents understand it for more than the curtain calls.

Rob Decina offers the realist's approach. "I think a career as an actor is about doing everything. It's about piecing together your theater, and your classes, and your commercials, and your auditions, and going to the library or the museum and reading. It's about keeping all those balls in the air, and trying to stay sane, because it's really not an 'If you do this, and you do this, and you do this, this will happen' business."

"Your passion has to be so enormous to take into rooms you've never been in before. Usually, in our culture, people don't share their passions," Fiona says. That, however, is the crux of our profession. And, as Mandy reminds us, "It's usually the moments when you are true, when something really speaks to you and you choose to do it, that end up bringing you what you want."

There's one more thing that will enable you to view your successes with ample pride and to chart your path forward.

Get a life.

Too often we hear stories of actors who forgot to live, who drove full steam ahead, sacrificing relationships for work. *This isn't my life,* an actor will think, *this is the path toward the life I will one day have.* If you still feel that way after finishing this book, then I haven't done my job. It is your life, and will always be your life. The pot of gold does not await, but the next audition, the next temp job, and the next regional gig do. You must accept that you will, perhaps forever, be in an unstable and unpredictable profession.

Do not put off personal choices because of this. Do not be afraid to tell an agent that you don't want to go out of town, or that a personal event in your life is more important that the job. Care for your craft as you see fit, and never let anyone else dictate how you should express this. Far too often, people will manipulate an actor by questioning his sense of commitment to a project, or to his career. Don't be afraid to tell people that you have a life outside of your work, and that you value it. It will make you a better actor.

We all cater, we all temp, and we all act. That's the way it goes for a very long time. But never, for one moment, allow anyone to take from you the fact that you are an actor. Measure your own success. Don't let those who work in business or finance or law or medicine do it for you. They measure success in dollars and promotions and partnerships. You measure it in inconceivable ways.

"The people who are crazy enough to get into this profession really deserve respect," Jon says, when I ask his final thoughts on our world. "It's a soul-wrenching, gut-turning profession. And the one thing is that, no matter what stage you get to, there's never a point where you sit back and relax and say you've gotten there. And that's both the best thing about it and the worst thing about it. It's great to be a dreamer, it's great to always have your dreams ahead of you, but everybody in this is insecure, everybody in this is scared, and everybody in this is struggling. And unfortunately, the very business itself, and the people who run the business, do almost everything they can to perpetuate that struggle and perpetuate that insecurity. Because, in a way, it keeps us hungry."

Once in a while, make sure you stop to ask yourself one simple question. Ask the one Patch asked me when I sought his advice. "Do you enjoy it?" he said. "I mean, that's why we aren't businessmen, because we thought this would be a more fun way to spend our lives. So hopefully, we're right."

"The only thing that is *absolutely necessary* in this business is the actor," Jon concluded. It's been proven historically. There were actors before there were directors, before there were playwrights and producers. For two thousand, five hundred and forty years, actors have been the driving force in this business.

One day it will come. A day where you find that acting—a dream of a profession, an ethereal mystery of a career—is actually a form of employment. And when that day comes, acting won't be auditioning, classes, agent mailings, or open calls.

On that day, acting is a job.

APPENDIX:
The Actor's Dictionary

An *aside* is different from a *side,* and *upstage* used to literally be higher than *downstage.* Mom is excited that "you're on a *shoot,*" but doesn't want you to get squeezed by the *grip.* The *talent* is hopefully talented. You've been *released* from that *industrial,* but you're sticking around for *pilot season* hoping to *book* a sitcom. And if you don't know what a sitcom is, you didn't buy this book.

13-episode guarantee—Also known as a bought series. This means that the network has committed to making that many episodes. Doesn't mean they'll air them all, though.

13-week cycle—For a commercial, holding fees are paid for each thirteen-week period a commercial runs, for up to two years. Then a contract must be renegotiated.

AEA—Actors' Equity Association. The professional union for stage actors and stage managers.

AFTRA—The American Federation of Television and Radio Artists. AFTRA is the union for performers working on television shot in any medium other than film (i.e., video). They also cover broadcast journalists, newscasters, game show hosts, talk show hosts, and recording artists.

Agency (advertising)—The advertising agency. Its creative department wrote the commercial.

Agent—The actor's connection to jobs. Technically an employment agent, the agent represents the actor, submits him for work, and handles negotiations, contracts, and other responsibilities.

Aside—Talking directly to the audience.

Avail—In the voiceover world, an *avail* is a check of your availability, kind of like being placed on hold in the on-camera world.

Backstage—The trade publication for actors in New York. It lists open calls, and gives pretty standard information about the business.

Booking—A job.

Booking out—Telling your agent that you're unavailable to audition over a certain period of time.

Breakdowns—The cast list for any project. Breakdowns are put out daily, and they are the backbone of the casting process. Agents read them and decide which clients to submit for which roles, then call the messenger.

Cable-only—A classification for commercial usage, whereby the commercial can only run on cable.

Callback—The second, third, or (worst-case scenario) seventh audition. Every time you return to audition for the same role, it's a callback. Unions regulate how many callbacks an actor can go on, depending on the contract. Callbacks are an indicator of success.

Casting directors—Are responsible for almost every aspect of casting. They put out breakdowns, sort through submissions, bring in actors to audition, hold auditions, and make selections for directors. Then, once a director or producer has cast a role, they make the offer.

Chorus call—An open call for chorus roles in musicals.

Client—That's you, to your agent.

Client (advertising)—The marketing people for the brand being advertised. If you're doing a Burger King commercial, Burger King is the client of the agency.

Co-star—The official union term for a day player role that does not get top-of-show billing.

Confirm—Telling your agent that you can make it to an audition.

Creatives—The people who wrote the commercial.

Copy—The script for a commercial.

Dry blocking—Blocking for on camera in a space other that the set.

Downstage—The front of the stage, or portion closest to the audience.

Episodic—Any television show with more than one episode.

EPA—The Equity Principal Audition. An open call for Equity members to audition for shows that they couldn't audition for at the real audition.

Equity—See AEA.

Extra work—If you are in a television show or movie and you have no lines, this is you. Also know as *background player,* because that's what they yell right before they say "Action." A referendum was once submitted to SAG that Extras no longer be called Extras, but instead become known as "Future Stars." I'm not kidding.

First refusal—Or *on hold.* This means that the commercial has the right of first refusal on you, which means you cannot take another job until they release you.

Fringe festival—A theater festival that takes place in the fringes of the theater world, both geographically and artistically.

General meeting—Meeting with a casting director, or producer, or director for no one specific project. A get-to-know-you kind of situation.

Going to network—Appearing before network executives to audition for a television show. This means you're really, really close.

Going to producers—Auditioning before the producers of a television show. This must happen before any major episodic role is cast.

Guaranteed release—An assurance that you will be done shooting by a certain time, in order to make your theater call time.

Guest Star/Guest Lead—also known as "Top of Show," a Guest Lead usually appears in several scenes in a television show, and gets paid more than a Co-star.

Hold—Being reserved for use in a show, on television, in a film, or on a commercial. Usually several people are placed on hold for each role.

Industrial—A sales video. Basically, anything shot on film or video that is not for broadcast purposes.

Leagues—The showcases for the top grad programs in the country, e.g. NYU, Yale, Juilliard.

Legit agent—The legitimate agent, which means nothing as far as ethical legitimacy goes; rather, this is what the industry coins television, theater, and film agents.

LORT—League of Resident Theatres. The official group for regional theaters, though there are a few theaters in NYC that operate under the LORT contract.

Major markets—Big-city usage for commercials. Cities like Chicago, Los Angeles, and New York.

Managers—Traditionally offer more personal attention than an agent. They act like agents, though they are not franchised by any unions.

Marcel Marceau—The most famous mime of them all.

The Method—The American version of Stanislavski's acting method, made famous in the fifties with Brando.

More remunerative work—The clause in a theater contract that allows one to take a higher-paying job without breaking contract.

National—The best, and best-paying, commercial usage. A national spot goes up on the network satellite feed and therefore plays everywhere.

Off-book—Having your lines learned.

Open call—An audition for anyone who shows up. Also known as a cattle call, or a nightmare.

Per diem—An additional allowance to your salary, say, $40 a day. A per diem is given when an actor is away from her home base for employment, e.g., working in Chicago when you live in New York.

Pilot—The first episode of a new television show.

Pilot season—January through April, when pilots are made.

Prescreen—The audition before the audition. These happen either when the casting director is unfamiliar with an actor, or if he's unsure if the actor is right for a role.

Previews—The performance of a show before the official opening night.

Quote—An actor's rate. A quote is determined by how much you've been paid for previous, similar employment.

Reader—The person reading with you in the audition.

Recurring—Appearing in the same role in more than one episode, but not contracted as a Series Regular.

Released—You didn't get the job. And you've just been released from your "hold."

Revival—A play or musical that has been previously performed.

SAG—Screen Actors Guild. The union for actors performing in anything shot on film. SAG covers movies, television, and commercials.

Scale—The minimum an actor is paid for work, as determined by the union

Script—All the pages of a film, television show, or play. Not to be confused with sides, which are excerpts from the script.

Series Regulars/Series Leads—The actors who appear on a show week in and week out.

Showcase—There are two types of showcases. One is the AEA-approved term for a play with union actors who are not getting paid. The other is the kind many graduate programs perform in New York to "showcase" their graduates. Another term for this is the leagues.

Shoot—Vernacular for work on a film set.

Sides—The excerpts from the script used for the audition.

Slate—Stating your name before an on-camera or voiceover audition.

Stand-in—An actor who looks kind of like the real actor in size and coloring. Stand-ins are used for camera blocking in film and television in lieu of the person who's really playing the role.

Submission—What you hope your agent does. The process of sending pictures and resumes to casting directors.

Talent—That's what some call actors behind their back.

Tech—The period of rehearsal where the technical elements are added.

Test deal—If you are going to network or testing for a pilot, you will sign your contract, or test deal, before you audition.

Testing—Going to network, or studio, or producers for a film or television show. A screen test.

TOS—Top of Show. Billing an actor's name in the opening credits.

Tryout—What a show that performs in another city before reaching its final destination in NYC is doing.

Under 5—Having five lines or fewer of dialogue, and getting paid as such.

Understudy—Or *standby;* goes on if the regular performer is unable to.

Up-fronts—The week where networks announce their seasons for advertisers, and advertisers buy ad space.

Upstage—The furthest point from the audience on stage.

Wild spot—A commercial usage that involves buying in random markets.

INDEX

Books from Allworth Press

Allworth Press is an imprint of Allworth Communications, Inc. Selected titles are listed below.

Making It on Broadway: Actors' Tales of Climbing to the Top
by David Wienir and Jodie Langel (paperback, 6 × 9, 288 pages, $19.95)

Acting–Advanced Techniques for the Actor, Director, and Teacher
by Terry Schreiber (paperback, 6 × 9, 256 pages, $19.95)

Improv for Actors
by Dan Diggles (paperback, 6 × 9, 246 pages, $19.95)

Movement for Actors
edited by Nicole Potter (paperback, 6 × 9, 288 pages, $19.95)

Acting for Film
by Cathy Haase (paperback, 6 × 9, 240 pages, $19.95)

Acting That Matters
by Barry Pineo (paperback, 5 1/2 × 8 1/2, 240 pages, $16.95)

Mastering Shakespeare: An Acting Class in Seven Scenes
by Scott Kaiser (paperback, 6 × 9, 256 pages, $19.95)

The Art of Auditioning
by Rob Decina (paperback, 6 × 9, 224 pages, $19.95)

An Actor's Guide–Making It in New York City
by Glenn Alterman (paperback, 6 × 9, 288 pages, $19.95)

Promoting Your Acting Career, Second Edition
by Glenn Alterman (paperback, 6 × 9, 256 pages, $19.95)

The Best Things Ever Said in the Dark:
The Wisest, Wittiest, Most Provocative Quotations from the Movies
by Bruce Adamson (7 1/2 × 7 1/2, 144 pages, $14.95)

Please write to request our free catalog. To order by credit card, call 1-800-491-2808 or send a check or money order to Allworth Press, 10 East 23rd Street, Suite 510, New York, NY 10010. Include $5 for shipping and handling for the first book ordered and $1 for each additional book. Ten dollars plus $1 for each additional book if ordering from Canada. New York State residents must add sales tax.

To see our complete catalog on the World Wide Web, or to order online, you can find us at
www.allworth.com.